Mr. Cronin, who is the son of A. J. Cronin, the novelist, lives in England. After studying at Ampleforth College and Harvard University, he received an honors degree in *Lit. Hum.* at Trinity College, Oxford in 1947.

A PEARL TO INDIA

By Vincent Cronin

THE GOLDEN HONEYCOMB

THE WISE MAN FROM THE WEST

THE LAST MIGRATION

VINCENT CRONIN

A Pearl to India

The Life of
Roberto de Nobili

New York
E. P. DUTTON & COMPANY, INC.
1959

Cronin, Vincent.   A pearl to India; the life of Roberto de
Nobili. New York, Dutton, 1959. 297 p. illus. 21 cm.
Includes bibliography.   1. Nobili, Roberto de', 1577–
1656. I. Title. BV3269.N6C7 1959 922.254 59–5815 ‡
Library of Congress

Contents

45063

Illustrations

SOUTHERN INDIA

GOA

Bhatkal
Basrur
Coondapur

IKKERI

NAYAK

Karkala
Ullal &
Bangher
Mangalore

COORG
Mysore

MYSORE KINGDOM

TODAS

Cannanore
Tellichery

CALICUT

Tanor

Ponnani

CRANGANORE

Angamalei
Vaipi I. Palliporto
COCHIN Ernakulam

Uttamapalayam
Kaduturutti

Purukad

Kayankulam

Quilon

Tiruvidankode
Kolachel

SERINGAPATANAM

Bangalore

NAYAK

Cauvery R.

Coimbatore

Sattiamangalam

Erode

Karur

Palghat
Dharapuram

Peryakulam
Uttappanayakenur

Tirumangalam

Manamadurai

Kamanayakanpatti
Kajetaro
Shenkotta

Tirineveli

Kottal
C. Comorin

Tirupati
CHANDRAGIRI
Pulicat

SAN THOME
(Mylapore)
Conjeevaram

VELLORE

Chengam
GINGI
Tiruvannamalei GINGI

GINGI NAYAK

Maramangalam
Salem

Tegnapattinam
(Devanampatnam)
Porto Novo Tivu Kottai
Chidambaram Devi Kottai

Sandamangalam
Tottiam TANJORE
Srirangam Cauvery Tranquebar
Allitorei TANJORE
Tiruchirapalli Nagapattinam
Kadavur Kandelur
NAYAK
Dindigul
Ammayanayakanur
Kilaneri Devakottai

MADURAI Tondi

Jaffna

Pogalur
Vambar Panben Rameswaram
Vaypar
TUTICORIN Manaars I.

Tunicael
Manapad

CANARA

MALABAR

MALABAR

COROMANDEL

Palar R.

Ponnaiyar R.

Palar R.

CEYLON

Miles
0   50   100

✠ Fortress town

Preface

ROBERTO DE NOBILI belongs to the generation after Matteo Ricci, whose life was recounted in *The Wise Man from the West*. Like his fellow-Italian, Nobili entered the Society of Jesus and sailed for the East, where he was able to make progress only after he had discarded European for Oriental dress and adopted Oriental ways. Like Ricci, he was a pioneer in adaptation; that is, he tried to bridge sixty-five degrees of longitude by a combination of theology, love and good manners. But there the resemblance ends. Because each missionary strove to identify himself with his chosen country, Nobili's life is as different from Ricci's as India is from China.

It seems to me that the adaptation of Christianity, devoid of unessential trappings, to Eastern customs, imagery and ways of thought, far from being a subject of limited historic interest, can claim to be one of the most urgent needs of our time. Nobili's approach which now, after three centuries, appears to be the only kind of approach the East will respect, is more than a missionary venture to increase the numbers of his Church. If moral and political opinions are largely influenced by religious beliefs, what Nobili did is one of the best ways of at last making for the world a garment without seam. Christendom, on her side, stands to gain by the spiritual forces to be found in India. Some will argue that such a love-match is too difficult to arrange, but Nobili would have disagreed. He held that East and West can meet—as arms in the upright of the Cross.

Fr Augustin Saulière, fifty-four years a missionary in the Madurai mission, placed at my disposal his valuable manuscript Life of Nobili, transcripts from the Shembaganur archives and translations of some of Nobili's writings. He also answered many questions about local customs and missionary history. Without his unfailing generosity this biography could not have been written. But Fr Saulière bears no responsibility whatsoever for any errors of fact or interpretation which may have crept into the following pages.

My thanks are also due to the Rockefeller Foundation for a grant towards research.

1. *The Roman Nobleman*

ROBERTO DE NOBILI was born in Rome in September 1577. His family, which claimed descent from the Emperor Otho III, had begun to make a name at the beginning of the eleventh century when Manente de Nobili became governor of the rock fortress of Orvieto. For fifteen generations the Nobilis were important figures in Orvieto as Governors, Consuls and "Capitani al governo" until 1460, when Guido de Nobili inherited a large property at Montepulciano and went to settle with his family in the Tuscan hill town.

Roberto de Nobili's grandfather Vincenzo—a grandson of Guido de Nobili of Montepulciano—had been created Count of Civitella and General in the Papal Army; and Roberto's father, Count Pier Francesco de Nobili, continued the family's military tradition. At the age of twenty-one Count Pier Francesco was appointed Colonel in a papal expeditionary force sent across the Alps to help the French Catholics against the Huguenots. So bravely did he fight at the battle of Moncontour and Poitiers that, in recognition of his services, he was made Chevalier of St Michel by the Duke of Anjou.

Shortly after the young Colonel's return to Rome, Pius V, alarmed at the steady advance of the Turk, sent a ringing appeal to the princes of Europe to rally in defence of Christendom. During the ensuing campaign Pier Francesco de Nobili was given command of a troop of infantry and sent to relieve the hard-pressed Knights of Malta.

After the victory of Lepanto, Pier Francesco returned home and married a noble Roman lady, Clarice Cioli. He was given command of the pontifical troops stationed at Bologna, proved an excellent officer and was soon raised to the rank of General.

Roberto de Nobili, the first child of Pier Francesco and Clarice, was named after his uncle, popularly known as "the little Cardinal". This uncle had been a prodigy of learning and virtue. At the age of ten he could speak Latin and Greek fluently, and before he was eighteen he had written a treatise *de Gloria Caelesti* and several panegyrics of saints. Such was his childlike piety that Pope Pius IV used to say of him that he was "an angel incarnate". At the age of thirteen he was raised to the purple by his uncle Pope Julius III, but instead of accommodating himself to the hunting and gambling of the papal court he led a strict life, fasting often, sleeping on a board and wearing a hair-shirt. At a time when Cardinals were expected to patronize artists, to sit again and again to such painters as Vasari and Titian, young Nobili from motives of humility would not allow his portrait to be painted even once. He repeatedly thought of renouncing the dignity of Cardinal and retiring into a religious order, but his confessor dissuaded him. After a painful illness, he died with the most perfect resignation at the age of eighteen.

Roberto de Nobili never knew his famous namesake, but during his early years he often heard about him. Men like Charles Borromeo, Robert Bellarmine and Baronius venerated "the little Cardinal" as a saint. It was generally agreed that he had been "too good for this world". Roberto's parents, therefore, were pleased to see their eldest son showing traits in his character which reminded them of Cardinal Roberto. True, he did not recite psalms while dressing, but he had the same gravity of manner, the same earnestness in his studies and the same inclination to piety. In the hope perhaps that he would one day be an ornament of the Sacred College, they joined with Roberto's aunt Caterina to give him the best possible education.

The Dowager Countess Caterina Sforza was the widow of Ascagno Sforza, Knight of the Golden Fleece, lately commander of the papal expeditionary forces in France. She was rich, pious and influential. Her daughter Costanza, the wealthiest heiress of Italy, had married Giacomo Boncompagni, Duke of Sora, son of Pope Gregory XIII, and had a son, the Marquis Gregorio Boncompagni who was the same age as Robert. Gregorio Boncompagni and Roberto were educated together under the watchful eyes of the Dowager Sforza, first by private tutors and then at the best school in Rome, the Roman College, which owed much to the munificence of Gregorio's grandfather, Pope Gregory XIII, and was beginning to be known as the Gregorianum.

Under the admiring gaze of three younger brothers and two sisters, Roberto learned to thrust with a filigree-handled sword and to conjugate Latin verbs from a grammar embossed with the family crest. In the fashionable quarter of Rome where he lived distinction was not always made between social and supernatural graces. Damask cushions softened the prie-Dieus and during Lent gloved footmen served heaped dishes of well-spiced carp and mullet. Society assumed that Roberto too, destined by his family to become a prince of the Church, would discreetly combine the best of this world and the next.

The Dowager Contessa Sforza's spiritual adviser was a remarkable French Cistercian, Jean de la Barrière, who exercised a great influence, through her, on young Roberto. Roberto's father had come to know and admire him while serving in France. Jean de la Barrière had then been abbot of a monastery in the diocese of Toulouse, where he had introduced severe reforms, including abstention from wine, fish, eggs, butter and salt, and the abolition of tables and beds. In 1587 the Feuillants, as the monks of Barrière's abbey had come to be known, were summoned to Rome. There Roberto's aunt spent a fortune building them a monastery and a church near the Baths of Diocletian: S. Bernardo alle Terme.

One of Roberto's early memories was of passion and persecution as a result of divided loyalties within the abbey, reflecting the political division of France. While the majority of his religious declared for the League, Barrière remained loyal to Henry III. As a result Barrière was condemned by his monks as a traitor to the Catholic cause, deposed and forbidden to say Mass. This was a great blow to his spiritual daughter. The Dowager Countess went to Cardinal Bellarmine and gave him no peace until, with the Pope's consent, he took the affair into his hands and reconciled the ascetic abbot to his monks.

The first eight years of Roberto's life coincided with the last

years of Gregory XIII's pontificate. It was a time of revival in
the Church, when saints, scholars and artists vied with one another
to restore the spiritual beauty which excesses during the Renaissance had so badly tarnished; it was the age of Teresa of Avila,
John of the Cross, Philip Neri, Charles Borromeo and Francis de
Sales; of Robert Bellarmine and the historian Baronius; of
Federigo Barocci and Annibale Carvacci; of Palestrina and of
Torquato Tasso, whose challenging war-cry against the Turk,
Gerusalemme liberata, was the most popular poem of the day. Old
religious Orders and Congregations were being reorganized and
reformed; new ones were being founded. Schools, colleges and
seminaries were being opened in almost every country of Europe,
where priests could be trained not only to lead the Counter-
Reformation but to be sent as missionaries to the new countries of
Asia and America which, it was believed, had been discovered
precisely to compensate for those nations of Europe lost to
Catholicism.

As though expressing the new mood, Rome was changing from
a Renaissance into a baroque city. As schoolboys Roberto de
Nobili and Gregorio Boncompagni walked down broad new roads
driven over the Quirinal, Viminal and Esquiline Hills; played
in wide-colonnaded piazzas, an obelisk at their centre; they
watched new churches being built, such as S. Maria ai Monti and
S. Girolamo degli Schiavoni, modelled on the severe lines of the
Gesù. And out of school they did not have to seek far for amusement: Rome and her visitors provided that.

"The most cosmopolitan city in the world," wrote Montaigne
of Rome during Nobili's childhood. "The Roman people do not
stare when they see French or Spanish or Teuton dress, and some
of the beggars ask for alms in our own language." Not only were
there European pilgrims—in the holy year, 1600, more than a
million came, seven times the population of Rome—but a constant
succession of embassies from a world continually growing in size.
In 1578 Armenians, Jacobites and Maronites; in 1581 and 1582
Russians in scarlet tunics and scarlet mantles, high boots and tall
sable hats, but whose manners were less distinguished than their
dress: when a secretary was slow in handing a letter from the

Grand Prince, the Russian struck him in the Pope's presence. On another occasion the guns of Castel San Angelo boomed salvos of salute to welcome an embassy from the Shah of Persia, promising troops against the Turk—always the Turk.

But the embassy which most impressed the Romans during Roberto's youth was that of four Japanese princes representing the Christian sovereigns of Bungo, Armia and Omura. After a journey of three years they made their solemn entry into Rome on the morning of 23rd March 1584, mounted on fine palfreys with black trappings, wearing their national dress—white silk coats embroidered in gold with birds and flowers, open in the front and with wide sleeves, a rich scarf over their shoulders, crossed on their breasts and tied as a girdle. In their right hands they bore a scimitar, in their left a dagger in a lacquered sheath. When they dismounted to present their credentials to Gregory XIII, their short stature was commented on—and also their polished manners. Later, because the Romans made such fun of their national costume, the ambassadors wore European dress, discreetly provided for them by the Pope.

To Roberto these embassies doubtless seemed living illustrations to the short booklets which his parents bought and read and recounted to him as a child: collected extracts from the Annual Letters—yearly reports sent to the General by the heads of the various "provinces" into which the Society of Jesus was divided —published to stimulate interest and support. The sections dealing with mission fields in America and Asia were the most interesting, for they described strange peoples, customs and sights, heroic martyrdoms and acts of self-sacrifice; gave statistics of a growing body of Christians—150,000 in Japan alone—and always made clear the increasing need for dedicated missionaries.

By the age of seventeen Roberto was convinced that he had a vocation to become a Jesuit missionary: to respond to the call of the embassies and the Annual Letters. His father had died the year before, entrusting the management of his family affairs to the Dowager Contessa Sforza's son, so that Roberto, in order to follow his vocation, had to obtain permission from his new guardian.

Cardinal Francesco Sforza, who loved the world, could not understand why his young cousin should wish to leave it to become a Jesuit. Roberto bore a great name, he was related to two Popes (including Julius III, the uncle of Roberto's grandfather, Vincenzo), he owned property in Rome, Montepulciano and Civitella, he was good-looking and intelligent: the world lay at his feet, the highest honours were his for the plucking. If he absolutely insisted on a religious career, let it not be in the Society of Jesus, whose members were forbidden, unless in exceptional circumstances, even to accept a bishopric.

Cardinal Sforza not only did all he could to dissuade Roberto from what he considered a foolish step, but he mobilized against it the opposition of his family and relations: the Boncompagnis and the Ciolis as well as the Nobilis and Sforzas: the richest and most influential people in Rome. The permission which Roberto wanted so much was firmly refused.

Roberto's spiritual advisers, unwilling to offend the powerful Cardinal, dared not champion his cause. They left the general's son to fight this battle alone. Alone, that is, with a famous precedent. One of Roberto's relatives, Fabius de Fabiis, was supposed to be the last and only descendant of the famous Fabius Cunctator who had saved Rome in the days of Hannibal. In the teeth of violent opposition, he had entered the Jesuit novitiate, and when his ordination was drawing near, his relatives rose up in protest to prevent what they considered a catastrophe, since his ordination would mean the extinction of the illustrious Fabian race. Pope Gregory XIII was persuaded to intervene, but Fabius de Fabiis had resisted even his opposition, and was now a prominent Jesuit superior.

Roberto lived up to his kinsman's heroic example. Since he could not follow his vocation in Rome, he decided to leave. He felt sure God was calling him, and to those who tried to bar his way he replied, "When God calls, no human consideration should stop us." Without telling his family, he travelled south and crossed the frontier into the kingdom of Naples. He had no preconceived plan and trusted in Providence to guide him. Eventually he arrived at the house of a certain Lady Anna Carafa,

Duchess of Nocera. He told her his story, not the whole of it, but as much as he could tell without betraying his identity and bringing on his heels the search-parties which the Nobilis, the Sforzas and the Boncompagnis had already set on foot. The Duchess was favourably impressed by Nobili's manner and intrigued by his story. She trusted him, tactfully refrained from indiscreet questions and promised to help him to complete his education.

For almost two years Nobili lived in Nocera—holiday resort of ancient Rome—where the Duchess provided him with good teachers and treated him like a son. When, occasionally, she visited Naples, Roberto would accompany her as a member of her household, but he was careful to confine himself to his room and to avoid all social calls.

One day, however, when he was hearing Mass in the Jesuit church at Naples, Roberto was recognized by one of the Roman emissaries who had been sent in search of him. He was accosted and questioned. In a few minutes his secret was out, and it seemed that his carefully planned scheme would be foiled. However, when she learned who her protégé was and his desire to be a priest, the Duchess Carafa, far from being displeased, entered still further into the spirit of the adventure and promised to become the champion of Roberto's cause.

Now the Duchess Carafa was a remarkable woman in virtue of her descent from Giorgio Castriota, who for twenty years, with forces never exceeding 20,000 men, held the Turk at bay in Albania during the fifteenth century. Army after army was sent against him and always repulsed, so that the Turks in grudging admiration called their adversary Alexander (Iskander) and added the title of "beg". As Scanderbeg, Castriota's memory was honoured throughout Italy.

With Scanderbeg's blood in her veins, the Duchess Carafa rallied to Roberto's defence. She wrote to his family, to Cardinal Sforza and to the Duke of Sora, putting forward exceedingly forcible arguments. Since the wishes of a lady of such ancestry could not be lightly set aside even by the greatest families of Rome, reluctantly Cardinal Sforza was persuaded to withdraw his opposition and Roberto was allowed to join the Society of Jesus.

Nobili did not return at once to Rome. Knowing his guardian's character, he considered it more prudent to stay in Naples, under the Duchess's protecting influence. At the age of nineteen, in 1596, he entered the novitiate at Naples, where he immediately found a kinsman and sympathetic supporter in the superior of the province of Naples—the Provincial—none other than Fabius de Fabiis.

During his first two years in the Society Nobili's vocation, and especially his humility, were tested by such drudgery as scouring pots and pans, washing floors and peeling potatoes in the college kitchen and tending the destitute sick in the local hospital. In the little time left to himself, he dreamed of becoming a missionary in the East. During his first year he wanted to go to India. Indeed, his novice-master, the historian Orlandini, prophesied that he would go to that country and do great things for the glory of God. And to India he now began to turn his thoughts, building up a picture of the country as his ancestors had known it chiefly from the scanty evidence of Greek and Latin classics.

Those books noted that India was the source of such luxuries as muslins, spikenard, tortoiseshell and pearls. Some bluish pearls were imported from Britain, but these could not compare with the big rose-tinted pearls of India—the favourite jewellery of ancient Rome. In fact, Romans preferred the pearl even to the diamond and ruby, because of its naturally complete beauty which could not be improved by cutting.

Direct trade with the East had languished after A.D. 217. But India had continued to sell, indirectly, her pearls and her spices to Rome—by way first of the Arabs and, after 1509, of the Portuguese: every Roman who had flavoured his salted beef with pepper and cinnamon knew something of the heat of India.

As regards the Indians' religion Rome until recently had contented herself with the few facts and many fancies brought back by Alexander's army from the Punjab and the rumours retailed in Alexandria: that India was populated by gymnosophists, by Pythagoreans, by men who burned their dead. Nobili knew a little more than that, for the Annual Letters had told him of missionary work in a hot, damp climate among a people naturally religious but exceedingly conservative of their traditional gods.

Throughout 1597 Nobili set his heart on India. The following year, however, Orlandini was succeeded as novice-master by Bernardo de Ponte, such an enthusiast for the Japanese mission that for a time there was a plan afoot for putting him in charge of a special novitiate for Japan. Bernardo de Ponte began to extol a country where the people were intelligent, vigorous and hardworking, and to describe the harvest waiting to be reaped there. Then came news which in Nobili's eyes gave the Japanese mission an irresistible attraction.

In 1596 the pilot of a stranded Spanish ship, in order to save his cargo from confiscation, made rash statements about the power of his king. He said Philip II was sending his priests abroad so as to convert the people as a prelude to conquest. These words were reported to Hideyoshi, a leading Japanese daimyo, who had formerly tolerated the presence of Christian missionaries. Seeing in Christianity a danger to the national unity for which he was striving, Hideyoshi condemned to be crucified six Franciscans, a Jesuit seminarist named Paul Miki, two Japanese catechists and fifteen other Japanese Christians. This sentence was followed by widespread persecution of Christians.

The prospect of danger and possible martyrdom seems to have appealed so strongly to Nobili that during 1599 he made known his desire to go to Japan. However, the persecution ended as suddenly as it had begun, with the death of Hideyoshi in 1598. Under his successor converts were being made at the rate of forty thousand annually. The good news reached Italy two years later. Nobili's chief motive for wishing to go to Japan had disappeared, and when the time came to put in his formal petition for a foreign mission field, he returned to his first choice: India.

In 1599 Nobili entered on his "philosophical" course, during which he studied logic, science, astronomy, metaphysics, psychology and ethics. The work consisted mainly in reading the writings of Aristotle, with his Christian commentators, and Nobili set about it with a will, for only men with good academic records were chosen for the coveted foreign missions.

In that same year Nobili's younger brother Vincenzo came of age, and Nobili had to make a formal abdication of his title of Count of Civitella in Vincenzo's favour. Cardinal Sforza, who had been appointed administrator of Civitella during the minority of his cousins, presided over the transaction. After this abdication the Cardinal proposed that Nobili should also renounce a sum of money bequeathed to him by his father to be used in almsgiving or any other way he pleased. Sforza explained his plan to Claudio Aquaviva, General of the Society of Jesus, and asked him to send an order to Brother Roberto to comply. This the General declined to do. "The Brother," he said, "must be quite free, but I am sure he will comply with your Eminence's desire."

Nobili, however, unlike his superior, felt no particular inclination to oblige His Eminence, who had done all he could to thwart his vocation. When he received the Cardinal's letter requesting him to surrender the disputed money, he did not even answer. Sforza, impatient of delay, complained to the General. This greatly annoyed Aquaviva, who feared lest he should be suspected of coveting the Nobili inheritance. To remove any such suspicion he wrote to Nobili that on no account would the Society accept a farthing from him. As to the disposal of his property, he had no order to give him; he could consult theologians at Naples and follow their advice, but care should be taken not to displease the Cardinal.

The theologians, being consulted, agreed with Nobili that his father's will should not be disregarded, that he need not give anything to his family, who were already very wealthy, and that he was quite justified in giving all he had to the poor. Nobili told the General and also wrote to the Cardinal, repeating for his benefit and instruction the arguments of the Neapolitan theologians and ending with a flourish not devoid of impertinence.

The Cardinal complained of this letter to the General, who wrote to Nobili that such forthright manners had caused him and the Cardinal keen displeasure. Realizing the futility of the unequal contest, Nobili asked the General to have a sheet of paper filled up as he thought proper and sent to him for his signature. When the draft reached Nobili, he noticed that he was expected "to declare that of his own free will etc. . . . . he bequeathed" the property in question. This wording roused Nobili's scruples. How could he say that he gave his property of his free will, when he had all along been determined to distribute it to the poor? He said he could not sign such a document.

When the General heard of Nobili's objections he nearly lost patience. On 27th November 1599 he wrote to the Provincial of Naples: "For God's sake take that affair in hand and explain to this young man that he can do with a free will a thing he had refused to do when the circumstances were different." Finally, on 9th March 1600 the affair was settled to everyone's satisfaction, even Cardinal Sforza's, who offered to let his cousin have, out of the disputed property, a small sum for the poor. On the same day the General wrote to Nobili that he was quite certain the whole trouble had arisen from his scruples and a desire to benefit the poor, but God who saw the heart would reward his charity, even though he had been denied the pleasure of exercising it on the lavish scale he had intended. This should be a great consolation to him, but it would be greater still if he had not written in that saucy manner to the Cardinal.

Two years of exile in the remote, closed household at Nocera had had their effect on Nobili; he grew up more slowly than his contemporaries and at the age of twenty-four, as his superiors at Naples noted, his character was still not fully mature. The General, nonetheless, thought highly of Nobili, and in 1600 invited him to Rome to begin the final part of his education—theology.

Nobili applied himself well under such masters as Cardinal Bellarmine—a close friend. He made a point of studying in detail all those arguments which he thought might be useful in refuting what little was known of Indian religions. He created such a favourable impression in his theological course that during 1603 he was allowed the distinction of being ordained priest before he had completed the final year of his three-year syllabus.

When it was known that the young priest intended to leave for India, Nobili's family again raised protests but, thanks to the intervention of Orlandini, Fabius de Fabiis and General Aquaviva himself, they withdrew their objections, and at the end of 1603

Nobili went to see his family for what both he and they knew would probably be the last time.

First he said good-bye to his mother, who was to live to an extreme old age and whose memory he treasured, turning to her in future trials with the "confidence of a son"; then to his five younger brothers and sisters. The eldest, Vincenzo, combined a religious vocation with a military career by becoming a Knight of Jerusalem. His second brother married and had a son, Roberto, last of the Nobili line. His third brother, Sforza, became a Monsignor and Vice Legate of Ferrara. He was thought likely to be made Cardinal, but died comparatively young before achieving that distinction. Of Nobili's two sisters, the younger, Clarice, married into the Cioli family; the elder, Ludovica, became a nun in the convent of the Noble Oblates of Tor Dei Spechi in Rome: she lived to see her missionary brother through his long career, and to help him with her prayers and austerities.

Having said good-bye to his family and friends Nobili shouldered the few books and belongings which were all he could take with him of Rome and set out for Portugal to learn the language of Camoens and await the ship that would carry him to India.

2. *Outside India's Walls*

NOBILI's voyage began from Portugal, because the eternal salvation of Indians, like that of his Portuguese subjects, was held to be the responsibility of the King of Portugal. No bishop could be appointed in India, no missionary could sail there, without permission of the King, and then only in a Portuguese ship. The King had the right of presentation to all benefices; even lay people employed by the Church were appointed entirely at his discretion. The King undertook to maintain all churches, chapels, monasteries, and provide them with the necessary mitres, crosiers, ornaments and holy emblems, chalices, patens, thuribles, vases, books, lights, organs and bells. The stipends of all missionaries and ecclesiastics, ranging from 650 ducats for the Archbishop of Goa to thirty ducats for canons, were provided from the royal treasury.

The royal patronage extended not only to India but to the whole Portuguese empire: Brazil, the African forts, Malacca, the Moluccas, China and Japan. Though since 1580 the Portuguese and Spanish crowns had been united, Portugal jealously guarded her own patrimony, refusing not only Spanish but all foreign traders entrance to what she still considered her own empire. She would have liked to evangelize all these lands herself, to crown the miracles of discovery and conquest with the miracle of conversion. This task was slowly destroying her. Her population, numbering only a million, was being steadily drained away, and so she agreed to let missionaries of other countries enter her empire. But very reluctantly. In 1585 the third provincial council of Goa, convened and presided over by Archbishop Vincente de Fonseca, had insisted on only Portuguese missionaries: at the most two Italians should accompany them each year. This concession had proved too meagre. Portuguese Jesuits numbered only 1,200, of

23

whom half were required at home. More and more Italians had to
be enlisted. But to satisfy Portuguese pride these missionaries
were considered vassals of the King of Portugal.

By the last week of April 1604 Nobili and fourteen other young
Jesuits—including seven Portuguese and four Italians—had
gathered at Lisbon. After Paris, Lisbon was the largest city of
Christendom—and the wealthiest. Its treasure came largely from
the India fleet, consisting this year of five carracks, now riding at
anchor on the Tagus. The carracks, of up to two thousand tons,
were the largest ships in the world. They had four decks, eight
feet high, with poop and prow overtopping the main deck by
twenty feet. No tree—unspliced—was tall or thick enough to
provide them with a mast. Two hundred men and two big
capstans were needed to raise the yard. Nevertheless, so dangerous
was the journey, only six out of ten carracks returned safely to
Portugal, and their average length of life was three years.

The carracks were laden with two sorts of cargo: silver belonging
to the King, and a variety of goods belonging to private merchants:
woollen cloth, hats, swords, arms and munitions, ironware, paper,
lead, mirrors, printed books, dried fruits, wines, Dutch cheese, oil,
olives and vinegar. After the cargo was stowed, the soldiers
embarked: gay youths who believed they were sailing to make
their fortune—about three hundred to a carrack.

Last of all arrived the nineteenth Viceroy designate of Portuguese India, a tall sallow figure with long uncurled moustache and
pointed beard, dressed in cloak, doublet and hose, a sword at his
belt. His Excellency Dom Martim Afonso de Castro boarded the
San Jacinto—the leading carrack—and insisted on taking with
him Nobili and two of his companions. The crew, soldiers and
missionaries then assembled on deck, and after the chanting of a
religious anthem anchors were weighed. On 28th April 1604 the
fleet glided down the Tagus into the Atlantic Ocean.

The fleet had orders to sail in convoy. Often the captains, being
gentlemen of rank, were unwilling to yield to the admiral, so each
went his own way—to be intercepted singly by Dutch or English
men-of-war, for both these countries were at war with Spain. But
with the Viceroy aboard the *San Jacinto*, all five stayed together,

each carrack priming her forty bronze cannon, weighing two tons apiece, against possible attack.

A week out of Lisbon the fleet passed Madeira; a week later they were off the Coast of Guinea. Here the carracks invariably ran into much thunder and lightning, many showers of rain and sudden gusts which meant lowering the heavy mainyard as often as ten or twelve times every day. The captains had to navigate carefully, for though a good sailor before the wind, the carrack was worth nothing on the bowline. Unless they exercised all their skill, a wind might carry the carrack not to the East but to the West Indies. Brazil had been discovered in this way, by Portuguese who had set out for the Cape and India.

The fleet in which Nobili sailed escaped this danger only to encounter a worse: the doldrums, where carracks lay weeks becalmed before a breeze swept them across the line and into the favourable winds of the southern hemisphere. This year the fleet suffered worse than usual under a tropical sun so hot it melted even the candles. Three of the five carracks, unable to make headway through the doldrums, turned back to Lisbon. Only the *San Jacinto* and the *San Phelipe* stuck to their course.

Like the other passengers, Nobili lived chiefly on dry biscuit and water so foul that it was usual to put a piece of cloth in the mouth to filter it of worms. On these voyages everyone fell ill at one time or another, and many died a lingering death from "the disease of the gums", as scurvy was called.

In these conditions the two carracks crossed the equator, lost the Pole Star from sight and rounded the Cape in full winter. Here the Portuguese soldiers on board had a custom of throwing their knives and forks overboard, as a sign that they had left behind their old way of life. Here too Dom Martim de Castro opened the King's sealed letters, for at the Cape his jurisdiction began. Not that the orders ever greatly varied: strengthen forts, guard the Malabar coast, build ships, manufacture gunpowder, found cannon, at all costs destroy the Dutch.

Turning northwards, the two carracks made for their first port of call, Mozambique. Despite a cool favourable wind, it was not yet plain sailing. Thirty leagues south of Mozambique stretched

a chain of atolls, called the Angoza Islands. Only one was inhabited, and between the desert islands lay a network of coral reefs
and sandbanks, covered during the spring tides, and so steep that
the lead was of little use.

Five months out of Lisbon, in the dead of night, both carracks
ran into a sandbank among this notorious group. The *San Phelipe*
struck harder: she soon split apart and sank. The *San Jacinto*
resisted the shock, but was so rudely shaken that her mast broke,
her rudder was smashed, and everyone on board believed their
last moment had come. While waves pounded the groaning
timbers, panic-stricken crew and passengers ran here and there
looking for Nobili and the other missionaries so that they might
confess their sins.

But the carrack did not break up. She remained wedged on the
rocks and sand. Soon after midnight a large wave set her afloat
again, but in the morning it was found impossible to make the
thirty leagues to Mozambique. The Viceroy gave orders to
abandon the ship with her valuable cargo of silver and make for
land—more than three leagues away—on boats and improvised
rafts. Leaving behind their belongings, soldiers, crew and passengers—Nobili among them—leapt overboard and, paddling
between the jagged coral reefs, beached their rafts on the palm-
lined African shore. Here they remained until the weather
improved. Then, despite dangers and difficulties, the crew
regained the *San Jacinto* and succeeded in refloating her. On 4th
October the battered carrack and exhausted crew, together with
the survivors of the *San Phelipe*, limped into Mozambique. But
they were too late to take advantage of the favourable winds which,
for thirty days in August and September, made possible the voyage
to India. They were compelled to winter in Africa.

Mozambique had been wrested from the Moors in 1507: a
town on an island with a small, safe harbour. It consisted of a
fortress, over thirty years old, poorly supplied with munitions and
men, and surrounded by four hundred straw houses belonging to
the natives: aborigines with bones thrust through their cheeks,
teeth filed sharp, and ivory tips to their weapons. Nearby gold-
mines made it one of the richest posts in the East, and crew and

passengers of the carracks who had been suffering from scurvy were able to procure oranges, apples, lemons, bananas and plenty of fresh meat. But foggy mists and the extreme heat of summer made the island an unhealthy place: the Cemetery of the Portuguese, it was called.

Nobili might well have had to spend a whole year in this miasmal island—until the next annual fleet arrived, for the *San Jacinto*, in spite of extensive repairs during the next six months, at the end of that time was not yet seaworthy. However, Dom Ayres de Saldanha, the outgoing Viceroy, anxious about the fate of his successor, had dispatched fast galleys to the Coast of Melinda to make inquiries. Dom Martim de Castro decided to continue his voyage in one of these galleys, whose oars made them independent of the monsoon. Much as he would have liked to do so, he could not, for want of space, take all the missionaries with him; but he found room for Padre Roberto, with whom he had become very intimate during the long voyage and their stay in Africa. Escorted by one of the two caravels which had just arrived from Portugal, they made a dash across the Indian Ocean.

On 20th May 1605 the Viceroy's galley sailed up past the island of Bardes, where the big carracks unloaded, to the port of Goa. All that day church-bells rang, music of trumpets and clarions was played and thousands of salvos of cannon fired. To the applause of welcoming crowds Dom Martim landed on the quayside, in front of the mint and cannon-foundry, and was led in state through a series of triumphal arches to his palace—more imposing without than within, since it was customary for the outgoing Viceroy to strip it bare of furniture.

Nobili, for his part, was led to the College of Saint Paul's, one of the finest buildings in Goa. Here he was welcomed by his fellow-Jesuits, who were known throughout the East as "Paulists". At the tailor's shop in the college it was usual to set out great tubs of warm water and aromatic herbs for newly arrived missionaries. Having washed off the salt and grime of his voyage, Nobili dressed in a new light-weight black soutane. When the college barber had shaved his beard, and trimmed his hair and tonsure, he was taken off to be given rich strengthening food.

For the next five months Nobili lived at the College of St Paul's, becoming acclimatized, continuing his theological studies and coming to know the city which controlled Portuguese trade and Christian missions in India.

Golden Goa, capital of Portuguese Asia, stood on an island of the same name—fertile, well-watered and full of trees—about fifteen miles long and ten wide, separated from the mainland by a mere river. The city was enclosed by low walls, strong on the river side only. Each gate was guarded by a warder—a cripple who got the place by way of compensation: this warder printed a mark on the arm of natives wishing to visit the mainland for provisions, for entry to the island was carefully controlled. In fact Goa was more like a rich Portuguese trading carrack anchored off the coast than a part of continental India.

Goa's buildings, of simple laterite, with tiled roofs, were in Portuguese style. The markets were heaped with pineapples, mangoes and jackfruit, with shad, sole, crabs, mussels, oysters, and shrimps so large a dozen made a meal. At the cross-roads vendors sold goods from the four corners of the world to richly dressed Portuguese merchants and soldiers who paraded the town with their slaves. And offshore rode at anchor the carracks on which such abundance depended: loading for China silver, wines, red scarlet, glass and crystal ware, clocks and jewellery; others returning with gold in ingots, gilded woodwork, lacquered and varnished, silk, musk and civet, Malaya tin, porcelain, cabinets inlaid with ivory, mother-of-pearl and precious stones; the whitest and smoothest paper in the world; quicksilver, hard white sugar, wax and honey. Portuguese fidalgos surveying the port from the shade of parasols could boast that never had their city been so rich as when Nobili first saw it.

Pepper and souls—the fidalgos could also claim that Portugal had not neglected her spiritual mission. In almost every street stood a church, monastery or convent, richly equipped and adorned with reliquaries of chased gold and silver, pearls and rubies. The fidalgos could justly point out that in Goa, as in the other small islands, peninsulas and beachheads under Portuguese domination, most of the Indians were Christian.

A close observer, however, such as Nobili was, would have noticed that the mass of these Indians, being servants and slaves of the Portuguese, were Christian in name only.

The situation had changed little since one of the first Italian missionaries in India, Niccolò Lancilotto, had written to Ignatius de Loyola:

"The people of this country who become Christians do so purely from temporal advantage, as is inevitable in a land where slavery reigns. Slaves of the Moors or Hindus seek baptism in order to secure their manumission at the hands of the Portuguese. Others do so to get protection from tyrants, or for the sake of a turban, a shirt, or some other trifle they covet, or to escape being hanged, or to be able to associate with Christian women. The man who embraces the faith from honest conviction is regarded as a fool. They are baptized whenever or wherever they express a wish for the sacrament, without any instruction, and many revert to their former paganism. . . . This country is so vast that a hundred thousand priests would not be sufficient to evangelize all of its population."

The greatest of Nobili's predecessors, Francis Xavier, had encountered another, no less formidable difficulty: corrupt Portuguese officialdom. "Everywhere and at all times," he complained, "it is rapine, hoarding and robbery . . . I never cease wondering at the number of new inflections which, in addition to all the usual forms, have been added in this language of avarice to the conjugation of that ill-omened verb 'to rob'." Xavier wrote to the Provincial of Portugal, telling him that he should never agree to any of his friends being sent to India as an official; however upright a man might be at home, they all fell into dishonourable ways in India. Finally he wrote to King John III that he would "flee" to Japan, so as not to lose his time on the coast of India; it was a "martyrdom" to see everything destroyed which had been built up with so much trouble—destroyed, that is, by Portuguese immorality and greed.

The half-century since Xavier's death had brought no improvement. Goa was still more concerned with enriching her churches and monasteries than with building new ones on the mainland. Two small missions had been admitted inland, one to Agra in the

Muslim north, another to Chandragiri, east-south-east from Goa. But both were accredited to a royal court, and the missionaries acted as unofficial ambassadors. Christianity lay entrenched without the walls of India. Within lay one hundred and forty million Indians. By his own efforts no Christian missionary had yet succeeded in scaling the walls.

Nobili's studies at the College of St Paul's were interrupted— as a result of the change of climate—by a "terrible illness". But he passed his examination in theology and by the end of 1605 was free to start his missionary work. In Rome he had met and favourably impressed an Italian named Alberto Laerzio, a missionary in India since 1579, and at that time on a recruiting tour. It seems likely that Laerzio had settled with the General at Rome that Nobili was to join his own province.

A short voyage of eight to ten days down the coast brought Nobili to Cochin, headquarters of his new superior. Ralph Fitch, a Londoner who visited Cochin in 1583, had this to say:

"All the inhabitants here have very little houses covered with the leaves of the coco-trees. The men be of reasonable stature; the women little black, with a cloth bound about their middle hanging down to their hammes, all the rest of their body be naked; they have horrible great ears, with many rings set with pearls and stones in them." Since Fitch's day, the second largest Portuguese base in India had grown to include a cathedral, bishop's palace, churches and monasteries, residential quarters for the Portuguese traders, and large warehouses to store pepper and cinnamon.

In Cochin's College of the Mother of God Nobili met his new superior. Laerzio was then forty-nine, twenty years Nobili's senior, an energetic Italian from the Pennine Alps whose gentle manner hid a determined and daring spirit. Though he had his limitations as an administrator, few could match his missionary zeal. Above all he was broad-minded. These were qualities Nobili admired; and at once he and Laerzio were laying the foundations of a lifelong friendship.

But the torrid heat of Cochin proved too much for Nobili and soon after his arrival he suffered a serious relapse. On 20th January 1606 he rallied enough to dictate a letter to Aquaviva:

"I am writing this letter from Cochin, where I arrived from Goa. From what I hear I am destined for the Fishery Coast; since yesterday I am in bed with a high fever which prevents me from writing to your Reverence with my own hand. I cannot find words to express to you my gratitude for the great kindness you showed me in sending me to this country where I feel an intense desire to serve God and the Society. Since this desire is due to your Reverence's prayers, I have no doubt that it will one day be fulfilled in spite of my weakness and incapacity."

After a short description of the voyage he goes on: "From this your Reverence will understand that those who come to India will not lack occasions to suffer for the love of Our Lord Jesus Christ. When I reflect on it, I regret I did not store up a larger capital of virtue, nor insist earlier on obtaining this holy mission. That is why I shall never forget the special favour you conferred on me when you granted me a boon which so many Fathers and Brothers had asked so eagerly, but in vain."

Even the mere dictation of a letter was too much for Nobili. The next day his fever rose so high that his life was almost despaired of.

"On the third day I was advised to make myself ready for death, as I had only five or six hours to live. I did as I was told, but apparently in that particular year God did not make a harvest of sinners, for He did not take me, no doubt to give me time to prepare myself better."

In the first week of March, when Nobili was almost completely restored to health, an unexpected visitor came to Cochin: Dom Martim de Castro himself. Usually a viceroy spent the first year of office getting to know his work, his second year amassing a fortune, his third visiting key forts. But a special alvara of the King dated 15th March 1605 had recently arrived, ordering Castro to proceed in person to Malacca and the Moluccas, where the Dutch were attacking in force. Castro had come to Cochin to collect reinforcements for his fleet. When he visited the College, he invited Nobili to come with him, but Nobili, looking upon the offer as an honourable sinecure, declined it with thanks. As he explained in a letter, "I no longer desired to live in high society;

had such been my wish, I should not have left Rome." Perhaps, also, he declined the post because he thought it entailed no risk. If so, he was mistaken. Castro sailed in May with three thousand men and seventy ships. Of the three Jesuits who accompanied the fleet, two lost their lives in the naval battle of 29th April 1606. Although the siege of Malacca was raised, the Portuguese suffered such severe losses that Castro considered he had failed. Nobili never saw his friend again; the nineteenth viceroy died in Malacca in 1607—from grief, so it was said.

With his new superior Nobili now began to consider his future. He had arrived in Cochin on the morrow of a very important change. Throughout the sixteenth century the lands between the Cape of Good Hope and the Moluccas had formed the province of Goa. It was the one centre from which missionaries were sent as far afield as Malacca, Pegu, Bengal, Agra—capital of the Great Mogul—Tibet, Abyssinia and the Fishery Coast of South India. The province contained no fewer than 169 churches. Since this made for slow, clumsy administration, in his visit to Rome Laerzio had succeeded in detaching South and East India and Indonesia, which in 1601 were formed into a separate vice-province. But Goa, with so many other interests, did little to help her new vice-province. To remedy this, in 1605, it was given full independence and known henceforward as the province of Malabar. Laerzio, as Provincial, could assign Nobili a post any-where within its huge area, which took three years to visit, and which included the Fishery Coast, Pegu, Bengal, Ceylon, Malacca and the Moluccas.

But first the new missionary must learn an Oriental language. It was agreed that Nobili should join the eight Jesuits working among the Paravas, or pearl-fishers, of the Fishery Coast, to learn Tamil. This would equip him to minister to converts on the east and west coasts of South India or in Ceylon.

At the end of March Nobili sailed from Cochin round Cape Comorin and up the eastern coast, a short voyage by no means without danger. Three years previously four ships sailing from Cochin had been attacked by the Dutch, captured and plundered. Among the booty the Dutch sailors discovered a cassock belonging

ROBERTO DE NOBILI

This, the only authentic likeness, is the work of
Baltazar da Costa. It portrays Nobili in sannyāsī
dress, somewhere between the ages of sixty-three and
sixty-eight

A GATE-TOWER OF THE MADURAI TEMPLE

to Laerzio. One after another, they put it on and ran about the ship looking for the missionary: they said they wished to discuss theology with him.

In Goa and Cochin Nobili had been sheltered by colleges, libraries, fine churches and the Portuguese language. Now, on the Fishery Coast, he left these behind. He lived in a thatched hut overlooking long beaches of white sand, where the surf rolled in to groves of palm trees. But he was still in Portuguese India. The twenty thousand Christian pearl-fishers were people of the sea— therefore subject to the Portuguese masters of the sea—separated by their calling from the rest of India.

When fishing was permitted, some five hundred boats protected by two galliots would set out in April for the oyster banks. The divers, bodies oiled, baskets strapped to their backs, went down in six to eight fathoms of water, using diving stones. Pearls revealed their presence by the distorted shape of the shell. Each diver had a separate compartment of his boat where he tipped his catch, paying the owner the produce of one dive. The pearls were sold at the annual pearl-fair in Tuticorin, brokers being appointed by the Nāyak of Madurai, who levied four per cent from the seller. The pearls were passed through sieves and graded into seven sizes, the smallest being used for antacid electuaries, the largest sent to Europe as jewels. The pearls worn in ancient and Renaissance Rome had been fished by Paravas on this coast.

Christians for two generations, the Paravas received, along with their Portuguese baptismal names, Portuguese "protection". The Captain appointed every three years no longer claimed 400 gold pardaos[1] "for the Queen of Portugal's slippers", as he had done before Francis Xavier stopped it, but he insisted on getting as much or more under other pretexts. The Paravas' overlord, the Nāyak of Madurai, resented seeing his profits disappear in this way. In 1604 he had intervened with troops, the Portuguese had retaliated, and pearl-fishing was now at a virtual standstill.

In this troubled atmosphere, still suffering from fever and sickness which he seemed unable totally to shake off, Nobili set about learning Tamil, not from grammar or textbook, for there were

[1] About £270 (all sums in footnotes are in modern equivalents).

none, but from the sturdy pearl-fishers, whose vocabulary was better adapted for grading pearls than naming the seven deadly sins.

His task was further complicated in that Tamil bears no structural or verbal resemblance to any European language. It belongs to the Dravidian group—the half-dozen languages spoken by Dravidas, an old name for South Indians—of which it is the most highly developed and most widespread. Its alphabet contains thirty letters (as well as a few borrowed from Sanskrit): twelve vowels (called "souls") and eighteen consonants (called "bodies"). Seventeen of the bodies can be modified by souls, giving 204 different characters. With the thirty original letters, Nobili had 234 different signs to learn, all in a script bearing no relation at all to Italian.

At the time when Nobili learned Tamil, the language was evolving from the poetic stage. Nearly all the literature consisted of lyrics and hymns. Nevertheless, it was capable of long and complicated phrases and extreme subtlety. Its richness in honorifics and the fact that the polite plural was used in the third person as well as in the second suggested that some at least of those who spoke it were a courteous and highly civilized people.

After seven months with the pearl-fishers, Nobili could speak and write Tamil adequately. The nine years' training which had begun in Naples was now complete. He was acclimatized to the burning sun, he knew something about Portuguese India and the problems of the Paravas. He was ready for work, and work, so it must have seemed, would consist in treading well-worn ground on the fringes of India.

Then, in November 1605, Alberto Laerzio arrived back on the Fishery Coast from a long tour of his province. He went at once to visit Nobili. Too long, he decided, had conversions been made in the islands and along the beaches, protected, if necessary, by Portuguese guns. The time had come for the cross to outstrip the flag. The walls of India—what were they but fear of the unknown? The time had come for someone to penetrate the interior and convert those living in the heart of Southern India. The man Laerzio had chosen for this experiment was Roberto de Nobili.

3. *The Closed Door*

IN Madurai, the town selected by Laerzio as the site of his new experiment, a priest had been stationed for the past eleven years, serving those few Paravas from the Fishery Coast who had occasion to visit or live in the capital of their overlord, the Nāyak. This priest now happened to be visiting the Fishery Coast and was summoned by Laerzio to meet Nobili.

Gonçalo Fernandez was sixty-five. Born in Lisbon, he had sailed to India as a private soldier. In 1560 he had served under the viceroy Dom Constantino de Braganza, who, after failing to punish the Rājā of Jaffna for a massacre of Christians in Ceylon, seized the small island of Manar, off the north coast of Ceylon. While serving in the fort of Manar, three Portuguese soldiers of the garrison came under the spell of a Jewish Jesuit named Enrique Enriquez and vowed to become priests. One of the soldiers was Gonçalo Fernandez. He became a Jesuit in 1562, studied at Goa and worked for many years among the Paravas on the Fishery Coast.

They were not well matched, the old and ailing ex-private soldier who had originally dedicated his life to the Portuguese flag: and the young, highly educated Roman nobleman. But Laerzio evidently had confidence in Nobili's good nature to offset any differences of temperament and upbringing. So it was that on 10th November 1606 a little group of explorers set out from Tuticorin for Madurai. It consisted of Alberto Laerzio, his Socius (or assistant) Jerónimo Gomez, Gonçalo Fernandez and Roberto de Nobili. Madurai is eighty-three miles from Tuticorin as the crow flies, but in November, with the monsoon unchained, every path turned into a torrent and every hollow into a pool, the distance is easily lengthened into a hundred miles—at least five days' journey on foot.

Their route lay due north, at first through a barren sandy plain, patches of thorny acacias overhung by hardy palmyras. Later the track was occasionally bordered with margosa, tamarind, coconut and immense banyan trees. Swinging on the aerial roots which hang from the boughs of the banyan monkeys would scramble to pilfer from the unwary traveller.

A distinctive feature of the countryside was the number of extensive tanks, where rainwater lay stored until the dry season, when it would be released to irrigate rice-fields. Birds which flocked to these artificial lakes were caught in an ingenious way. After floating inverted water-pots on the lake, the Tamil fowler waited till the birds grew accustomed to them. Then, inserting his head in a pot pierced with eye-slits, he would move underwater, catch his prey by the legs and quickly pull it under.

Villages consisted of houses of four mud walls, thatched with straw, surrounding a courtyard, with a hearth on the south-west side. There were no temples: the chief sign of religion was a small enclosure with a few rough stones and sometimes the remains of a sacrificed cock or sheep. The larger villages boasted a public building—a sort of caravanserai. Here, doubtless, the four missionaries spent their nights, in a windowless room, under the curious eyes of villagers who had never before seen white men.

The four Europeans penetrated deep into the kingdom of Madurai, which extended east for a journey of eight days to the kingdom of Tanjore; and north from Cape Comorin an eleven days' journey to the kingdom of Mysore. Partly because the country's wealth came from the pearls fished on her eastern coast, partly in recognition of her spiritual resources, the kingdom of Madurai was known to Tamil poets as "The Kingdom of Pearls".

Gonçalo Fernandez's letter of recommendation from the Nāyak allowed the travellers to pass freely, mostly through dry lands sown with millet, cotton, cummin, garlic, ginger, gum-lac and capers. On the way they may have passed merchants transporting the famous cotton cloth of Madurai on oxen to the coast, where they exchanged it for salt, areca nuts, pepper, copper and iron. About the fifth day the travellers saw the high towers of the temple of Madurai, a landmark for miles around, and came up under the fortified stone walls of the city, which stood on a gently sloping plain beside a river.

Nobili and his companions entered the crowded outskirts. Cloth-dealers, coppersmiths, flower-sellers, vendors of sandal-wood, goldsmiths, painters and weavers—each trade had its own district. The people's complexion varied from dark to golden and even to almost white; they had black, glossy hair and regular, pleasing features. Women generally wore one piece of seamless coloured cloth some twenty feet long, covering them from feet to throat and allowing their arms full freedom. Men and women sparkled with jewels: silver rings on the toes and ankles, gold chains round the neck, bracelets on the arms, precious stones or pearls in the nose and round the ears, the lobes of which were stretched. Even the very poorest wore ear-ornaments and armlets of glass.

Nobili, who had grown up in the magnificence of early baroque Rome, found Madurai "a beautiful and densely populated city". The windowless houses were built round an open court, paved but not roofed. Most were of one story, and built as low as possible, that the dwellings of the gods might tower high above those of man. A rush mat served as bed, chair and table. A few earthen and metal pots, round as a cannon ball, and a box for clothes and jewels formed the whole of the furniture.

Students crowding the temple porticoes, expensive goods for sale, gaily caparisoned horses and elephants—these suggested an important centre. In fact, Madurai had been a flourishing city before the time of Christ, capital of the Pāṇḍya Kingdom, with its own Academy and university. The emblem on its coins was a fish, suggesting the importance of overseas trade. This trade had been backed up by embassies including one to Augustus Caesar. At the end of the thirteenth century Marco Polo called the wealthy Pāṇḍya kingdom "the finest and noblest province in the world".

Early in the fourteenth century a dispute arose about the succession to the throne of Madurai and one of the claimants appealed for help to the Muslim emperor of Delhi, the leading power of northern India. As a result the Muslims invaded South India: the first appearance there of a foreign invader, for though the South had traded widely it had been protected by the ocean and an almost impenetrable barrier of hill and forest.

For forty-eight years the Muslims ruled in Madurai, until a great new Hindu kingdom based on Vijayanagar, a month's journey north of Madurai, rallied the once independent kingdoms of the South (including Madurai) under its overlordship, drove out the Muslims, and for the next two centuries stemmed the tide of invasion. Vijayanagar, though past its heyday, was still able to hold back the Muslims, who were divided among themselves, and no longer powerful enough to exercise effective suzerainty over the Nāyak of Madurai. Though nominally a vassal, the Nāyak in fact acted as an independent king, and Madurai was for all practical purposes a soverign capital city: the finest in South India.

The four travellers made their way to the outskirts where the Paravas lived and reached Fernandez's mission house, built of clay, whitewashed inside and out, and roofed with tiles. There, after a restful night, such as Madurai can provide in November when the monsoon has cooled the air and blown away the mosquitoes, Nobili began to take stock of his new home. The mission in Madurai was then eleven years old. In addition to the fine house it consisted of a small neat church, an elementary school for boys under a Hindu master and—pride of the mission—a small dispensary. Here Fernandez gave free treatment to poor patients of the town.

The Portuguese—as Nobili had found in Goa and Cochin, and had cause to be grateful for—prided themselves on their high standards of medicine. At Goa they maintained the Hospital del Rey Nosso Senhor, the finest in the world, better than even that of the Holy Ghost in Rome. Physicians, surgeons, apothecaries and bleeders visited the sick morning and evening; the staple article of diet—chicken—was served in dishes of China porcelain; and linen was changed every day. The hospital was reserved for Europeans, but Indians—those who bore Christian names—were given treatment in a lesser hospital apart.

The dispensary attached to the Portuguese mission in Madurai was on a much smaller scale but it was well patronized, for South India had no hospitals, either privately endowed or attached to temples, monasteries and educational institutions. Doubtless its medicines proved at least as effective as the mixture of herbs prescribed by local doctors, for a Tamil proverb joked, "He who has killed a thousand men is already half a doctor."

When not dispensing medicines, Fernandez looked after the Paravas' interests. With the Nāyak he was on friendly terms. Though the status of the Paravas remained in dispute, Madurai and the Portuguese had other economic grounds for accord. The Nāyak bought horses (there were no native horses in South India) imported by the Portuguese from Persia by way of Ormuz; in return he sold large quantities of saltpetre, which the Portuguese desperately needed for gunpowder against the Dutch and English. Fernandez, who could speak Tamil, was a useful go-between in such business.

The buildings were there, the missionaries were allowed to enter and remained unharmed, good will existed between the court and the mission: superficially there was much to gratify a newcomer. But Nobili had been appointed to make Indians Christian and as he looked round the neat compound he noticed one fatal shortcoming. Apart from a hundred Paravas from the Fishery Coast, strangers in the city, who had broken with Indian customs, there were no new Indian Christians. Not one in all Madurai. In his eleven years in the prosperous capital city Fernandez had been unable to make a single convert.

Not that Fernandez had been remiss. On several occasions he had asked to be allowed to expound before the Nāyak and his court the principles of Christianity, but every time permission had been refused. Whenever he tried to introduce that subject into his conversation, the king would at once find some pretext for retiring to his inner apartments. Once however of his own accord he put a question to Fernandez regarding religion, and a great hope surged in the missionary's heart; but before he could make a reply, a spiritual adviser touched the arm of the king who, taking the hint, at once dropped the conversation. On another occasion an officer of the court warned Fernandez that he should never speak of religion. Fernandez retorted that if he could not speak of religion and make converts he had better leave the town. His

words were reported to the Nāyak who, highly offended, sent word
to Fernandez that if the object of his presence in Madurai was to
turn his subjects into Christians, the sooner he retired to the Coast
the better.

Every year had been the same: no progress to report. And every
year, as now, Laerzio inspected the house, the church, the school,
the dispensary; he checked the account books, scrutinized the
parish registers and found everything correct. But he did not find
the cause of that stagnation he was so anxious to remedy.

Nobili, also, set about seeking the reasons for Fernandez's
failure, for he had no wish to spend his life ministering to the
spiritual needs of occasional Christian pearl-fishers and Portuguese horse-traders. Until then, the door of India had been closed
to Christ. To open that door now became Nobili's fixed purpose.
Henceforth the words *"aperire portam"* recur often in his letters,
as though he had taken them for the motto on his banner.

Nobili's first Indian acquaintance at Madurai was the schoolmaster employed by Fernandez. Intelligent and well-versed in
Hindu theology, he held the title of guru (spiritual teacher) in his
own sect. He was a strict vegetarian and sincere inquirer after
truth, but he had such a poor opinion of Fernandez and his
religion that it never occurred to him to seek the missionary's
advice.

Nobili set about winning the school-teacher's friendship by
asking his help in his Tamil studies. Little did he get at first, for
the teacher thought highly of himself and was rather reluctant to
communicate his knowledge to a foreigner. Gradually, however,
as he came to know better the man he had to deal with, he dropped
his conceit and became quite friendly. In the course of long
conversations, dimly at first, through a language he had not yet
mastered and because the school-teacher used many new words
which had to be defined, Nobili came to understand the repug-
nance which kept most Hindus away from Christianity. He did
not come to understand it in a day nor even in a week, for it was a
complex problem, arising chiefly from something totally unfamiliar:
the organization of Indian society into castes.

All mankind, according to the Indians, are divided into groups

called by the Sanskrit word *jāti*, meaning primarily birth. The
Portuguese translated *jāti* as *casta*, meaning breed: as exact a
term as can be found in a European language, for it implies what
the Sanskrit implies: that men can be grouped according to their
hereditary natures. A man is born into his caste, he is maintained
in it by observing certain customs when he eats, when he marries
and when he happens to become defiled. He must marry within
the caste, and his children will belong to the same caste as he.
Normally he dies within his caste. Often he practises the same
trade as other members of his caste, but this is not always so,
hence caste is more than a guild.

The system posits that some men are born alike, and like must
always live with like. But the nature of man, though usually
unalterable, is not necessarily so. It cannot be raised to a higher
level, but it can fall away to a lower. This lapse will show itself
in actions. If he does not conform to the customs which charac-
terize his caste, a man shows that he no longer belongs, whereupon he has to be punished or expelled. Judgment is by the caste
council, commonly spoken of as a *panchāyat*—a body of five men,
but in practice usually much larger. Evidence before a caste
panchāyat is given on oath: by Ganges water or the sweet basil
plant, or by holding a cow's tail. The accused may have to under-
go an ordeal: to extract a coin or pebble from a boiling liquid, to
grasp a piece of red-hot iron, to walk barefoot over red-hot
embers. If he comes through the ordeal an offender is usually
reinstated.

But for certain offences such as eating cow's flesh or repeatedly
breaking a caste rule there is no reinstatement. The official
punishment, amounting to expulsion, is to deprive the guilty
person of the right to receive water from the hands of his fellow-
castemen, and to forbid them to receive water from him. This
automatically prohibits food cooked in water. For practical
purposes he is excommunicated. He cannot enjoy the services of
the Brahmins, should they conduct ceremonies for his caste, nor
of the barbers who shave for it, nor the washermen who wash for it,
and if he die under the ban his corpse must lack the funeral rites
which ensure continued existence and subsequent reincarnation

Nor can he accommodate himself to a caste lower than that from which he is expelled. He must remain an outcaste: a living creature who is treated socially as dead, or worse than dead.

New castes are continually arising. A new occupation often means the creation of a new caste. Sometimes the well-to-do elements in a despised caste try to cut adrift from their humbler-caste brethren and raise themselves in the social scale by finding a new name and a dubious origin associating them with some higher caste. In general, the higher the caste, the stricter its way of life, the more often it washes, the more closely guarded it keeps its women, the stronger the ban on the remarriage of widows.

The three highest castes, as established by the Code of Manu— the most binding Indian legal authority—are the Brahmins (the sacerdotal and learned class, whose members may be, but are not necessarily, priests), Kṣatriyas or Rājās (warriors) and Vaiśyas (husbandmen or traders). The Brahmins are said to be born from the head of God, the Kṣatriyas from his shoulders, the Vaiśyas from his thighs. The fourth caste enumerated by the Code of Manu is the Śūdras (serfs)—said to be born from the feet of God. By Nobili's day the Śūdras, comprising the bulk of the population, had become divided into more than a thousand castes (subcastes would be a more logical word), carefully graded.

Since, in Nobili's day, caste was a basic category of Indian thought, the first thing that had been asked about the Portuguese when they arrived in India was "To what caste do they belong?" The Indians watched their behaviour, how many times they washed daily, how they treated women and, in particular, what and how they ate. The Indians soon concluded that the Portuguese observed no caste rules and so belonged beneath the lowest Śūdras, with outcastes and untouchables. To the beef-eating outcastes in foreign dress the Indians gave the name of Parangis. Fernandez was a Parangi; and it was the first name given to Nobili in Madurai.

The word "Parangi" had a strange history. Since at least the time of the Crusades, Europeans had been known throughout Asia as Franks. Thus, in a Chinese notice of the fourteenth century the horses taken by Marignolli as a present from the Pope to the Great Khan are called "horses of the Kingdom of Fulang" = Farang, or the country of the Franks. In Sanskrit it is written Phitanguin and in Persian Feringhee: Baber, in describing the Battle of Panipat in 1526, calls his artillery Farangiha. Parangi is the South Indian version of the word, which it had been thought was particularly appropriate to the Portuguese, with their guns and horses.

The Parangis were considered polluting, like the Paraiyans and the Pallans. What, in practice, did this mean? The Paraiyans, for instance, who were slaves in all but name, going about naked or in rags, living from hand to mouth as hired labourers, were forbidden even to cross a street in which Brahmins lived. Should they do so, the Brahmins had the right, not to strike the Paraiyans themselves, because that would produce defilement, not even to touch them with the end of a long stick, but to order them to be severely beaten. Speaking to other castes, a Paraiyan must hold his hand before his mouth, lest his breath contaminate. If a Brahmin appeared on the road, he was obliged to flee or hide. He dare not enter the house of another caste. If employed, a door was purposely pierced for him. He had to work with his eyes on the ground, for if he glanced at the kitchen, all the utensils would be polluted and would have to be broken.

In some parts the Paraiyans were compelled to use a special language when referring to themselves or their possessions. When speaking, for instance, of their eye or their ear to a superior, they had to prefix it by the epithet "old". They had to call their children "calves", their silver "copper" and their paddy "chaff".

The Pulayans were even more degraded. They had to call their rice "dirty gruel" and their children "monkeys". They were forbidden even to build huts. They lived in forests of the Malabar coast in a lean-to, supported by four bamboo poles and open at the sides. Most made a sort of nest in branches of the thickest trees, where they perched like birds of prey. On a road, if they saw anyone coming, they were bound to utter a certain warning cry, for even the sight of them, at less than a hundred paces, polluted those of a higher caste. They were forbidden the use of gold or even silver ornaments, and of wearing clothes above the waist. Known to worship demons, they were forbidden to approach within a certain distance of Hindu temples.

Such was the destiny of polluting outcastes. But, in Hindu eyes, the Parangis merited even more contemptuous treatment, for they would not keep their distance and, being strong and well-armed, could not be forced to do so. Then again, the Parangis were seen to drink wine and to stagger drunk through the streets: an absolutely revolting practice to Indians, whose caste rules forbade them alcohol. It was also said that the Parangis ate dead horses and gave their daughters in marriage to the Paraiyans. They were known to kidnap children—to make them slaves, and worse. When Fernandez went out for a walk, as soon as women saw his black cassock they seized their children and drew them to safety. He would hear the women say that Parangis had a variety of recipes for frying children in butter, to make of them a more palatable meal. Anything that was vile was associated with Parangism. Anyone going about in trousers and wearing a coat and hat, whether born on the banks of the Tagus or in the backwaters of Travancore, was considered a Parangi: by their dress you shall know them. Parangism became, in the eyes of Hindus, the refuge of criminals who had fallen foul of the laws of their country, of social rebels who sought to shake off the discipline of caste and the Hindu rules of decency: the vilest word in their language.

The Portuguese, though unaware of the full opprobrium attached to that name, knew that it was used contemptuously. But, secure in their power and pride, they were far from resenting it. Rather, they welcomed the name as a means of swelling their ranks and strengthening their hold on their followers. They would not trust the sincerity of their converts unless it was guaranteed by a participation in their meals, loss of caste, change of name and dress, and the adopting of Portuguese customs. Once a man had become a Parangi he was irretrievably compromised in the eyes of his own people; he was looked upon as a traitor, ostracized and cast away; he had no choice but to cling to the Portuguese.

Nobili now began to see why Gonçalo Fernandez had failed.

Fernandez, who had fought under the Portuguese flag, was perfectly certain that no name was more glorious than that of Parangi, which to him was merely the Tamil translation of "Portuguese". He used it, without the least qualm of conscience, to describe his religion. He translated the phrase "Do you want to become a Christian?" by *Prangui kulam puguda venumo*. Since *kulam pukundaven* was the recognized phrase for degradation, a Hindu understood Fernandez's question to mean: "Do you want to fall down among the outcaste Parangis and become Parangi?" From the very start, the Gospel was identified with an inferior, polluting group.

Similarly, Fernandez called Christianity *prangui markkam*. Now the Tamil word *markkam* is derived from the Sanskrit *mārga*, meaning way or manner of living. *Markkam* in Tamil suggests caste rather than religion. But, as Nobili was beginning to learn, a god specially worshipped by outcastes could not be worshipped by caste Indians. Fernandez, by calling the Christian God "God of the Parangis", implied that no one could adore that God unless he joined the Parangis.

Fernandez would, in his most ingratiating way, invite high-caste Hindus to adopt the Parangi religion and, when his invitations were met with contempt, he could find no other explanation than the ignorance of those poor people who could not appreciate what was good for them. Indian customs and Indian ways were to him, as to the Portuguese missionaries and theologians who had trained him in the capital of Portuguese India, nothing but a bundle of superstitions which were to be carefully avoided. To have suggested that they could go very well with a sincere profession of Christianity would have sounded blasphemous to him. The more Indians discarded their ancestral customs and the closer they adhered to Portuguese ways, the better Christians they would be.

So much Nobili learned in his first few weeks in Madurai from the school-teacher employed by Fernandez. He was not slow in drawing his conclusions. He had come to India to fulfil not the first but the second half of Lope de Vega's couplet:

Al Rey infinitas tierras
Y á Dio infinitas almas.

Making people change their national customs and lose their caste, as a token of the sincerity of their conversion, struck him as a crying injustice. One of Nobili's first steps, therefore, was to call Christianity not the religion of the Parangis but the true religion (*sattya védam*).

But this repudiation was by itself insufficient. Nobili was an educated man devoted to religion; he spoke Tamil; his manners were impeccable, yet when he tried to associate with educated Hindus of Madurai (all but the school-teacher, a high-caste Sūdra) they would not let him enter their houses, and if he happened to touch them, they went to rid themselves of their defilement by washing and prayer.

This fear of defilement, with a consequent shrinking from impure matter or persons, was unknown to European history and correspondingly difficult for a European to understand. No seminarist recoiled from a copy of the *Decameron*, no hypochondriac from a sick-room, more horror-stricken than a high-caste Indian from a Parangi. Nobili, instead of treating such incidents as a personal affront, decided to come to terms with this horror of defilement underlying all Indian social life. He saw that if he were to mix freely with Indians, he must at all costs avoid being irretrievably classified as a Parangi. He had to act promptly. Touching untouchables was the mark of a Parangi—well, he would avoid it; Hindus bathed often and sat down cross-legged—well, out of courtesy he would do the same. He had to experiment as he went on, avoiding all that stigmatized a man as "polluting", watching Hindu reactions. His theological knowledge told him what could be conceded without detriment to the faith; his tact and courtesy suggested the rest.

While pursuing this makeshift change of manners, Nobili considered the possibility of a more radical adaptation. He had by his religious vows dedicated himself to a life of penance and chastity: was there a group of Indian men who led the same sort of life, whose name would be more appropriate to him than Parangi?

As the weeks passed, from his own personal experience and from further questioning of the school-teacher, Nobili discovered that the way of life most resembling that of a Christian priest was practised by a small group of men called sannyāsīs. The word was Sanskrit and meant "one who resigns or abandons all". In Tamil poetry the sannyāsī was called *ponnasi* = he who is without gold; *mannasi* = he who is without his own land, a pilgrim; and *pennasi* = he who is without a wife. Traditionally, it was the fourth and last stage of life recommended for Brahmins. First, as a youth, the Brahmin studied; then he married and founded a family; thirdly he withdrew into the forest; lastly, he became a sannyāsī. As such, he wandered, living on alms, devoted to the contemplation of God and the problems of philosophy.

Other men, aspiring to the same ideal, realized it in a somewhat different way. Instead of roaming, they generally lived in monasteries, spending their time in prayer, study, the practice of austerities and the training of disciples. Since they renounced all mundane things, caste included, their mode of life was open to non-Brahmins as well as Brahmins.

Traditionally, the sannyāsī took his vow of poverty in a simple ceremony, during which he was presented with ten pieces of cotton cloth such as are worn on the shoulders, four of them dyed dark reddish-yellow for his own use, the rest to be distributed as presents. This reddish-yellow colour, rather than white, was considered the sign of nakedness and deprivation. He was also given a bamboo staff with seven knots or joints, some small silver and copper coins, flowers, aksatas and sandalwood. The officiating guru then ordered him to don one of the yellow cloths and, in token of his renunciation of his caste as well as of the world's vanities, to break his thread and allow his tuft of hair to be shaved off—the thread and tuft being distinctive signs of the three upper castes, from whom sannyāsīs were recruited. Afterwards, the sannyāsī went away with his bamboo, his gourd full of water and his antelope's skin—all he was allowed to call his own.

Among the rules which he had to observe were to take only one meal a day of rice and herbs, during which he must not be seated; never to look at a woman; to live entirely by alms—though he had a right to ask for them, it was more proper to receive them without asking; when travelling to carry only his bamboo, gourd and antelope's skin; to avoid the defilement of walking barefoot, he must wear wooden sandals, held to the foot by a wooden peg, which comes between the first and second toes. By such austerities, by prayer and meditation he hoped to destroy any feeling of attachment for the world and its pleasures, as a means to final reunion with God.

Though there was much in such a life to make a European flinch, it offered Nobili two advantages. First, it might allow him to escape the stigma of Parangism. A Parangi sannyāsī: an impure pure man, so low as to be incapable of worship, yet dedicated to God: that was virtually a contradiction in terms. Secondly, as a sannyāsī, he would be translating the religious life to which he was vowed into terms Indians could understand: a courtesy no less necessary, say, than speaking in Tamil instead of in Portuguese. Nobili came to the conclusion that to adopt the sannyāsī's dress, diet and manner of living would prove the best means of opening the door of India. However, such a major change could be made only with the sanction of his superiors, of whom the most immediate was Alberto Laerzio.

Nobili's suggestions were not only daring, they were revolutionary. For three generations thousands of missionaries had worked in India as Parangis, teaching the religion of Parangis, wearing the black cassock of Parangis. The vast majority had not penetrated far enough into Indian thought and customs to know precisely what a sannyāsī was. To mix oneself up in that sort of thing was dangerous, tainting—so thought the Portuguese. The proper thing was to turn Indians into Portuguese subjects, and here was an Italian who wanted to turn himself—and with him, doubtless, before long, his Portuguese colleagues—into Indians. That, thought the Portuguese, was the one certain way to lose an empire.

But Laerzio was an Italian. Although he had been twenty-eight years a missionary in India, he was not fixed in his ways. Partly this was because he had grown up in the heyday of the Renaissance and, like Nobili, was heir to a culture which, from being pagan, had flowered into Christianity, gaining, not losing thereby. He was of the same race as Aquinas, who had taken Aristotle as his mentor in the realm of metaphysics, and of Dante who had taken Virgil as his guide in the underworld.

Laerzio, therefore, when he heard Nobili's plan, did not dismiss it as the raving of a lunatic. He was broad-minded enough to see its merits. Nevertheless, there was something breath-taking about the idea of a Christian missionary, almost the only white man in the centre of India, head shaven, preaching in Tamil, living on rice and herbs. Such a picture clashed with every conventional idea, not only of what Christianity was but of what it had been during sixteen centuries. Christianity was nothing if not traditional, and what priest had ever worn a couple of scant red ochre cloths? Laerzio wanted to convert Indians—but was it absolutely necessary to go to such prodigious lengths? Laerzio decided that he could not himself give Nobili the permission for which he asked. He told Nobili that he would refer the innovations to the Archbishop of Cranganore in whose diocese Madurai lay.

4. Styled a Rājā

When Vasco da Gama and his party visited a Hindu temple in Calicut in 1498, the year of the discovery of India, they firmly believed that St Thomas the Apostle had evangelized the subcontinent. Seeing such familiar things as statues, altars, lights, flowers and holy water, da Gama and his officers prayed to the Christian God. In the words of the chronicler, "Only one, Juan de Sa, who had some doubt of the matter, in making his genuflexions said 'If this be the devil, I worship God', which made da Gama smile."

The belief in St Thomas's evangelization was strengthened by the discovery in Malabar of a sect of 200,000 Christians. Though the sect was supposed by experts to have been founded from Syria or Persia in the eighth century, the Portuguese called them St Thomas Christians. It was these, the largest group of Indian Christians, who formed the bulk of the archdiocese of Cranganore.

The archbishopric had been created only two years before, in 1605, and was filled by a remarkable man, Don Francisco Ros, a Spaniard from Catalonia, a master of the Syrian and Chaldaic languages, as well as of Tamil. Ros, who had been working for many years among the St Thomas Christians, knew their piety, their orthodoxy as regards most doctrines, and the tenacity with which they had guarded their faith in Indian dress. When, therefore, Laerzio presented Nobili's request, no longer to call himself a Parangi, and to dress in Indian style as an Indian holy man, Ros naturally considered it in terms of the St Thomas Christians. This sect ranked as a distinct caste, treating Indian outcastes as polluting and untouchable. They spoke the language of Malabar (though their holy books were written in Chaldaic) and adorned their brows with sandal—a distinctively Indian practice. They dressed in Indian style, and their priests wore loin-cloths and cotton shawls: never in such a climate would they exchange them for heavy black serge. Most important of all, they were known as Nazarinis: never had anyone dared call them Parangis. Against this background Nobili's proposals to repudiate the name Parangi and become a sannyāsī sounded reasonable, and Archbishop Ros, after consulting Alexeio de Menezes, Archbishop of Goa, gave them his approval.

Comforting though this was, Alberto Laerzio wanted to be absolutely certain that he was acting correctly. On such a weighty matter he decided to secure the support of his consultors. To these venerable Jesuits the word "sannyāsī" evidently called to mind certain vagabonds who performed publicly feats of self-torture, such as staring at the sun till they were blind, standing on one leg or on their heads, or keeping an arm stretched high till it dried up. These self-styled sannyāsīs went about, some half-naked, some stark naked. "Let Fr Robert call himself as he pleases," the consultors decided, "choose any diet he likes, frequent whomsoever he fancies but, for heaven's sake, let him not dress as a Hindu sannyāsī!"

Laerzio, though somewhat disappointed, did not insist. This question of dress might be reconsidered later. In the meantime a beginning could be made in the way of adaptation. So he hastened to inform Nobili of the Archbishop's favourable attitude and of the changes he was allowed to make. His encouraging letter arrived none too soon, for things were not running smoothly at Madurai.

Already Nobili had begun in small ways to try to shake off the stigma of "Parangi". Gonçalo Fernandez had been quick to notice his abstinence from beef, his keeping aloof from Portuguese visitors to the parish house, the care with which he avoided speaking Portuguese, the efforts he made to speak the purest Tamil, which the Portuguese called "Court Tamil". Evidently this young Italian, less than half his age, after only a few months in Madurai, was leaving the beaten track for a path of his own. He imagined he was going to teach his Vicar, with eleven years' experience in Madurai and almost fifty years in India, how to run his parish! What was the meaning of these novelties? Abstinence from beef was a cowardly concession to the prejudices of the gentiles; his keeping aloof from the Portuguese sheer arrogance. As for his attempt at speaking Court Tamil with its poetical conceits and Sanskrit borrowings, it was ridiculous pedantry.

Despite Fernandez's reproaches, Nobili continued his experiment. These attempts at Indianization might be clumsy and inadequate but their meaning was not lost on those who observed them. The schoolmaster was delighted and made no secret about them when after school he returned home to his own people. So the rumour spread among the high castes that the stranger was not a Parangi at all, and a few Hindu Śūdras no longer felt any scruple about visiting him.

Nobili's innate courtesy and kindliness made them feel at home. He spoke well, without any mixture of Portuguese, and he said things worth hearing. He listened too with close interest to what they had to say. When they narrated to him their Purānic stories he would never brush them aside with a contemptuous "Nonsense". He became specially popular with some of the younger men, who would come and converse with him. He was struck by their deep sense of religion. With them religion was not a cloak which they only occasionally put on. It was ingrained in their very life, in their thoughts, in their words and in every action. He found them extremely sociable and kind-hearted. They would explain to him their customs, and knowing he was most anxious to conform to them, would warn him against false steps and give him useful advice regarding Hindu etiquette. Thus many things which had been pointed out to him by Fernandez as absurd now appeared to him as not only very reasonable but full of wisdom.

No longer an outcaste, Nobili began to see India not as the country of his voluntary exile, but as his own country, the country of *his* people. Madurai—almost from the very beginning—was his own town and he took a patriotic pride in its "beauty, wealth and large population". Tamil was his language and he regarded it as "copious, elegant, most beautiful". He loved it and studied it thoroughly, trying to discover behind the words the mentality of "his people".

This patriotic partiality was sometimes put to severe tests; but instead of dwelling on the dark side, he would point out whatever

was admirable in the strange practices. An instance took place a
few weeks after his arrival, in December 1606, when the body of
Muttu Krishnappa, Nāyak of Madurai, who had died a few days
before, was publicly burned, and certain of his wives showed themselves *sati*, or faithful, by being consumed with their lord and
master.

Suttee is a very ancient practice, but it has not always existed
in India, for there is no mention of it in the *Ṛg Veda*, oldest of
Indian texts. Even in later sacred books such as the *Atharva Veda*,
examples of widow-burning are exceptional. The *Rāmāyaṇa* is free
from suttee; the lawgiver Manu commends but does not command it.

No one knows how the practice originated. Diodorus Siculus
says suttee was adopted to deter wives from poisoning their lords.
But in the Punjab and Rājasthān sometimes a mother consumed
herself on her son's pyre. This, known as *mā-satī*, mother-suttee,
was considered the highest kind of self-immolation and received
special honour. More probably, then, suttee had arisen as a proof
of courage and loyalty in the caste of Rājās, who prided themselves on those virtues; to this caste and to the widows of kings it
was now almost exclusively confined. Since in the highest caste
widows were obliged to shave their hair, abstain from wearing
ornaments and participating in even the mildest amusements and
forbidden to remarry, suttee might well appear the lesser of two
evils. Its glory was endorsed by such texts as these:

"Accompanying her husband, she shall reside so long in Swarga
[paradise] as are the thirty-five millions of hairs on the human
body.

"As the snake-catcher forcibly drags the serpent from his earth,
so, bearing her husband (from hell), with him she shall enjoy
heavenly bliss.

"Dying with her husband, she sanctifies her maternal and
paternal ancestors; and the ancestry of him to whom she gave her
virginity."

A contemporary account describes the practice:

"We found a pit ten or twelve feet square, and about a man's
height deep, full of wood and burning charcoal, as hot as a burning

furnace. Thence we were conducted to the widow, in front of whom men were dancing and playing. She ate betel with a cheerful countenance, and we had a few words with her there, trying to dissuade her, but she answered that it would be a great disgrace if she did not accompany in the next world the man who had loved her so much. Then she rose and gave us betel, and went to the river, where she bathed, and put on a cloth dyed with saffron; she distributed her necklace, ear-rings, and arm-rings among her relations, came close to the pit, round which she walked once, speaking to each of her acquaintances, and then, raising her hands, jumped with a cheerful face into the fire. Immediately she was covered with some hurdles and large logs, which were ready for the purpose, and some pots of oil were thrown on the fire, so that she should be burnt more quickly. As soon as she jumped into the fire, the relations and others, both men and women, embraced each other, and raised a great outcry, which lasted for about a quarter of an hour. She looked to be about twenty-four years of age; she left a baby three months old."

Not once only, not twice, but all through a long day Nobili saw the rite of suttee enacted as no less than four hundred of the Nāyak's wives, holding a mirror in their right hand and a lemon in their left, chose to unite themselves with their lord Muttu, the Pearl, in flame and ash.

Every European who had ever witnessed suttee had thrown up his hands in horror. A "barbaric" custom, comparable to human sacrifice in Mexico, which heightened his own sense of superiority. In North India the Muslims had banned the practice: so too had the Portuguese in the territory of Goa. Suttee went to show how essential it was for Indian converts to turn their backs on India.

Four hundred women were consumed by fire; Nobili had only a month's knowledge of India proper. But he did not yield like everyone else to facile condemnation. He tried to wrench himself free from European categories of thought. He forced himself to see the rite within its context. What struck him was the courage of the women who showed their fidelity in such a heroic manner; theirs, he said, might be a mistaken ideal, but their courage in striving after it was none the less magnificent. Should he ever succeed in inspiring them with his own Christian ideal, they would show themselves, if the test came, heroic martyrs.

By giving this gage of tolerance, Nobili showed his willingness to enter Indian society. Nevertheless, he still stood outside. Since he could not prove by red-ochre clothes that he had become a sannyāsī, no one knew exactly what he was. Hence suspicions lingered, and the stigma of Parangi might be reapplied. To discover his position in Indian society, he must continue inquiring of the Indians.

They, too, were anxious to discover. They plied Nobili with questions, some very personal, perhaps indiscreet, but he would never draw himself up to reply proudly that there were questions a gentleman would not answer. He knew they were kindly meant and he answered them in the same spirit. Thus they came to know of the high social standing of his family in Rome—he doubtless had to specify that he was not one of the Turks of Constantinople, who throughout the East were known as Rumè. This, combined with his noble manner and unfailing courtesy, led them to the conclusion that he must belong to the caste of the Ksatriyas or Rājās. They explained to him what that meant.

In the Vedas the Rājā was the overlord of a confederation of clans, each of which had its own chief. The Sanskrit word was *rājan*—a petty king, cognate with *rex*. The office was hereditary, and its holder dependent on the advice of the clan council; he had no assigned revenue, but received a share of the booty gained in a successful foray. In later times his power increased: he occupied a central domain, provided with a fort, in which he lived with his family and dependants, and stored his goods and cattle. The traditional duty of a Rājā was protection: in wartime fighting, in peacetime governing.

There was no exact correspondence between the social structure of Italy and South India, but in so far as correspondence was possible, the nobles of Italy were the Rājās of India. Indeed, Italian nobles were as jealous of their position as any Indian caste. A Portuguese nobleman might stoop to trade, not an Italian: he would never devote himself to anything but government, arms or books.

Not every king was a Rājā: the Nāyak of Madurai, descendant of a general, was merely a Śūdra. Nor was every Rājā a king or a member of a royal family, but, his informants pointed out, Nobili could satisfy those purists who claimed that every true member of the Rājā caste must have royal blood in his veins, for his family was directly descended from a King—the Emperor Otho III.

Nobili, having considered the matter carefully, concluded that if he must have a caste, that of Rājā was the only one he could honestly accept, for it was the only one that corresponded to his social status in the world. And it had this advantage, that by accepting the name, he could still become a sannyāsī at a later date, should his Superiors give permission, for sannyāsīs were recruited from the three highest castes.

Early in 1607 Nobili proclaimed to the people of Madurai that they had been mistaken in thinking that he belonged to the Parangi caste. He did this by accepting the style of Rājā—and by organizing his house on strictly Indian lines. He could claim to be a Rājā only by behaving like one. Since the three highest castes were set apart from the rest of Indian society, he could not, for the moment, consort with the mass of the people. He could no longer speak to Paravas who might happen to visit Madurai. Every day he must be scrupulously careful to wash.

Particularly important as a sign of caste were the food a man ate and the way it was prepared. To eat flesh defiled a high-caste man in two ways. First it was a condonation of the taking of life; secondly, flesh (and even eggs) by becoming part of the man who ate them partially dragged him down to animal level: in direct opposition to the whole purpose of high-caste life, which was to combat the animal side of humanity.

But even vegetables and rice could be rendered impure if handled, or even seen, by a low-caste man. According to the generally-held corpuscular theory of vision the low-caste man being inferior, the matter or subtle substance proceeding from his eye and mixing with the objects he saw must necessarily be inferior and bad, so that the food, in virtue of these pernicious rays, would contaminate a man of high caste. Brahmins—men of the highest caste, who could not pollute—were therefore usually employed as servants in high-caste households.

Nobili, therefore, was obliged to engage a Brahmin cook and a Brahmin boy to serve his meals of rice and herbs on a plantain leaf. Italians were the daintiest eaters in Europe—they surprised English travellers by using both a knife and a fork. Nobili now had to unlearn these habits. Seated on the ground, he must take his rice with the tip of the fingers of his right hand (the left hand, used for impure purposes, was never used for eating), and carry it to his mouth in the approved Indian style. Gone were the days when he might sip sweet canary or the famous red wine from the Nobili estates at Montepulciano. Now he must drink water once only, when he had finished eating, pouring it into his mouth from a distance, so as not to sully the water-pot with his saliva, considered by Indians an extremely impure substance. After his meal, with his left hand he poured water out of the drinking vessel to wash his right hand clean. At first this way of life proved awkward, but soon he became used to it. He knew that he was being carefully watched and he, in his turn, was waiting to see the effect of his new manners.

To give Nobili's experiment a fair trial, Laerzio decided to send Fernandez for a time to the coast. A triple stigma attached to the old Portuguese, first as a self-confessed Parangi, secondly for living and working among the Paravas, whom their Hindu neighbours despised as "reeking with the stench of fish", and thirdly because competence to haggle about the price of saltpetre, horses and fish went, in Hindu opinion, with utter incompetence to deal with spiritual subjects.

The departure of Fernandez meant that Nobili was no longer associated in Indian minds with a polluting Parangi. He continued scrupulously to observe the rules of the Rājā caste. For a time nothing happened. Then men of the three highest castes—the best educated in Madurai—began to come and speak to Nobili: at first only one or two, at rare intervals, then in groups. Those who had formerly spat contemptuously as he passed or uttered a pious prayer to avert ill omen now came to see him in a friendly spirit. Though he was more dignified than his old colleague, he gave them the impression that he was nearer to them, that he was one of themselves. They began to address him deferentially as "Aiyer", the Master of the House. For the first time in almost two thousand years—since the day when another young Rājā, Alexander of Macedon, conquered, pardoned and restored to his throne a Hindu king—a European had succeeded in winning the respect of high-caste Indians.

5. Guru ana Sannyāsī

SOME of Nobili's visitors wore painted on their forehead a trident composed of three lines, one red and perpendicular, two white and oblique, meeting at the base. The trident proclaimed them Vaiṣṇavites. Like most Hindus they believed in the *Trimūrti* or three aspects of God: Brahmā the creator, Viṣṇu the preserver, and Śiva the transformer and destroyer, but declared Viṣṇu to be the chief of the three. They represented Viṣṇu as the Milky Ocean of Immortal Life, out of which the transient universe arises and back into which it again dissolves. But Viṣṇu was also the most human of the triad, and under the form of Kṛṣṇa had given to man the most tender and charitable of Indian scriptures: the *Bhagavad Gītā*.

Vijayanagar had been a great Vaiṣṇavite centre, and the Nāyaks of Madurai, originating in Vijayanagar, had brought their religion with them. After the fall of Vijayanagar to Muslim troops in 1565, the Nāyak's court and army had been flooded with more of the same sect. Vaiṣṇavas were known for their tolerance—they even admitted Paraiyans to their ranks—and the Nāyak made no attempt to impose Viṣṇu as the state god.

A second group of visitors wore three horizontal lines on their brow, the sect mark of Śaivism. They believed that the supreme god of the triad was Śiva, who destroyed even other gods and wears their skulls as his necklace, to symbolize the successive dissolution and regeneration of the races of mankind. Śiva also personifies nature's eternal reproductive power, and in this character is worshipped under the symbol of the lingam. He is a wild, jovial, wine-drinking hunter addicted to dancing and jollity. Yet he is also the great ascetic and self-mortifier, sitting naked, motionless, with ash-besmeared body, matted hair and beggar's bowl under a banyan tree.

59

Most people in Madurai were Śaivites: indeed the city was a centre of Śaivite pilgrimage, by virtue of its temple, dedicated to Śiva in his form Chockanātha or Sundara, "the beautiful", and to his wife Mināksī, "the fish-eyed". This temple, one of the largest and most beautiful in Southern India, was bounded by four high stone walls, enclosing a nearly rectangular space of about 830 by 730 feet, within which lay a labyrinth of store-houses, cloisters, galleries and shrines, a sacred tank and, in the centre, surrounded by other walls with gateways and towers, the inner shrines of Śiva and his goddess. The pyramidal *gopurams*, or gate-towers, 150 feet high, each a jungle of intricately carved statues, dominated every part of the city. Here and on the temple columns an attempt had been made to crowd infinity into finite forms, to express some of the multiple characteristics of Śiva. A favourite portrayal was with three eyes (insight into past, present and future) and eighteen arms (the divine omnipotence), poised on tiptoe, knees bent, dancing the universe in and out of existence.

Such was the god worshipped by most of Nobili's visitors, including his friend the school-teacher. About February 1607 Nobili had opened a course of religious instruction for those young men who had gathered round him and were eager to hear him. Naturally curious to know how his Tamil pupil was conducting his class, the school-teacher inquired from those who attended it, and when he heard the praises they bestowed on Nobili, he decided to attend the course also. It did not take him long to discover that his pupil was a past master in the art of teaching. What pleased him most was the elegance and the clearness of Nobili's exposition. But soon his attention was absorbed not so much by the language as by the doctrines.

The school-teacher was not altogether ignorant of Christianity, for Gonçalo Fernandez had given him to put into good Tamil a pamphlet on the Creed which he had written in his own imperfect and halting Tamil. The sketchy outline in that book had made no impression on one versed in Hindu theology. "I believe in God" —easy to say, but what is God? "Creator of heaven and earth"— but what is creation? "and life everlasting"—who knows anything about it?

Now, however, he heard Nobili explain some of these terms with eloquence and fervour, bent not only on convincing the mind but also on winning the heart. The school-teacher began to argue with Nobili, and seeing that reason was not always on his side, he began to show himself more humble and respectful. But he remained uncommitted.

Then came the solar eclipse of 25th February 1607. Eclipses were fairly accurately predicted in astrological almanacs, and aroused deep religious awe, for sun-worship, practised at the time of the composition of the Vedas, had not totally disappeared, and almost every Hindu sect venerated the sun as well as the moon, the seven planets observable by the naked eye, as well as Rāhu and Ketu, the ascending and descending nodes of the moon. As the moon's disc slowly obliterated the sun, the people of Madurai bathed (for bathing on this occasion purified a man from sin) and prayed aloud in the midday darkness.

Nobili met the school-teacher as he was returning from the ceremonial bath prescribed during eclipses, and they entered into a friendly talk which soon drifted from eclipses to religion. "We agreed", wrote Nobili to the General of the Society, "to go on studying our respective religions, and so we did during twenty days at the rate of four or five hours a day; and your Reverence must know that these people are not so ignorant as some men imagine."

The first doctrine about which Nobili argued with the school-teacher was the unity of God. Now in Tamil India there seems always to have been a belief that religion meant loving self-devotion to a single God; and in Nobili's day the Śaivites approached nearer to a thorough-going monotheism than any other Hindu sect. According to the *Canam*, one of their sacred poems, "The supreme being, whom we call Śiva, and others call Viṣṇu, is the only one we recognize as all-powerful; he is the principle of the five elements, of actions and movements which occasion life and time. . . . This God alone has created the universe by his productive power; he maintains all by his conservative power, and destroys all by his destructive power; so that it is he who is represented under the name of the three gods, Trimūrti."

Some such belief the school-teacher doubtless already held and on the very first day of their twenty-day course, Nobili, by arguments drawn from the perfection and absolute independence of the Divine nature, was able to convince him of the unity of God. The discussion then went on to the second article of the creed: "Creator of heaven and earth".

The school-teacher did not believe in creation out of nothing: there was no evidence in the world of nature to support such a theory. Instead, he believed in the existence from all eternity of (1) Pati, the Lord: Śiva himself, (2) Paśu, the flock: Śiva's flock—all the souls which, by his grace, he wills to conduct to blessedness, (3) Pāśam, the bond: that is, bodies: the aggregate of all those elements which bind souls, hindering them from finding release in union with God.

Nobili began by pointing out that whatever exists must owe its existence either to itself or to something else. "Your Paśu exists," he argued, "therefore its existence must depend either on God or on itself."

"Paśu does not depend for its existence on God—or on any other thing," replied the school-teacher.

"In other words," said Nobili, "your Paśu is God."

To this, reports Nobili, the school-teacher did not know what to answer. Perhaps he did not accept Nobili's premise that all existent things must necessarily be dependent; perhaps he agreed that Paśu is, in a sense, God, for he believed that the soul, freed of its bonds, actually becomes a Śiva, equal to the deity in power and knowledge, but still dependent on him rather than identical with him.

Seeing that the school-teacher was not satisfied, Nobili proved the same thing "with a more palpable and obvious argument drawn from divine omnipotence". If God could not create anything out of nothing, he would not be more powerful than nature which produced trees out of seeds, nor than water, which with heat and other accidents produces frogs and other imperfect animals, nor would he be more powerful than a carpenter who with pieces of wood makes a bench, and cannot do it without wood. Nobili added that for God to be omnipotent, it was necessary that his power should not be limited or defective. Now to be incapable of creating without Paśu, as the school-teacher said, was a defect and an imperfection; hence either God's power was not infinite or He did not require matter to create the world.

This line of argument was not totally new in Madurai. The Śaivite God had often come under attack, especially from the Brahmins, precisely because Paśu seemed to impose some such limitation. The school-teacher conceded the point and ended by accepting Nobili's conception of a Creator out of nothing.

On the second day Nobili found himself in difficulties, when the debate turned to transmigration. Transmigration had been considered a self-evident truth from very early times. Already, in one of the Vedic hymns, souls "return again [from the gods] to that ether, from ether to the air, from the air to rain, from rain to the earth. And when they have reached the earth, they become food, they are offered again in the altar-fire, which is man, and thence are born in the fire of woman. Thus they rise up towards the worlds, and go the same round as before."

The fully developed doctrine was found in the *Bhāgavata*: "The Supreme Being, before creating anything which now exists, began by creating souls, which at first animated bodies of fantastic shapes. During their union with these bodies they either committed sin or practised virtue. After a long abode in these provisional dwelling-places, they were withdrawn and summoned before the tribunal of Yama, who judges the dead. This divinity admitted into Swarga [paradise] those souls which had led virtuous lives; and he shut up in Naraka [hell] those souls which had given themselves up to sin. Souls which had been partly virtuous and partly sinful were sent to earth to animate other bodies, and so to endure proportionately the pain due for their sins and to receive the reward of their virtues. Thus every new birth, whether happy or unhappy, is the result of deeds practised in previous generations and is either the reward or punishment for them. We may thus judge by the condition of a person in an existing generation what he has been in the previous one. Nevertheless, those who die in holiness are no longer exposed to new births; they go straight to Swarga."

Transmigration had been generally accepted for so long that it received (and indeed could receive) no formal proof. But the following considerations were adduced: The self is eternal; it is also in fact known often to be embodied. It is inconceivable that this should be uncaused, for we realize the endless chain of cause and effect as in the series of seed and shoot; nor can there be a single cause, for the effects are various, and so must be their causes.

Evidence for previous embodiments was seen in the fact of instinct, as when a child sucks without being taught, and in memory of past births—a power which some holy men enjoy, and which exist in most men as impulses and potentialities lying hid beneath our normal selves, and explaining the infinite possibilities of our nature.

When the school-teacher explained this belief, which he shared with the vast majority of Hindus, Nobili recognized it as "Pythagoreanism" and called it by that name in his letters to Europe. Pythagoras had probably learned it in Egypt, a clearing-house of Oriental religious ideas; Plato too had held the doctrine in a modified form and from the neo-Platonists, in the second and third centuries, it had come close to being adopted by the Church. With the decline of neo-Platonism it had been a dead letter in Europe, and so Nobili was singularly ill-equipped to deal with it. The scholastic authors he had read in Naples and Rome rarely bothered to refute it, for the theory was incompatible with their premise that the soul is the form of the body, giving it its specific essence and able to be united only to that particular body. If the theory was broached in European textbooks, two arguments were considered adequate to refute it: why do we have no memory of a previous life? And if we have no such memory (as Aeneas of Gaza argued), how can there be punishment?

"The school-teacher's strongest argument," writes Nobili, "was the variety of the conditions of man, which, he claims, can only be explained by admitting merits or faults before the present life. He proved himself a subtle Platonist, maintaining that the soul was not the form of the body but rather like a bird in a cage, or a chicken in the eggshell. It was not difficult to prove to him how wrong that opinion was.

SARASVATĪ
A statue of the goddess of literature, music and the
fine arts in the Madurai temple

A statue in the Madurai temple

" 'The cage,' said I, 'does not grow while the bird is in it, but the body grows while it is united with the soul. The bird can beget other birds even when out of the cage, while the soul without the help of the body can beget no children.' The soul is not therefore in the body as the bird in a cage, and I explained it was there as the form and life of the body, and that the two combined to make one being which we call man."

Nobili went on to say that since the soul and body commit sins together, it was not just to punish the soul in a different body. Moreover, since sin had an infinite malice, it must be punished by an infinite penalty, lasting for ever. This condition would not be satisfied if the soul were to remain in the body of a dog, as Hindus claimed, for that would be the end of the punishment.

The difference, argued Nobili, between rich and poor, Brahmins and Paraiyans, happy and miserable, came from secondary causes whose action God is not obliged to suspend; that He wants thereby to show how contemptible are the glory, riches and joy of this world in comparison with those that He reserves for us in the next, and which we deserve by the good use of gifts and patience in evil.

"I added", concludes Nobili, "that in every well-regulated society some form of subordination was necessary: if everyone were a king, they would be phantoms of kings without subjects, generals without troops; in the human body, if all the limbs were heads, the result would be monstrous. Finally I concluded with an argument *ad hominem*: 'You say that God drew the first Brahmin from his head, the first Rājā from his shoulders, the first Paraiyan from his feet, and so on. Now the first Brahmin, Rājā and Paraiyan could not possess any merit or fault before being produced: therefore the doctrine of karma, or deeds, is not universally applicable. Here I borrowed from St Paul the comparison of the pot of clay in the hands of the potter: just as one pot is used on a king's table, and another for washing feet, so by an eternal decree of the will of God, one man is made a king, another a trader, and no one can explain why they are given that particular status and not another."

"No one can explain": in place of transmigration Nobili could offer only a mystery. But at the end of six hours the school-teacher accepted the mystery.

This was the first religious debate between a European and a Hindu to be conducted on terms unfavourable to the European. Nobili lived now alone, unprotected by the Portuguese, in the heart of South India. He was at a disadvantage in having to speak a language whose theological terms were unfamiliar, weak from lack of food and living day after day shut up in a windowless room. He had nothing to offer in the way of Portuguese guns or horses, exemption from taxes or an official sinecure. He had nothing to offer but what he believed to be the truth.

At the end of twenty days the debate ended—the debate in microcosm for the soul of India. "Liberation from the miseries of life and the round of reincarnation"—like most Indians, that is what the school-teacher sought. Now he had found a religion which taught that miseries were merely a privation and put an end to reincarnation not with a technique of Yoga but with the single statement that man is a unique compound of one body and one soul. He declared himself satisfied on all points and asked to be allowed to join the sect which professed "the true religion".

Aware, doubtless, that he was baptizing the first convert in the interior of the peninsula since its discovery more than a century before, and aware too of the tens of millions still waiting, Nobili solemnly poured the salted holy water over the school-teacher who had taught him all he knew about India and who had ended by being his pupil. He gave him the name of Albert—no doubt as a compliment to Laerzio.

Albert's example was soon followed by a young man, Alexis Nāyak who, it was hoped, would be instrumental in converting his mother and brother. Then came the turn of Ignatius Nāyak and Eustace Nāyak, and Albert's brother, who was given the name of Francis. No doubt some of these first conversions were brought about less by Nobili's arguments, for he was still a beginner in Indian philosophy, than, under God, by his extraordinary personal attraction. They had heard him speak, they loved him, and because they loved him wanted to be like him. And the way to be like him was to become a Christian.

Since coming to India Nobili had been known successively as

Paulist, Parangi, Rājā and Aiyer. With his first converts he now received a new title—that of guru. Guru means both spiritual teacher—one who imparts knowledge—and spiritual master—one whose life is a model. Indians prefer a highly unequal relationship between master and pupil, priest and flock; so that by accepting Nobili's teaching, Albert and Alexis and the rest looked upon themselves as disciples of Nobili.

If the disciple humbled himself, it was because he expected much of his guru. Ideals varied according to caste and sect, each of which had their own gurus, and the new converts from Śaivism doubtless adapted the following description to the new doctrines and exigencies taught by Nobili. "A true guru", according to the Śaivite *Vedānta Sāra*, "is a man who is in the habit of practising all the virtues; who with the sword of wisdom has lopped off all the branches and torn out all the roots of sin, and who has dispersed, with the light of reason, the thick shadows in which sin is shrouded; who, though seated on a mountain of sins, yet confronts their attacks with a heart as hard as a diamond; who behaves with dignity and independence; who has the feelings of a father for all his disciples; who makes no difference in his conduct between his friends and his enemies, but shows equal kindness to both; who looks on gold and precious stones with the same indifference as on pieces of iron or potsherd, and values the one as highly as the other; whose chief care is to enlighten the ignorance in which the rest of mankind if plunged. He is a man who performs all the acts of worship of which Śiva is the object, omitting none; who knows no other god than Śiva, and reads no other history than his; who shines like the sun in the midst of the dark clouds of ignorance which surround him"; he is a man who has made pilgrimages to all the sacred places, Rameśvaram, Śrīrangam, Sringeri, Gokernam, Kalahasti and other spots consecrated to Śiva, performed his ablutions in all the sacred rivers, bathed in all the sacred springs and tanks, left his footprints in all the sacred deserts and woods. He must be acquainted with all the observances for penance, perfectly versed in the Vedānta, astrology, medicine and poetry. "This is the character of a true guru; these are the qualities which he ought to possess, that he may be in a position to show others the path of virtue, and help them out of the slough of vice."

Now no man could have two gurus. By taking Nobili as his new master, Albert had to reject the authority of his former guru, a pandaram sannidhi; that is, a non-Brahmin Śaivite spiritual leader. This famous pandaram, Dakṣṇamurti by name, a kinsman of Albert's, returning from a visit to his disciples, learned with horror that his relative had become as they put it, a Parangi. He went about complaining so bitterly of what he called Albert's meanness and treason that Nobili began to fear lest the man, who was very influential and had a large following, should appeal to the Nāyak or stir up a riot. As he was wondering how he could avert such a blow, the pandaram himself came to seek an explanation.

Such men wore reddish-yellow dress, a long necklace of nutmeg-like seeds, and carried a bronze gong and a large conch, which they sounded when begging alms. Nobili's visitor was more richly dressed than most, in red silk and jewellery. He was received with such courtesy and treated with such rare consideration that he at once dismissed the idea that Albert's new guru could be a Parangi. A long discussion followed, at the end of which the pandaram was convinced that this new guru was the most distinguished and scholarly master he had ever met. As he left the house, seeing that some of his disciples reproached Albert for disgracing his family by having become a Parangi, he silenced them with these words: "I have inquired into that case and I declare that Albert has adopted an excellent religion." Then, taking his kinsman aside, "You have done well," he said. "Don't be afraid, I will stand by you and help your guru to spread his doctrine. I must speak to him again and settle what is to be done."

The pandaram sannidhi did in fact become a frequent visitor and on each visit he urged Nobili to remove his black cassock, and adopt the costume in use among the gurus who professed to teach religion. Since Indians distinguished with difficulty voluntary from involuntary poverty, many gurus surrounded themselves with all the exterior pomp of wealth. Far from being scandalized, Indians were most ready to praise and admire the privations which they imposed on themselves, though they had all the money necessary to enjoy life. Some rode on an elephant or in a palanquin; others had an escort of cavalry; and when they travelled incense and perfumes were burned in their honour.

When the pandaram suggested that Nobili should wear red silk and ornaments, Nobili objected that that was incompatible with religious humility. "Do you suggest," he said, "that I should take back willingly what I have rejected with scorn?"

With a smile the pandaram replied, "If it is only a question of your own salvation, retire to the desert where you can live stripped of everything. But if, as you claim, you really have the salvation of the Indians at heart, you must—in order to preach the truth—add to, rather than subtract from, the trappings of which I spoke to you. The spiritual man is a corpse: all things are equal to him: silk and the coarsest cloth, riches and poverty, honour and shame."

As days went by, Nobili became increasingly aware that his black cassock and leather shoes were compromising his work. Those who lived in his immediate surroundings and knew him intimately could overlook them, being perfectly aware of his orthodox habits; but for the majority they remained the badge of the hated Parangis, and caused him to be shunned. So he wrote again to Alberto Laerzio asking permission to put on Indian dress —not the red silk of a powerful guru but the red-ochre cloth of the sannyāsī—and among the arguments he gave in favour of the innovation, he did not forget the pandaram's advice.

Laerzio again put the request before his consultors, this time with a new argument drawn from another mission field.

In 1583 Matteo Ricci, an Italian Jesuit, had entered China with a companion, both proclaiming their priesthood by dressing as Buddhist bonzes in ash-coloured coarse cloth, heads and faces shaven. For eleven years Ricci failed to make much progress, because Buddhist bonzes at that time had a very low reputation. As a bonze, he could not associate freely with mandarins, the best educated men of China and his most likely converts. To do so, he would have to change his status in Chinese society and the dress which proclaimed that status: his ash-coloured rags for the plum-coloured silk and tall black hat of a mandarin.

One good precedent could be invoked for the change Ricci

desired: Francis Xavier, on his first journey in Japan, travelled very simply in a black cassock, but finding that the Japanese despised him for his poverty and foreign appearance, on his second journey he wore the silk clothes of a Japanese sage.

In 1594 Ricci was finally given permission to adopt mandarin dress and habits, which included growing long hair and travelling in a palanquin. Since then a dozen other missionaries had adopted plum-coloured silk. Taking these facts into account, the consultors now approved Nobili's request.

Despite the precedent invoked, Nobili's change and the motive behind it were as different from Ricci's as the values of the two countries. In China the most respected men were state officials, trained in the humanities, elegant, worldly-wise, bent on enjoying life, whereas the Indian élite were the Brahmins, trained in theology, often poor, disdainful of mundane pleasures. To associate with mandarins, Ricci had to attend luxurious dinners and plays, to exchange fans inscribed with polite verses, to visit palaces and converse with members of the Government. But to win the respect of Indians, Nobili would be obliged, on the contrary, to adopt an even stricter life than formerly: to give up all amusements, to eat only one meal a day, to fast and do penance on the Indian scale; he would have, above all, to lead a hidden lonely life.

The consultors' approval reached Nobili in November 1607, a year after his arrival in Madurai. At once he discarded his black cassock and leather shoes. He had his hair shaved close to the skull and, since Indians considered a bare brow naked and indecent, he made a rectangular mark on his forehead with sandal. This, known as the mark of science or learning, could be worn by any well-educated man, especially by one proficient in philosophy. His body he draped in three pieces of red-ochre cloth, two round his shoulders, the third round his loins and extending below the knees. Sannyāsīs usually wore only a scanty loin-cloth, but Nobili modified the fashion for his own dress. On his feet he clamped high wooden sandals. Though the light red-ochre cloths proved more comfortable in hot weather than his black cassock, the sandals were meant to be awkward and penitential. He obtained a water-gourd to carry in his left hand when he went out, and a bamboo stick with seven knots to carry in his right hand. In Indian eyes Nobili was now what he claimed to be, an ascetic, his life devoted to serving God: a beggar clothed in the sunrise.

But aware of difficulties ahead, remembering how, during his early days as a Jesuit, he had found a scanty diet so injurious to his health that his superiors had dispensed him, one Lent, from all fasting, Nobili bound himself by a solemn vow to continue as a sannyāsī for the rest of his life.

6. Discovering the Vedas

SHORTLY after Nobili's change of dress, Gonçalo Fernandez returned to Madurai. He was deeply shocked by what he saw, not least by Nobili's converts, who repudiated the Parangi name. For Fernandez, Parangi meant Portuguese. He himself had served under the seven fortresses of the Portuguese flag and was doubtless justifiably proud that Portugal had emerged as a Christian nation *par excellence* through five centuries of battle with the infidel. What Nobili was doing must have seemed very much like surrender. As for his red-ochre clothes, his wooden clogs, his frequent washing: these were even more disquieting to one who believed that Indian beliefs and practices were a tangle of superstitions, aberrations from the light. The old man dashed off a letter of indignant protest to Laerzio.

There was nothing unusual in Fernandez's attitude. It was shared not only by his fellow-Portuguese but also, for instance, by the English. Ralph Fitch, who visited India from 1583 to 1591, has this to say: "Here in Patenana I saw a dissembling prophet which sate upon an horse in the market place, and made as though he slept, and many of the people came and touched his feete with their hands, and then kissed their hands. They tooke him for a great man, but sure he was a lasie lubber. I left him there sleeping. The people of these countries be much given to such prating and dissembling hypocrites." And thirty years later Thomas Coryat addressed an Indian Muslim in these terms: "Yea, I wold have thee know (thou Mahometan) that in that renouned kingdome of England where I was borne, learning doth so flourish that there are many thousand boies of sixteene yeeres of age what are able to make a more learned booke than thy Alcaron."

No, it was Nobili's attitude which, in that country, was considered eccentric, and he did his best to explain it to Fernandez. But in vain did he try to reconcile the old man to his reforms and induce him to adopt a vegetarian diet. For a few weeks the ill-assorted couple carried on, taking their meals separately. While Fernandez sat at his table eating meat with knife and fork, his assistant sat on the floor in the corner of the house before a plantain leaf on which his Brahmin cook, bare to the waist, ladled out rice and curry. Evidently this could not go on. With Laerzio's permission Nobili began to look for another house where he could lead in peace the life of a true sannyāsī.

It happened that among his Hindu friends was a young Āndhra —a Telugu-speaking northerner—by name Errama Setti, whose brother Nagaya was one of the chief poligars or Lords of Madurai. The whole country was divided into seventy-two palaiyams or baronies among these poligars. As long as they paid their tribute, which consisted of a third of their income, and spent another third on the maintenance of a military contingent to serve the Nāyak in time of war, they might use the rest as they pleased, and administer their territories as they thought fit. Apart from the government of his palaiyam, each poligar was responsible for the defence of one of the seventy-two bastions which guarded the ramparts of the capital, and for the administration of a ward within its walls called the "town palaiyam".

When Nagaya Setti Nāyak was told by his brother that a sannyāsī, from a remote country, had come to Madurai and needed a quiet place where he could lead a penitential life, he agreed to help, for this was a recognized way of sharing in a holy man's merits. In his town palaiyam of Chinaxauta there happened to be a vacant plot, well situated on one of the main streets. This he readily offered. In the centre of the plot stood a dilapidated cabin, which could easily be repaired and used as a temporary hermitage or āśram, as the abode of an ascetic was called.

The hut stood near and slightly to the north-east of the temple of Śiva. Nobili found it suitable; secluded enough to be peaceful, yet central enough to make it easy for visitors to call on him. He thanked the poligar for his kind offer and, at the end of November 1607, after saying good-bye to Gonçalo Fernandez, moved from the Portuguese-style mission house, with tiled roof, to the little hermitage.

A few days later he wrote to his friend Cardinal Bellarmine:

"I am now living in a cabin with earthen walls and a thatched roof, which is more useful to me and makes me happier than if it were a rich palace. It is certain—and your Eminence may say it to anyone you please—that in this world there is no consolation to be compared with the one which the Lord gives me in this holy, voluntary and most pleasant exile, working and suffering for His love. It is quite true that I suffer and at times I wonder whether I shall be able to continue very long in this life of hardships, without ever taking any rest.

"But when I look up to Heaven and remember what your Eminence used to tell us when explaining the words of David: '*Qui posuit fines tuos pacem*' [Who hath placed peace in thy borders], I feel happy and comforted, for I realize that if such a rest is in store for us in heaven it is not reasonable to wish to enjoy it on earth.

"The way of life which necessity has compelled me to adopt is this: I always remain confined to my little cabin. After rising and saying Mass and commending myself to the Lord, I admit anyone who wishes to come to talk or discuss with me. The rest of the time, which is very short, I devote to writing refutations of some of the chief doctrines of these people, in their own language, which is very beautiful, copious and most elegant. As I never stir from my house and the nourishment I take is not very substantial, I am always ill, and rare are the days when I do not feel some pain in the stomach or in the head. My food consists of a little rice— abundant in this country—with some herbs and fruit; neither meat nor eggs ever cross my threshold. It is necessary to observe all this, for if these people did not see me do such penance, they would not receive me as one who can teach them the way to heaven, because that is the way of life their own teachers observe. Some of them lead an even more austere life, abstaining even from rice, which means a good deal, for your Eminence must know that here we use neither bread nor wine, except at the Holy Sacrifice, so that if we do away with rice you may imagine what remains.

"As for me I do not venture to go so far, because my abstinence from meat, fish and eggs is enough to persuade these people to receive me as their master. I hope from the Divine Mercy that, without considering my sins, He will deign to make use of this clumsy instrument, for I know that the more worthless and incapable I am (and so I am, indeed) the greater will be God's glory."

As the fame of the Rājā sannyāsī spread, more inquirers began to break in on his solitude, some merely idle and casual. "As I do not want to waste my time," Nobili wrote to the General, "I have told them clearly that, except for questions and arguments which regard the soul, I do not wish to treat of any other philosophical subject. This has proved very useful to me, for these people, being very curious, are now asking only such questions as I desire—that is, about religion."

As many inquirers told him that if they had the Nāyak's permission they would become his disciples, he thought of asking that permission. "I shall go and visit the Nāyak as soon as I can offer him some presents which Fr Provincial will not fail to send me, and if by God's grace he receives me well, even if he does not give me clear permission to make Christians, that will be enough for the moment. May Our Lord in Whose hand are the hearts of kings touch this Nāyak so that he may not oppose the true Faith."

To be admitted to the Nāyak's palace, with its guard of elephants, was by no means impossible. A visiting Jesuit had been invited ten years before, and as a mark of favour presented with the royal turban. He reported that a Brahmin stood close by the Nāyak, continually repeating the name of his god: "Rannāthan" (a form of Viṣṇu). When one Brahmin was tired, another took his place, so that the Nāyak never lacked this reminder, even if he sat five or six hours at his tribunal of justice.

Nor was the difficulty primarily one of religion. The Nāyak, despite his snub to Fernandez, did not really object to a new religion being preached in Madurai; what he could not tolerate was that the preachers of this religion should turn his people, particularly those of high castes, into Parangis and so cause an erosion of all that was noble in his kingdom. Furthermore, once Parangis, the Portuguese might well insist on taxing them, and the

Madurai treasury would suffer. The case of the Paravas remained in dispute and the Nāyak was still imposing a ban on their pearl-fishing.

Now in principle Nobili was in perfect agreement on this and other points with the Nāyak. He would, on no account, rob his subjects of their culture, their good name and traditions; he only sought to enrich them with a new faith. If he could convince the king that his teaching, far from tampering with the loyalty of his people, would strengthen it with supernatural motives, the Nāyak would surely give it his approval. But taxation and the limits of Portuguese jurisdiction were exceedingly far-reaching questions, interwoven with passion and prejudice; Nobili may have thought it prudent not to antagonize the Portuguese any further at present.

A still more important reason for delaying his visit to the Nāyak was this. In 1607 a new Jesuit mission was on its way to the Nāyak's overlord, the Emperor Venkata, whose court, now that Vijayanagar lay in ruins, was installed at Chandragiri. One of the objects of this mission was to obtain official approval by Venkata's vassals—the Nāyaks—of Christian missions, present and future, in their territories.

The history of the Chandragiri mission brings out by contrast the originality of Nobili's approach. Missionaries had first arrived at the Emperor Venkata's court in 1598. Venkata received the Jesuits well and promised them an annual income of a thousand pagodas[1] for the construction and upkeep of a church. During their first audience, the Emperor asked them about the King of Portugal. The missionaries happened to have several small pictures of Dom Sebastião and his predecessors. These they showed to Venkata, who was very much struck by them and asked whether there was a good painter at their residence in San Thomé. The missionaries were prepared for Venkata's interest: it was well known that he patronized literature and the arts. They answered Yes, and showed a painting done at San Thomé representing Dives and Lazarus. The Emperor liked it.

In 1600 the artist who had painted the Dives and Lazarus, an English lay-brother by the name of Alexander Frey, arrived at

[1] £1,050.

court. Brother Alexander offered the Emperor a choice of subjects and painted those which specially interested him, including the Adoration of the Magi and the Descent of Christ into Hell. The Englishman became a great favourite of the Emperor, who spoke to him quite informally. One day, while the Emperor was watching, Brother Alexander happened to say that he could not always procure the colours necessary for his work. At once the Emperor left the studio, went to his apartment, and returned with a hundred gold pieces, which he gave to Brother Alexander for paints.

Brother Alexander Frey spent two years at Venkaṭa's court, and his canvases were largely responsible for interesting the Emperor in Christianity. Though a fervent devotee of Viṣṇu, Venkaṭa had so far shown himself an eclectic in religion. Almost every day he held disputations in Sanskrit with his Brahmins about God, philosophy and mathematics, and he liked to speak to the Jesuits on these subjects.

Jesuit hopes of converting Venkaṭa were set back for a time in 1606, when the Portuguese at San Thomé rioted against Indian soldiers of the governor. Venkaṭa was furious at this challenge to his vassal and asked the Jesuits to withdraw. But peace had recently been restored at San Thomé and now the Jesuits were back, this time with a young Italian painter named Bartolomeo Fontebona. The embassy worked with a new sense of urgency. The Dutch were seeking permission to set up factories along the coast in Venkaṭa's territory and so break the Portuguese trade monopoly. Venkaṭa, the Junta at Goa decided, must somehow or other be persuaded to withhold this permission. Indeed, there was only one certain way of guaranteeing Portuguese interests in South India—by converting Venkaṭa to Christianity.

Nobili must have known of these moves at the court of the Nāyak's overlord and he deemed it prudent to postpone his visit. But the Nāyak heard of Nobili and invited him two or three times to the palace, saying that he would be glad to speak with him. He wondered why the stranger did not accept his invitation, and was told that the new sannyāsī was so chaste that he never left his hermitage, lest his pure eyes should fall on a woman.

That hermitage, with the growing numbers of inquirers, soon

began to prove too small. In December 1607 Nobili laid the
foundations of a real house with several rooms to accommodate
visitors, and a little chapel where he could say Mass. He thought
these buildings would be finished in a few weeks, but in fact he
was unable to occupy them before May 1608. They were temporary structures with walls of clay and roofs of palm leaves; the
floors, like those of all high-caste South Indian houses, had to be
made of lime plaster, stone or earth, because these materials were
non-conductors of pollution. For the same reason no carpets
could be spread; instead, the floor was plastered every week with
a mixture of cow-dung and water. The old dilapidated hermitage
which he called his *"retiro"* Nobili preserved as a souvenir.

During 1607 and 1608 Fernandez, with his tiled house, his
school and dispensary, but still without any converts, continued to
act as semi-official representative of the Portuguese authorities at
Madurai. A Portuguese ship had recently been wrecked off
Tuticorin. Jesuits from the college had waded in to help with the
rescue work; the Rector had spent seven nights without sleep
guarding what was salvaged. But there remained a number of
chests, full of valuables, at the bottom of the sea. These some
expert Parava divers undertook to recover, on condition that they
were given a fourth part of the salvage as a reward.

The salvaged goods, worth thousands of pounds, aroused the
interest of the Nāyak of Madurai who, as overlord of the Fishery
Coast, claimed his share in the wreckage. Fernandez, therefore,
was constantly on the move between Madurai and Tuticorin, trying to settle the affair to everybody's satisfaction. His work was
complicated by the fact that the Portuguese authorities, when
they saw how quickly the divers did their job, requested the
Jesuits in charge of the Paravas mission to intervene and obtain a
rebate. Laerzio, unwilling to deprive his flock of their well-
earned reward, refused to interfere, but the Portuguese Jesuits at
Goa sided with the authorities. One of them, a theological expert
but obviously not a diver, declared that it would have been quite
enough to pay three per cent. Long negotiations followed until
finally the owners of the ship resigned their claims into the hands
of Archbishop de Menezes, then acting Viceroy. Menezes asked

Laerzio to persuade the Christians to give up, out of the profit they had made on the wreck, 10,000 cruzados[1] towards the state funds. Laerzio succeeded in this unpleasant negotiation and a document signed by Menezes was delivered to the Paravas exonerating them from all further obligation regarding the salvage.

On his visits to the Coast, Fernandez did not speak only of the wreck. He had also much to say about his former curate's experiments, which he found extremely dangerous. It was no small comfort to him that the Jesuits on the Coast, who lived in European style and never entered the hinterland, agreed with him that Nobili's method was scandalous. They too thought that it was time the Provincial put a stop to it.

Laerzio, knowing that Fernandez was given to exaggeration, had not so far paid much attention to his letters, but when his complaints came supported by experienced missionaries of the Fishery Coast, he began to fear that Nobili had gone too far, and he became alarmed. He wrote to Nobili not to admit any more Indians to baptism until he had clarified certain doubts regarding his way of dressing, taking his meals, etc., which he intended doing on the occasion of his next periodic visit to Madurai.

Laerzio arrived at the end of August 1608 and spent nearly a month in Madurai. He wished not only to set his conscience at rest but also to be in a position to refute the complaints he had heard about Nobili with well-authenticated facts. Instead of living European-style at Fernandez's mission-house, and making do with second-hand information, he went straight to the hermitage. There he donned a red-ochre gown and shawl like Nobili's, shared his meals and behaved in all things as if he had been his disciple. Later he summed up his impressions in a report to the General at Rome.

"*The dress of Father Robert* consists of a long gown of a pale yellow colour reaching down to his feet; over it he wears a rochet of fine linen of the same colour as the gown. On the rochet, and thrown over the shoulders, he wears a cloth either red or pale yellow. As for his head-dress it consists of a cloth of fine white

[1] £3,750.

linen which he wraps round his head, so as to give it the shape
of a round biretta.

"Since the Brahmins, who are the teachers of these people,
wear round their neck, as a badge of their status, a *thread* made of
three strands, Father Robert, to assert his position as a teacher
of the Christian law, also wears a thread in the same manner.
However, it consists not of three, but of five strands. Of these,
three are of gold, and symbolize the Holy Trinity, while the two
white ones represent the Soul and Body of Christ Our Lord. To
this thread he attached a cross which represents the Passion and
Death of Jesus Christ. So his thread is a symbol of the mysteries of
the Holy Trinity, Incarnation and Redemption."

It was Archbishop Ros who, after consulting the Archbishop
of Goa and the Inquisitors, had given Nobili permission to wear
the thread. This was slipped over the left shoulder on the bare
skin so as to reach the right hip where the knot joining its two
extremities was tucked in under the loincloth.

Nobili made a mistake by putting on the thread, for most
sannyāsīs discard it as a sign that they have renounced all worldly
things. Modification of the thread, though ingenious and pious,
was none the less another mistake, for it changed the nature of the
thread, which must be of plain cotton. And when Nobili further
tampered with it, by putting it round the neck to suspend from it
a crucifix, it practically lost its significance as a caste emblem. As
yet, however, no one noticed this, for Nobili used to cover his
torso with a cloth called *aṅga vastram*, so that the thread could
hardly be seen.

"His *house*", continues Laerzio, "is in a street where only the
high castes may dwell, and to obtain greater credit he does not go
out of his house; nor does he allow people to see him at any time
they please. It is only when visitors have called two or three times
and begged his interpreter to let them speak to the Aiyer that he
allows them to be introduced, and have speech with him. (Aiyer,
which means 'Signore' is the name they give him.)

"The visitors find him sitting on a raised platform, covered
with a red or yellowish colour, in front of which is spread a mat of
fine straw. All—even the noblest and highest personages of the

court—bow to him, raising their joined hands to the forehead, then lowering them in a profound inclination, to indicate that they desire to be his disciples. After repeating this ceremony three times, they prostrate themselves on the ground and, rising up, remain standing in front of him.

"The Father speaks the purest Tamil and pronounces it so well that even the most fastidious Brahmin scholars cannot improve on his diction. He has already read many books, and learned by heart the essential passages of their laws as well as many verses of their most famous poets, who are held among them in great honour. Many are the hymns he has learned by heart, and he sings them with such perfection and grace that all listen to him with pleasure and unconcealed admiration."

Laerzio came to know some of Nobili's friends and studied closely his methods of conversion. At the end of his month's stay he was entirely satisfied. "I was so pleased", he wrote to the General, "with Father Robert's way of dealing with those gentiles, that I thought I had good reasons to encourage his fruitful work among them, and therefore I gave him full permission to preach openly and baptize all those who were called by God, without any fear of what might happen, for I felt that God has chosen him for that enterprise and that we must rely on His Divine help and protection."

Nobili doubtless heard his superior's decision with deep relief, for it meant not only that he could continue his present mission among educated Indians but also that he could embark on an entirely new and much more ambitious course: nothing less than an apostolate among the Brahmins.

Ever since his arrival in Madurai he had been struck by the extraordinarily privileged and respected status of the Brahmins. It was easy to recognize one in the street by his swagger and the freedom of his behaviour, to which superiority of birth, rank and education gave him a right. A Hindu of lower caste would greet him by joining both hands, touching the forehead, then putting the hands above the head and saying, "*Saranam, ayya*", "Respectful greeting, my lord". Talking to the man, the Brahmin would stand with his hands behind his back—the attitude of contempt.

His language was concise and elegant, enriched with many Sanskrit words, interspersed with proverbs and allegories, lengthened with endless polite and flattering terms.

The Brahmin ate no meat—neither beef nor the flesh of game-bird or horse—no fish and no eggs. He also rejected any vegetable whose root or stem grew in the shape of a head, such as onions, garlic, and mushrooms. His dress was not peculiar except for the thin white thread of three strands, hung from the left shoulder and falling on to the right hip—a distinction shared with the castes of Rājā and Vaiśya. He might often be poorly dressed in rags, for Brahmins were not the richest section of the community and, by virtue of their meagre diet, certainly not the strongest. They held their position by reason of their caste (of which the thread was the outward sign) and that caste religion and tradition had sanctioned as incomparably the highest.

According to the Laws of Manu, the Brahmins had been appointed by the Brahman-divinity lords over all that the world contains. The word Brahman appears to be derived from the root b—r—h, to be strong, and originally was equivalent to "sacred power". The caste of Brahmins were then, as their name proved, men united to this Power. From this premise, it followed that they were to be venerated as godlike beings. A Brahmin boy of ten must be respected as if he were the father of a hundred-year-old member of the Rājā caste. The murder of a Brahmin was the most heinous of crimes: the murderer must expiate it with death and would be born again as a savage beast. Anyone who seized a Brahmin by the hair was to have his hands cut off; anyone stealing a cow from a Brahmin was to have one foot mutilated.

On the other hand, if a Brahmin committed every kind of crime he could not be condemned to death, only to banishment. The killing of a Śūdra by a Brahmin was equivalent merely to the killing of a cat, a mongoose, a blue jay, a frog, a lizard, an owl or a crow.

To serve a Brahmin learned in the Vedas was the highest duty of a Śūdra. If he served well and humbly he might be reborn in a higher caste. He was obliged to give alms to any Brahmin who entered his house and demanded them. If he died without natural heirs, his property went to the Brahmins.

In return, the Brahmins were expected to be without avarice, arrogance or guile, to be hospitable and kind. Above all they must keep themselves from bodily and spiritual defilement, for in their "cleanliness" resided their ascendancy over other castes. An ignorant Brahmin was castigated as a useless creature, comparable to an elephant carved out of wood.

As was fitting to men learned in the Vedas and guardians of tradition, the life of a Brahmin was hedged with complicated ritual and prayers deriving from the Vedas. This started even before birth. During the *Pumsavanam*, a male-producing ceremony, in the seventh month of the first pregnancy the pregnant woman fasted, and her husband squeezed into her right nostril a little juice from the fruit and twig of the Bengal fig, saying "Thou art a male child". The twig had to be one pointing east or north, with two fruits. Later it was placed on a grinding-stone and a girl, who had not attained puberty, was asked to pound it. The pulp was then wrapped in a new silken cloth and squeezed to express the juice.

In the ninth month of pregnancy took place the *Sīmantam*, or parting the future mother's hair. After oblation to the sacred fire, the husband took a porcupine quill, to which three blades of dharba grass and a twig with fruits of the aththi tree were attached, and passed the quill over the woman's head from in front backwards, parting the hair.

When the child was born, if a boy its tongue was smeared with ghee and honey, to the accompaniment of verses from the *Ṛg Veda*: "O long-lived one, may you live a hundred years in this world, protected by the gods. Become firm as a rock, firm as an axe, pure as gold. You are the Veda called a son; live a hundred years. May Indra bestow on you his best treasures. May Savitṛ, may Sarasvatī, may the Aśvins grant you wisdom."

As he grew up, a naming ceremony, a food-giving ceremony, a tonsure ceremony and a ceremony of initiation into the art of writing were performed. But the boy was not yet a member of his caste—he was referred to jokingly as a low-caste fellow, a Śūdra— and could not take part in ceremonies requiring the repetition of Sanskrit formulae. Though he learned to obey rules of cleanliness, he could yet be ritually polluted by a death or birth in his lineage or by the touch of low-caste men. If he died, no pollution would be observed for him, the bones of the cremation would not be collected nor offerings made to his spirit.

In addition to ceremonies marking stages of growth, Brahmins observed precisely defined daily rites. They got up at the time called Brāhma Muhūrtam in the hour and a half before sunrise. After cleaning their teeth with a mango leaf or acacia twig, they had to bathe in a river or tank, standing knee-deep in the water, saying: "I am about to perform the morning ablution in this sacred stream, in the presence of the gods and Brahmins, in order to remove guilt resulting from act, speech and thought, from what has been touched and untouched, known and unknown, eaten and not eaten, drunk and not drunk." After the bath the Brahmin had to wipe his body with a damp cloth and put on his cotton madi cloth, which had been washed and dried. If the cloth had been touched by anyone, it was polluted and a silk cloth, which cannot be polluted, put on instead. The madi or silk cloth had to be worn until the close of the morning ceremonies and meal.

Then followed a service of prayer, which involved touching twelve parts of the body in a certain order, holding the breath by three distinct methods, drinking water and saluting the sun. Meals, visits, worship—each event of the day was governed by rigid rules and accompanied by symbolic ritual.

So elaborate a ceremonial and an outward manner of disdain had antagonized Europeans, who believed the Brahmins were the proudest and most superstitious of all Hindus. According to Francis Xavier: "They are the most perverse people in the world, and of them was written the psalmist's prayer: *De gente non sancta, ab homine iniquo et doloso erue me.* They do not know what it is to tell the truth but for ever plot how to lie subtly and deceive their poor ignorant followers ... Were it not for these Brahmins all the heathen would be converted."

In Goa force had been used to stamp out Brahmin ceremonial. "As the Fathers had heard from their neophytes that the pagans were going to hold a feast called *Ganessa Vinacociti* and *Vinaico*[1],

---

[1] Probably Vināyaka, like Gaṇeśa, one of the numerous names of Vighnesvara, the god of obstacles.

so called from the names of the idols, they went suddenly and discovered an idol in the house of a Brahmin. All who were present were punished, the Brahmin being sentenced to hard labour for life and, at the command of His Highness [the Viceroy], all his property confiscated. The same night we went to the house of a Brahmin and discovered there people engaged in idolatrous worship, which we stopped, and took away three idols called *Salgramma*.[1] The Brahmins had fled and could not be detected. Orders were issued to arrest them. Their idols were painted on leaves with motley-coloured eyes and fastened with threads."

As with suttee, towards the Brahmins a tradition of righteous anger had grown up. Once again Nobili declined to continue it. From Albert his first convert he knew that behind the "pagan idols" on the temple of Chockanātha lay a highly developed Śaivite metaphysic. The Brahmins, by common consent, were the *élite* of Madurai. Before passing judgment on their ceremonial, he would try to understand it.

How could this be done? Brahmins kept to themselves and were forbidden to divulge their religious secrets. "A Śudra attempting to hear the sacred texts shall have his ears filled with molten tin or lac; if he recites the Veda, his tongue shall be cut off; and if he remembers it, he shall be torn limb from limb." Nobili, as a sannyāsī, might be able to learn some of their doctrines, were it not for the fact that their texts and commentaries were composed in Sanskrit, a language which they did not want castes other than the Brahmin to learn. No European had ever learned Sanskrit, or Grantham, as it was termed; no one even knew very well what it was. "The Latin of the Brahmins", Europeans called it, meaning that like Latin in Catholic Europe, so Grantham in India was the language of theology, philosophy and science.

For some months it seemed that Nobili, despite his accommodation to Indian manners, would be unable to pierce this inner bastion. Then, one day during 1608, a man called Śivadarma came to see him. He was a Brahmin of the Śaivite sect, whose native tongue was Telugu, a language as closely related to Tamil as Portuguese is to Italian, and he had a great reputation as a

[1] The Sālegrāma stone, an ammonite venerated by Vaiṣṇavites.

Sanskrit scholar. After questioning Nobili, Śivadarma came to the conclusion that if he could convert the strange sannyāsī to his way of thinking, Brahminism in Madurai would win a considerable victory. Hiding this motive for the moment, Śivadarma offered to become Nobili's pundit. Nobili was only too glad to accept.

He now began to learn Sanskrit, not at first from books, for there were no grammars of the language, but by word of mouth. It proved much more difficult that Tamil: not a language for communicating practical ideas or trivialities, but a vehicle for abstract truth. *Samkr* means to change or transform, to adorn, the opposite root being *prakr*, as in *prakrti*, meaning matter as it is at hand, presented in its raw state. Whereas the vernacular speech of the uneducated is *prākrta* ("Prākrit" in English), *samskrta* ("Sanskrit") is the classical ornate language. Some Indians even claimed that Sanskrit, the holy language of the Vedas, was not a historical tongue based on convention, but an emanation of Being in sound—hence the coercive power of sacred mantras and Vedic hymns.

Again, Nobili had to learn a language without textbook or grammar. His Tamil was little help, for although a large number of Tamil words, used to express abstract notions, were borrowed from Sanskrit, Tamil belonged to the Dravidian group and Sanskrit to the totally different Indo-European group. Although certain simple Sanskrit words, having the same root as Latin and Greek, were easily learned, religious terms presented grave difficulties, for their meaning had fluctuated in course of use in the world's oldest literature. One discovery Nobili soon made: Grantham was not, as Europeans thought, a name for Sanskrit, but merely the angular script evolved by the Tamils to write Sanskrit.

Nobili made quick progress. His memory was so retentive that he seldom forgot anything he had once heard, and so prompt that on the spur of the moment he could recall an apt quotation or recite a revelant passage. Śivadarma found it a pleasure to teach him, and Nobili, whose notions of the Brahmins was slowly being revised, felt the highest esteem for his tutor, his "carissimo maestro", as he called him in letters.

By the end of August Nobili could speak Sanskrit fluently and read Grantham. The Sanskrit prayers accompanying Brahmin ceremonial were now within his grasp, and Śivadarma, bent on conversion, had told Nobili something of what Brahmins in Madurai believed. But this did not satisfy Nobili. When an argument was carried to its conclusion, Śivadarma would invariably quote from the Vedas. Evidently to master Brahminism without studying the Vedas was as impossible as to master Christianity without studying the Bible. Nobili asked Śivadarma to provide him with the text of the Vedas.

For an Indian to make such a request would have been almost unthinkable, and it doubtless caused Śivadarma shocked surprise. Nobili was merely a Rājā, and the Vedas were the prized heritage of the Brahmin caste; in fact from knowledge of the Vedas flowed their exclusive power and status. To divulge the Vedas was strictly forbidden: if discovered in such a sacrilege, Śivadarma would be expelled from his caste.

Probably Śivadarma's first answer was an unqualified No. But Nobili persisted. Great might be Śivadarma's danger, but his own would be greater, adapting himself to a religion whose central texts he had not read. At last Śivadarma agreed, and that he risked degradation for so new a friend is a measure of Nobili's power of inspiring love.

"Your Reverence must know," wrote Nobili to Laerzio, "that these people regard the writing down of their law as a most grievous sin. Children must learn it by heart, a labour in which they spend ten or twelve years. But now I have a good opportunity of getting it written through my master .... As he is very learned in their religion, we must not let slip this excellent occasion of acquiring a knowledge of it. No doubt it must be done with close secrecy, considering the great personal danger involved; for if he were discovered they would certainly pluck his eyes out. But since it is very necessary and, under God, the chief means of converting these people, it should not be neglected. It is certain that God Our Lord will help him in all things and save him from all danger."

In this way, some two thousand five hundred years after they were composed, a European first had knowledge of the Vedas.

The oldest is the *Ṛg Veda*, a collection of over a thousand priestly hymns addressed to the old gods of the northern invaders from Central Asia. These gods are, in general, personifications of natural phenomena: one of the most important being Indra, god of rain. The hymns were recited during sacrifice, which consisted of oblations of intoxicating soma and libations of melted butter poured into the fire, personified as the god Agni.

The second is the *Yajur Veda*. These verses are concerned no longer with devotion to the gods but with the sacrifice itself and its mystic power. A crowd of priests (seventeen being the largest number) conduct a vast, complicated and painstaking ceremonial, believed to be coercive. Thus, the priest chants a formula for rain while pouring out a sacrificial fluid: rain, it is believed, cannot fail to come. From the moment when the priests seat themselves on the sacrificial ground, strewn with sacred grass, and proceed to mark out the altars on which the sacred fires are built, every act has its stanza or formula, every utensil is blessed with its own appropriate benediction, every flaw elaborately expiated.

The third, the *Sāma Veda*, is devoted chiefly to the worship of Indra, a blustering, boastful god, who has to befuddle himself with soma in order to slay demons. It also contains formulae of coercive magic.

The fourth, the *Atharva Veda*, is a collection of seven hundred and thirty hymns, many dealing with the World-Spirit or Brahman as a kind of pantheistic personification of holy thought and its pious utterance.

Now the Vedas, the religious books of foreign invaders, had been brought to Southern India comparatively late, about the third century B.C. By then their content had been codified and erected into a system, which the Brahmins gradually imposed in the peninsula. But the Dravidians had their own religious ideas, and while accepting many innovations from the north, including the belief that the first three Vedas were revealed truth, they declined to accept the authority of the *Atharva Veda*. This Veda, which extolled fertility cults, flagellation and ritual prostitution, they claimed was not genuine. Śivadarma, therefore, wrote down and expounded to Nobili only the *Ṛg Veda*, the *Yajur Veda* and *Sāma Veda*.

At first the mere text, a tissue of veiled allusions, must have posed as many problems as it solved.

> Three are thy powers, O Agni, three thy stations,
>   three are they tongues, yea, many, child of Order!
> Three bodies hast thou which the gods delight in:
>   with these protect our hymns with care unceasing.

From these typical lines of the *Ṛg Veda* even so perceptive a student as Nobili could hardly have gathered that Agni, god of Fire, is represented as the sun, lightning and the altar-fire: and that this was the earliest Indian triad. Despite Śivadarma's help, months of study must have been necessary first, through the various planes of mythology, to grasp the Vedas' meaning, then to relate this to Hindu religions as practised in Madurai.

To safeguard Śivadarma, Nobili had to be circumspect in his letters, but he shows himself aware of the importance of his discovery. He may have known that he had stumbled on the earliest detailed expression of man's religious thought, but he does not say so. His main interest in the Vedas was pragmatic. As he mastered their meaning, he was in a position to understand Brahmin ceremonial: a relic of Vedic coercive magic; Brahmin respect for water, the sun and grass: a relic of Vedic worship of natural phenomena; and how such varied doctrines as Śaivism and Vaiṣṇavism could claim to be orthodox, because the Vedic hymns themselves expressed developing religious views, and so lent themselves to widely varying interpretations.

Among the Tamilians *Védam* means both the three collections of hymns known as the Vedas, and also religion in general, without reference to a book. When inquirers asked Nobili what his religion was, they used the term "*Védam*". Nobili was able to turn to his advantage this loose use of the word, as he wrote to Laerzio in December 1608:

"I have found in their books that formerly four laws were preached in this country, three of which are still taught by the Brahmins, namely, the laws of Brahmā, Viṣṇu and Rudra (Śiva). The fourth was a spiritual law, which taught men to obtain salvation and a part of this law is mixed up with the other three; but the rest is lost, and there is nobody learned and holy enough to recover it . . .

"Moreover, the most learned among these people assert that it is written in their books that none of these three laws can bring true salvation, from which some conclude that there is no other life beyond the present one. I take occasion of this to tell them that they are indeed mistaken if they think they can be saved by any of those three laws, and I proceed to prove it to them by the very words of their books. As they are most anxious to save their souls, for which they undertake various works of penance and alms-giving, I tell them that I have come from a distant country for the sole purpose of teaching them that law which is said to have been lost. Thus I adapt myself to their ideas just as Saint Paul adapted himself to the ideas of the Athenians, regarding the unknown God. I tell them that if they wish to recover and learn that law, they must become my disciples. This facilitates conversions, for, once they have recognized me as their guru, they come willingly and even gladly to my instructions. This method is in conformity with the custom of this country where we find many sects all admitting the three Laws but each of them professing allegiance to a particular teacher. Being eager to receive the law of spiritual salvation, as they call the religion I teach, they first decide to be my disciples and receive from me the *tichei* [initiation] I give them."

By "the law which is said to have been lost" Nobili evidently meant the primitive religion revealed to mankind and obliterated by sin, which is embodied in and perfected by Christian Revelation. Thus he made a first attempt to adapt not only his dress and manners but his way of thinking to Indian preconception.

He had a precedent for such a method. In China Matteo Ricci went directly to the old texts of Confucius and extracted from them doctrines compatible with Christianity, such as the worship of a supreme divinity—doctrines which had fallen into abeyance or been whittled away by commentators. He also interpreted ambiguous texts in a sense which showed them to be compatible with Christianity. In this way Ricci had found common ground with the Confucianists he wished to convert. First he pointed to their own ancient texts and elicited their agreement of such reasonable propositions as the immortality of the soul and God as Creator; then he passed on to the Christian mysteries.

Nobili knew what Ricci had done and evidently hoped to apply similar methods in India. The task would be vastly more difficult, for while the texts of Confucius were comparatively straightforward and easily understood by Europeans, the Vedas belonged to a much earlier stage of human thought; clarity had been sacrificed to a mnemonic form, and ambiguity was sometimes intentional, part of the magic. On the other hand, the stakes were even higher than in China, where only a small *élite* regarded Confucian texts as authoritative. In India, if Christianity could be shown as the religion which crowned the Vedas, it would have a claim on every orthodox Hindu. With some such plan in mind, Nobili began to extract from approved commentaries of the Vedas a collection of texts and allusions best suited to serve as a basis of demonstration of the truth of Christianity.

7. On Trial

THE religion of the Vedas had been developed into the esoteric doctrine of the Upaniṣads, and the Upaniṣads by the Brahmins into a system called the Vedānta—the teaching contained at the end of the Veda, which the whole Veda has in view. It was doubly important for Nobili to master this system: first, because it would show how the Vedas were interpreted by Vedic specialists, and secondly, as the most important Hindu philosophy, it might, he hoped, provide a groundwork compatible with Christian revelation.

The Vedānta taught in Madurai had been formulated by Śankara, a South Indian Brahmin of the ninth century. Śankara had managed to combine, if not totally reconcile, diverse truths. The higher truth, imported by the Brahmins from the north, is that man, through knowledge of the identity of his own self with the Brahman or Absolute, should experience his unity with the Brahman and his freedom from the illusory world of the senses already in this life. The lower truth is the Dravidian belief that the everyday world is real, not illusory; that man even without true knowledge of the Brahman can, by good works and devotion to a personal God, attain eternal bliss after a cycle of rebirths.

The central doctrine of the higher truth is summed up in the formula "That art Thou", explained as follows in the *Chandogya Upaniṣad*.

A father is addressing his son, Śvetaketu:

" 'Bring hither a fig from there.'

" 'Here it is, sir.'

" 'Divide it.'

" 'It is divided, sir.'

" 'What do you see there?'

" 'These rather fine seeds, sir.'

" 'Of these, please, divide one.'

" 'It is divided, sir.'

" 'What do you see there?'

" 'Nothing at all, sir.'

"Then he said to him, 'Truly, my dear, that finest essence which you do not perceive—truly, my dear, from that finest essence this great sacred fig tree thus arises. Believe me, my dear,' said he, 'that which is the finest essence—this whole world has that as its self. That is Reality. That is Ātman. That art thou, Śvetaketu.'

" 'Do you, sir, cause me to understand even more.'

" 'So be it, my dear,' said he. 'Place this salt in the water. In the morning come unto me.'

"Then he did so.

"Then he said to him: 'That salt you placed in the water last evening—please bring it hither.'

"Then he grasped for it, but did not find it, as it was completely dissolved.

" 'Please take a sip of it from this end,' said he. 'How is it?'

" 'Salt.'

" 'Take a sip from the middle,' said he. 'How is it?'

" 'Salt.'

" 'Set it aside. Then come unto me.'

"He did so, saying, 'It is always the same.'

"Then he said to him: 'Truly, indeed, my dear, you do not perceive Being here. Truly, indeed, it is here. That which is the finest essence—this whole world has that as its self. That is Reality. That is Ātman. That art thou, Śvetaketu.' "

In other words, *Thou*, the individual soul, *art God*, contained within Him in absolute absorption. To realize this, the conscious personality must turn inwards to remerge itself in the Subconscious, with which it is really identical. Only so can man emancipate himself from the miseries of life. These must be fled, not conquered, for just as we may mistake a rope for a snake or mother-of-pearl for silver, so at another level we make the mistake of calling the world around us real. Nothing is real save only the impersonal Brahman, indivisible and without attributes.

Such in brief was orthodox doctrine in Madurai. Even to a well-read Italian of the seventeenth century it must have seemed totally new and extraordinary. European philosophers had denied the reality of the world perceived by man, but no one had ventured to deny at the same time the reality of the world, the ego, the senses and the mind, as did the higher truth of the non-dualist Vedānta.

Further reading and discussions with Śivadarma seem to have convinced Nobili that the Vedas were basically polytheist or pantheist and the Vedānta, as expounded in Madurai, inalterably monist. Now a monist theology leaves no place for the very core of Christianity: the union of the human person with the living God in a love which transforms but does not consume. Nobili's hope that it would be possible to present Vedāntism as a philosophy compatible with Christian revelation was proved an illusion. He therefore abandoned his short-lived attempt to base an apologetic directly either on the three Vedas or on the Vedānta.

He did not thereby cut away all common ground with the philosophers around him. A contemporary account lists no fewer than five different schools of thought in Madurai alone. "According to one opinion holiness consists in *Sāṁnidhyam*—in being in the presence of the god of their sect; according to a second opinion it consists in *Sāmīpyam*—in coming close to God; according to a third opinion, in *Sāyujyam*—in the mixing of the soul with God, as water with water; according to a fourth opinion, in *Sārūpyam*—the soul loses itself in God as fuel in fire; according to a fifth opinion in *Sālokyam*—in the clear contemplation of God."

Some of these schools were compatible with Christian revelation. Those that were incompatible Nobili tried to confound, no longer on the basis of Indian Scripture, but with arguments of the Christian schoolmen, adapting only his imagery and metaphors to Indian predilections. The schoolmen's arguments were of two main kinds. Those based on the authority of Scripture, as when St Thomas Aquinas argues that the body is not an evil prison-house by citing the passage from Genesis where God, after the creation of man, looks on the world and finds it good: such arguments as this would clearly prove useless in Madurai. But even arguments from "reason" could be expected to make only a limited impact. St Thomas Aquinas combats the theory that man is a soul "using" a body, as he would use a piece of clothing, by the argument that "animals and men are sensible and natural things, and this would not be so if the body and its parts did not belong to the essence of man and animal". This argument is merely an expression at the reflective level of a pre-linguistic apprehension or experience of the nature of man. Now, such experiences vary across the world in so far as they are, at least to some small degree, conditioned by early family life, education and local "climate of opinion". For example, Nobili was faced with an overwhelming Hindu tradition that the "real" man is the soul, or even simply the mind, which is doomed for a time to inhabit the prison-house of the body. This theory seems to have been evolved by thinkers who concentrated their attention on man's highest activities, such as contemplative experience. In Europe, on the other hand, at least since Aristotle conceded that a life of pure contemplation lies beyond man's powers, the practical has been given as much attention as the contemplative mind. Ship-building Europe had discovered India, and Vasco da Gama, master-mariner, cartographer and soldier, was none the less a Christian gentleman: even an ideal type of Christian—a crusader. Growing up in such a world, a European would normally apprehend that the human body, far from being a prison-house, actually perfects the nature of the soul, with which it forms one substance. But an Indian Brahmin could scarcely be expected to share such an intuition. Not, at least, without much understanding help.

Nobili had committed himself to help. For that he was living as an Indian, leading—after his 13,000 mile journey from the West—a totally static life in the hermitage, making concessions in dress, diet, language and manners.

He was committed to spreading the Catholic faith, not a system of European philosophy. Nevertheless, to preserve the faith intact, it would be necessary to retain certain basic apprehensions (for example, about the nature of divine love and of the soul) not normally perceived in India and, indeed, to communicate them. The comparatively easy task of becoming in all ways Indian was not open to Nobili.

He must communicate those basic apprehensions not only, or

even chiefly, by verbal arguments but, under God, by a good life, for Indians expected of a guru not so much information as transformation of character. Grace in him must act out the truth of his apprehensions. Between Rome and Madurai he himself must become the bridge of love.

While still adjusting himself to his new knowledge, towards the beginning of 1609 Nobili received a visit from two Brahmins who wished to betray him into some statement which they could afterwards use against him. Their first question was how man could attain emancipation from the miseries of this life: what Nobili, adapting himself to his European correspondent, calls "acquiring eternal glory".

"I answered them", writes Nobili, "with arguments drawn from their own books and proved to them that eternal glory could not be acquired by their religious practices. These arguments seemed to satisfy them. They next asked me why it was that some men were born of noble and others of low parentage. I replied that just as in the body, for unknown but excellent reasons, a diversity of members is necessary, so in this universe, which bears some resemblance to a well-organized body, there is a beautiful diversity of parts. We see that among its various kinds of men, some, for example the kings, are like the head of the body, while others, the labourers, are like the hands, and others again, that is, the lower classes, are like the feet."

Now this perfectly orthodox European doctrine that the king is the head of the state was at variance with the Brahmin belief in their own supremacy. When the Nāyak of Madurai—a mere Śūdra—offered a banquet to a thousand Brahmins, he could not even look at the dishes served to his guests. A small sample of his guests' food was shown to him for his approval, then thrown away as fit only for dogs and the lowest castes. And this stranger threatened to upset such arrangements! For the moment, however, Nobili's visitors hid their disapproval.

The Brahmins next questioned Nobili about the relationship between God and the soul. They believed that only a few men, with knowledge of the Vedas, were able to become united with the Godhead within them.

"When I told them", Nobili continues, "that God was present in the soul of every man, they objected that if it were so, all men would follow the same religion, and see Him with the eyes of their intelligence. And if God were present in the souls of men He would share all the sufferings of those souls. To this I replied:

" 'Although the sun moves with its light round the world, if I remain always in my house with door and windows closed, I shall not receive its light. In the same way, although God is present everywhere, if we shut against Him the door of the soul with our sins, we cannot see His divine light, which is His most holy religion.

" 'God is present in men in several ways, by His power, His essence, etc., yet they cannot see Him; for, as to see a man who is near or in front of me, I must have light, so to see and know God who is near me, it is necessary that I should have the light of His most holy religion.

" 'God is not so united with the soul as to form one composite whole with it. If it were so, He would share in its sufferings, just as when pain is inflicted on the body the soul feels it and is grieved, for it is united with the body with which it makes a whole, which we call man. But as God is in us in the manner described above, He cannot suffer.' With these answers they seemed satisfied.

"We imagine that these people are ignorant, but I assure you that they are not. I am at present reading one of their books in which I am learning [philosophy] over again; the terms they use are almost the same as ours, but, of course, their philosophy is fundamentally different."

Already, when Nobili claimed that the Christian religion gave true knowledge of God, the discussion had reached fundamentals. For the Vedānta could not be proved. Given a doctrine of absolute unity, the ordinary means of right knowledge—perception—becomes invalid, because there are no real objects to be perceived. The Vedānta, like Christianity, had to turn to Revelation. The Vedas were the word of God, and the traditional interpretation of the Vedas by the Brahmins infallible.

The Brahmins next asked Nobili about actions, good and bad. The Vedānta teaches that since man is identical with God, sin must be a negligible element, for it is impossible to conceive that sin belongs to the Absolute. As for good actions, according to the lower, exoteric truth taught by Śankara, even those incapable of true knowledge of the Brahman nevertheless participate in union with Him by fulfilling the duties of their state of life.

"My two visitors finally asked me what were good works and what was sin. In the course of my answer I explained that there are actions which, though good in themselves, do not merit heaven; such are the actions of those who do not know the true God; while there are others which, on the contrary, do merit heaven: for instance, the actions of those who know God and are His friends.

" 'But,' they objected, 'he who touches fire gets burnt, even if he does not know the nature of fire; so also those who do what is right, even if they do not know God, will be rewarded, just as a man will be benefited by a remedy even though he does not know its nature.'

"Here I had to explain how actions become different according to the diversity of intentions; acts are good or bad according to the motive of the will that inspired them, so that, though they may appear identical, they are very different one from the other. Therefore their example drawn from a remedy had no value, for its virtue is always the same. I went on to say that sin consisted in turning away from God to embrace a bad and forbidden object, and as I supported that definition with texts from their Sanskrit books, they were fully satisfied. May God do the rest."

In fact, the Brahmins only pretended to be satisfied. They were deeply disturbed. Were the towers which seemed to touch heaven and the thousand-pillared hall of the temple of Śiva to be undermined from a mud-walled hermitage, to totter and fall—not this time to Muslim soldiers, but to the slow, subtle encroachments of heresy? In spite of the stranger's friendliness and respect for their ways, his doctrine led to a complete overthrow of a thousand-year-old religious, philosophic and social tradition. The two Brahmins at once started an agitation to have Nobili and his pundit Śivadarma expelled from Madurai.

The Brahmin caste had power to pass such a sentence—or

worse—without reference to the Nāyak, merely by a condemnation of unorthodoxy in public assembly. A day was set aside for a hearing and invitations sent out: in view of the gravity of the charges, as many Brahmins as possible were urged to attend.

On the appointed day, no fewer than eight hundred Brahmins, young and old, rich and poor, assembled in the open air to hear Nobili's case. Had the Pope, the cardinals, the archbishops and bishops of Italy thronged the square of St Peter's to pass judgment on a Hindu who claimed the Vedānta as the one and only truth, the occasion could hardly have been more momentous. One of Nobili's two visitors acted as plaintiff, while Śivadarma was to speak for the defence. It was a very serious affair, "for", writes Nobili, "if by some misfortune our enemies had succeeded in proving their charges they would have torn our eyes out of their sockets.

"Our enemy began as follows:

" 'Be it known to you, O Brahmins! that we have in this town a man who calls himself a sannyāsī, though he is in fact a vile Parangi. Even a child can see at a glance the proof of what I say, for that man is white, the colour of the Parangis. But leaving aside his complexion, I now come to the blasphemous statements he made before me, in the presence of another Brahmin and of his pundit [Śivadarma] who is here present. First of all, he said that the laws of the Brahmins are a tissue of errors and lies; secondly that giving alms to them brings no merit; thirdly, that bathing in the sea at Rameśvaram or in the Ganges is not helpful for salvation; fourthly, that the Rājās are higher in nobility than the Brahmins; fifthly, that among the people of this country there is none who has any knowledge of the true God and can attain salvation.

" 'See for yourselves, Brahmins, the stupidities uttered by this man. He alone knows God; where then are those more learned scholars and doctors whom we held in such great honour because of their learning, who conducted so many famous disputations among us, whose disciples crowded our streets, whom so many sannyāsīs used to follow? Has this man alone the monopoly of salvation?

" 'He even went so far as to pervert some of my friends, but I did not allow them to accept his initiation; but for my timely intervention, they would have fallen into hell. To prove the truth of all I have said, I call on his master here present to bear me witness, and if what I have said is not true, let my tongue be cut out. If on the other hand, I have spoken the truth, let him receive the punishment he deserves.' "

With the addition of other insults and calumnies against Nobili, the plaintiff wound up his charge. The presiding Brahmin then expressed astonishment that Śivadarma—like his father, a man of great learning—should follow a guru who laid himself open to the accusations they had just heard. He called on Śivadarma to answer them and vindicate his master's conduct.

As he came forward, Śivadarma noticed his father trembling with fear at the outcome of the case. After bowing to the assembly, Śivadarma pointed out that he was young and of little learning, and begged them to forgive him if in what he was going to say he did not express himself in a way worthy of that distinguished gathering.

" 'This Brahmin', he continued, 'has alleged that I am serving a Parangi, and he proves it by saying that the Aiyer who is my master is white. But this argument has no value, for by the same method I could prove that he is a Paraiyan and of low birth. Since in this country men of high and low birth, Brahmins and Paraiyans, are found to be of the same colour, cannot the same be true of men living in other countries? Cannot those men, though belonging to different classes by birth, have the same complexion?'

"This retort", says Nobili, "pleased everyone, and the accuser himself declared he was convinced, but added that he did not rely so much on this argument as on the others. Śivadarma answered that he would give a clear refutation of them all, and taking up the first he said:

" 'The plaintiff and his friend asked my master whether a man living according to their mode of life would acquire glory. He replied that there were two kinds of life, one which consisted only in ceremonies, baths, anointings, pilgrimages and so forth; and this way of life he declared to be of no help for salvation; the other

45063

consisted in knowing, loving and serving God, and this, he said, is the only way to attain glory. Our accuser then asked what would happen to a man who, without knowing God, made pilgrimages to the Ganges and Rameśvaram.

" ' "He will not acquire glory in this way," answered my Aiyer.

" ' "It follows therefore," replied this Brahmin, "that our religion is false."

" ' "The law which maintains that a man can be saved without knowing God is certainly false," replied my master, and this he spoke truly, for in our law there is nothing contrary to it.

" 'The plaintiff's allegation that people bathing in the Ganges, even without a knowledge of God, can thereby obtain salvation, is most erroneous; it is a law of his own invention, of which our books make no mention. So all my master said was that the law alleged by this Brahmin was false, for it contained that gross error, that one can be saved without knowing God.'

"Śivadarma spoke with such force and grace that all applauded him. The chief Brahmin, turning towards the accuser, said to him: 'It is obvious that you are a great ignoramus, and did not understand the words of that sannyāsī. You are indeed a fool if you think you can save your soul merely by taking baths and rubbing your body with ashes. When that sannyāsī spoke as he did, he showed that he was a very learned man and well versed in our religion.'

"Then my Brahmin went on:

" 'Regarding the second point, which concerns alms, my master answered in the same way, that without a knowledge of God, they were evidently of no use for salvation; the same applied to baths taken at Rameśwaram and in the Ganges; they cannot procure glory, but if they deserve any reward they will receive it in this life.

" 'As to the fourth point, that the Rājās are more noble than the Brahmins, the Father did not say so, he simply said that the human race was comparable to a body composed of many members, of which the Rājās were the head, not by reason of higher nobility, but because they governed us who are the members of the body politic, for even we, Brahmins, are under their protection and subject to their government. Moreover the Aiyer said that in this land of ours, there were few, if any, who attained salvation, for very few know God, but he did not say that nobody knew God, or that he alone knew Him and would be saved.'

"'Thus spoke Śivadarma with all the authority of a recognized scholar. He told me later that he was astonished at his own boldness, for he is very shy by nature.

"When the discussion was over they were all quite satisfied, and they felt indignant against that perverse accuser, whom they treated quite roughly. The chief Brahmin called Śivadarma aside and asked him who I was and what I knew. He replied: 'This sannyāsī is a very learned man and his learning does not come from me, for he could not have acquired it within the four months I have been with him. If you don't believe me, you have only to go and talk with him; you will soon find out what sort of man he is.'

"The Brahmin answered that it was not necessary and that he believed him. 'But in future,' he said, 'don't allow your Aiyer to speak with men of no understanding and less conscience, such as your accuser of to-day. If this man has the audacity to retail any more nonsense about you and your Aiyer, I'll have him put in irons.' "

The eight hundred Brahmins who had assembled in a mood of antagonism dispersed with feelings of respect for the stranger sannyāsī. The plaintiffs had helped him by basing their case on a "popular" doctrine ill-considered in academic circles. Clearly they professed "the way of works": that sacrifices, general religious duties and pilgrimages can lead to liberation, even if performed entirely for selfish motives. This "way", traditionally opposed to the way of knowledge and the way of devotion, was frowned on by philosophers, who believed all action of whatever kind led to reaction and ultimately to rebirth. Nobili, as a sannyāsī, had, in Hindu eyes, passed beyond the way of works to the way of knowledge. By denying value to the way of works, if followed in ignorance of the true God, he was believed to be striking a blow for the way of knowledge, and so supporting the orthodox Madurai school. In fact, however, Christianity, as Nobili himself stated, contained all three ways, and was hostile to neither. The verbal sequence—"knowing, loving and serving God"—merely reflected a temporal sequence: without knowledge man could neither love nor serve.

Śivadarma's speech had won Nobili a resounding victory. Instead of being expelled as a Parangi he had been promised protection as a learned sannyāsī. More important still, the trial had shown that, irrespective of the Vedas and Vedānta, it was possible to find common ground with at least some of the Madurai Brahmins.

8. *The Problem of the Thread*

SHARED danger and the preparation of a joint brief brought Śivadarma and Nobili much together. As they studied their texts, they also studied each other. After some months, for the second time in Madurai, Nobili the pupil convinced his Hindu master of error. Śivadarma, who possessed a virtue rare among his caste—humility—was prepared to admit the consequences. He, a Brahmin, asked Nobili, a mere Rājā, to be his guru.

Nobili hoped to baptize Śivadarma on Easter Sunday 1609—about a year after their first meeting. But the baptism had to be delayed, for it raised a grave problem of principle. Should Śivadarma, after baptism, be allowed to retain two distinctive insignia? The first was the *kudumi*, or hair-tuft. The front and back of Śivadarma's skull were shaved, and the remaining hair gathered into a "pony-tail", which hung flat over the back of his head. Nobili believed that the *kudumi* was not a symbol of religion, but of the "twice-born"—the three highest castes. It was worn among the Paravas, and Francis Xavier had allowed the custom to continue. Nobili wanted Śivadarma and other high-caste converts to be allowed to retain the *kudumi*, and for this innovation he obtained Archbishop Ros's approval.

The second of the two insignia was the thread: simplest yet most exclusive of ornaments—a triple strand of white cotton. Hanging from the left shoulder across the breast and back and tied near the right thigh, though thinner than the gold band of a wedding ring, the white thread stood out clearly against a brown bare torso. Should Śivadarma, after baptism, be allowed to wear his cotton thread, which in common with all Brahmins he prized more than a European knight his cordon? To deprive him of it would be, in Indian eyes, to remove him from his caste: that is, condemn him to worse than ostracism, to a kind of living death.

Nobili did not want to demand such a sacrifice if he could help it; on the other hand, he must be scrupulously careful not to tolerate among his converts anything savouring of superstition. On the coast the thread, worn like a deacon's stole, was believed by the Portuguese to be a mark of the Brahmins' priesthood, and the wearing of the thread had been forbidden to Indian converts by four Provincial Synods of Goa.

The Synods' decisions, though based on the scanty information available in and around Goa, could not lightly be contested. According to decree 47 of the first Synod, those who permitted heathen rites to Christians were *ipso facto* excommunicated. On the other hand, Nobili had access to Indian sacred books, which threw a flood of new light on the thread; in particular to the long and complicated ritual by which the Brahmin was invested with his thread: the *upanayana*, or "leading a boy to his guru". Nobili's interpretation of this was to have the most far-reaching consequences.

The *upanayana*, the most important event in a Brahmin's life, whereby he became "twice-born" and fit to study the scriptures, took place when the Brahmin was between seven and nine, sometime during the spring, and lasted four days. A sacrificial fire was lit, in front of which sat the boy, his father beside him to act the part of the guru. First the boy's hair was shaved; then he bathed and approached the sacred fire. After melted butter had been poured on the flames, a bundle of palāśa sticks was handed to him. These he placed on the fire to the recitation of Vedic verses.

The thread was then produced. It was composed of three strands of cotton secured together by a knot of peculiar construction, called Brahma Granthi. In preparation of the thread ordinary cotton could not be used: cotton had to be picked by Brahmins and spun on special spinning-rods made of bamboo-stick weighted with lead or soapstone. The officiating Brahmin put the new thread round the boy's left shoulder, saying, "I make thee glorious and famous with the thread."

After the thread, a new cloth was given to the boy, then a girdle spun from grass was wound three times round his body and tied with a knot opposite the navel, while the celebrant recited: "This blessed girdle, the friend of the gods, has come to us to remove our sins, to purify and protect us, bring strength to us by the power of exhalation and inhalation. Protect, O girdle, our wealth and meditation. Destroy our enemies, and guard us on all the four sides."

A small piece of deer-skin was next tied on to the sacred thread. "O skin which is full of lustre because Mitra sees you, full of glory and one that is not fit for wicked people, I am now putting you on. May Aditi tuck up thy garment. Thou mayst read Vedas, and grow wise. Thou mayst not forget what thou hast read. Mayst thou become holy and glorious."

The boy sat next to the guru and said: "I have come near the spiritual teacher, my Āchārya. May the teacher and I become prosperous. May I also complete my Vedic studies properly, and be blessed with a married life after the study."

The guru sprinkled water over the boy and taking him by the hand said, "Agni, Soman, Savitar, Sarasvatī, Pūṣan, Aryaman, Amsuhu, Bagadevata and Mitra have seized thy hand. They have taken you over to them, and you have become friends."

The guru then entrusted the boy to the gods, with the words, "O boy, may you have children full of lustre and capable of becoming heroes."

After further Vedic ritual, the boy begged rice from his mother and other female relatives. With that the first day's ceremonial ended. On the second and third days the boy made the sacred fire flare with palāśa sticks and melted butter; on the fourth day he gave to his teacher the cloth with which he had been invested on the first day.

So went the *upanayana*. Clearly, by Christian standards, it was a superstitious rite. But then superstitious ceremonies took place at every important moment of a Brahmin's life. What Nobili had to decide was whether it was so essentially superstitious as to taint the thread.

When he later came to defend his decision, Nobili began by

restating principles laid down by St Thomas Aquinas. According to St Thomas an action, indifferent in itself, tends to become superstitious in the following ways: (i) materially—inasmuch as the nation is pagan, or (ii) because it stands as a civic distinction between Christians and pagans, or (iii) because it marks a religious distinction between Christians and pagans, either (*a*) as fulfilling a human need (for example, a priest's cassock), or (*b*) as fulfilling a specifically religious need (for example, a priest's stole). According to St Thomas, all these actions can be allowed, even iii*b*, if the emblems are honorific. For example, until the time of Gratian, the Christian emperors at Rome wore the stole used by the pagan pontiffs in their sacrifices.

While accepting St Thomas's principles, Nobili found it more useful to define new categories. An action, he asserts, can be tainted in three ways: (i) if it is to an equal degree civil and religious (for example, the dress of certain pagan priests), or (ii) if it is primarily civil and secondarily religious, or (iii) a purely civil action recommended by poets, who attribute to its performance divine rewards.

Nobili, basing himself on the theologians Azor, Bannez and Valencia, maintained that tainted actions of the second and third categories are permissible. As regards the third category, he asserted that, if forbidden, no Christian could stay in India. A Christian could not keep a cow because, according to the poets, that brings a heavenly reward. He could not wear a white loincloth because white is derived from the moon, in whose honour it is worn, and the loincloth is called *somen*, a name applied to the moon. He could not eat butter, the food of the gods, nor rice, which the poets say is a god.

The thread, Nobili claimed, belongs to the second of the tainted categories and is therefore permissible. It is primarily an emblem of caste, tainted because it incidentally entitles Brahmins to make religious sacrifices and to recite sacred texts.

His main argument for this claim Nobili borrowed from the Laws of Manu, where to the different castes threads from different materials are prescribed: to the Brahmins a threefold thread of cotton, to the Rājās a single thread of flax, and to the Commotis

(Vaiśyas) one of hemp. Hence it follows that the thread is not a religious token, for otherwise soldiers and merchants would be reckoned as clergy, which is absurd.

Manu also says that the belt of kuśa-grass, the staff, the thread and the water-jug, "all these things make a Brahmin grow in glory or splendour". Now the staff and water-jug are certainly "adapted to social purposes and tokens of rank". Therefore also the thread, which is mentioned together with them.

Another proof Nobili drew from the *Smṛti*, which ordains that "a Brahmin must receive the thread from the eighth year on, counting the years from the time of conception, a Rājā from the eleventh year, and the Commoti from the twelfth". Although, therefore, certain superstitious ceremonies take place at the giving of the thread—as on every other important occasion—the thread itself is but a token of rank, as it certainly is for the Rājās and Commoti here mentioned together with the Brahmins.

Besides, at the imposition of the thread, the guru tells the child, "I make thee glorious and famous with the thread", and according to the *Parāśara Smṛti*, "Just as a painting is completed little by little with brush-strokes given to the different parts of the subject, so the Brahmin is perfected and beautified by the different acts and signs proper to his caste."

A fifth argument was that the thread and the hair-tuft are given up by Brahmin sannyāsīs, whereas the trident, the mark of the Vaiṣṇavites, and the ashes, a Śaivite emblem, are kept. Now, were the thread and hair-tuft religious signs, they would be retained as well as the trident and ashes.

This and further evidence satisfied Nobili that the thread was a badge of rank, not of religion. As for the *upanayana*, he decided that, like the hair-tuft ceremony, it was bad *quoad modum*, in the way it is done, but not *quoad se*, essentially. He therefore asked his superiors' permission that high-caste converts should be allowed to wear the thread. But the old thread with which they had been invested at the *upanayana* would be replaced by a new thread, unsullied by superstition. Despite the ruling of the four Provincial Synods, Archbishop Ros, having obtained the consent of the Archbishop of Goa and the Inquisitors, gave his approval.

Nobili procured a new cotton thread and blessed it in the name of the Father, the Son and the Holy Ghost. This thread he gave to Śivadarma, who wore it in place of the thread he had received during the *upanayana*. Nobili also gave Śivadarma a small crucifix to wear round his neck tied to his new thread, so that it could be clearly seen. If Śivadarma wore the crucifix bravely and gave a good account of himself, he intended to baptize him at Pentecost.

As Pentecost approached, Śivadarma fell a prey to doubts and hesitations. One night he dreamed that a man came to him and reproved him sternly for his delay: "Why don't you listen to the sannyāsī and do as he bids you?" said the apparition. "But, sir," replied Śivadarma, "how can I become a Christian in this town where everybody knows me?" "Do as he tells you," insisted the strange visitor, "even here in this town."

These words and the fear of hell, which had begun to work on him, ended Śivadarma's hesitation. On Pentecost Sunday, 7th June 1609, Nobili announced the good news to Laerzio: "To-day I baptized my beloved Brahmin Master. It was a great joy and consolation to me, to him, and to all the Christians. I gave him the name of 'Diodato', in Tamil 'Śivadarma'. I hope that he will be of great help for the conversion of these gentiles, for he is a young man known throughout the whole town of Madurai. He belongs to a very good family and has the well-deserved reputation of a great scholar, learned in their laws and sacred books; and what raises him still higher in my esteem is that while still a gentile he was a man of excellent morals, modest and well-behaved."

Nobili had evidently decided that his Brahmin master's Tamil name was a suitable name for him to bear as a Christian. He had christened his first converts with Western names, such as Albert and Alexis, but already in the previous year he had given some Tamil names. Baptizing Alexis's brother, Viśwanāth, he had merely changed it slightly to Visuvāsam, meaning Faithful; and to another neophyte he had given the name Yesupatten, meaning Lover of God. Now he went one stage further on the road to adaptation, by retaining an appropriate Tamil name and hallowing it in baptism. This was in striking contrast with current practice in India, where all converts were given not merely the Portuguese form of a Christian name, but also a Portuguese surname, some-times the reigning viceroy's, sometimes that of his master—if the convert were a slave; sometimes that of a Portuguese godfather.

The baptism of Śivadarma was the culmination of eighteen months' work, during which the Sanskrit master had become the Christian pupil. Nobili could well look at his Brahmin with satis-faction. A few Brahmins had been baptized in Portuguese terri-tory, but for motives of gain, and in receiving baptism they had ceased to be Brahmins. The thread had been ripped from their shoulders, and with it their caste: they wore trousers and a hat and ate Portuguese food, they spoke the language of their masters. Forced to ape the Portuguese, they had ceased to be Indians.

But Śivadarma was a true Brahmin and a true Christian; he bore a Tamil name, not one borrowed from a Portuguese godfather, and he would continue to speak his own language. The waters of baptism had washed away his sins, not his colour, nor his nation-ality, nor all that was good in his former way of life.

While learning Sanskrit, studying the Vedas and Vedānta, and instructing Śivadarma, Nobili had continued to receive an in-creasing number of inquirers. They gave him no rest day or night. "The work", he wrote to Laerzio, "is so exhausting that I am afraid I shall not be able to carry on much longer and I feel it absolutely necessary to ask for a companion. But he must be a man of great courage, full of fervour, with a real desire to suffer for Jesus Christ." In spite of fatigue, however, Nobili's health had never been so good. He had become used to staying indoors, to his diet of rice, to the heat, and to the flies and the white ants which swarmed everywhere and gorged anything which happened to be left on the hermitage floor.

But he was not yet by any means accepted in Madurai. A series of sporadic attacks culminated at the end of December 1608. This was the monsoon season, and the *Kanyatchi* or manager of the temple of the great god of Madurai—Chockanātha, the handsome lord—called a meeting of Brahmins to find out why it did not rain: a matter of life and death to the farmers in and around Madurai. A lame school-teacher named Nondivāttiyār, who had been employed by Gonçalo Fernandez at the mission-school and later dismissed, decided to get his revenge by blaming Nobili. Chocka-nātha, he claimed, was so angered by the stranger's teaching that unless he was punished and expelled from Madurai, disasters were bound to occur. Some of the Nāyak's suite, including a eunuch secretary devoted to Chockanātha, were induced to join together and denounce Nobili. They were to explain to the Nāyak that the foreign sannyāsī was an atheist who did not acknowledge the Trimūrti, showed no respect for Chockanātha, nor for the lingam, that he had suborned disciples of the great pandaram Avexida, and yet, in spite of all that, he kept Brahmin servants and studied their law.

A new charge was also made. Basing themselves on Nobili's fairer complexion, and the fact that he came from Rumi, they claimed that he was a Muslim: a Turk: a particular irony for Nobili, whose father and uncle had fought to save Christendom from the Turk, and a particular stigma in Tamil eyes, for Madurai had been captured and ruled by Muslims less than three centuries ago, and even now Muslim kingdoms of the Deccan menaced the Vijayanagar empire.

In view of the gravity of the charges, Nobili's enemies asked for his immediate expulsion and insisted that his Brahmin teacher should have his eyes plucked out, his thread removed and his tuft of hair cut off.

Nobili's Brahmin servants, Tirumalai and Anen by name, were so terrified by the news that they refused to cook his meals and finally took to flight. This was more than an inconvenience: as a Rājā he had to have high-caste servants. He looked around for a protector and remembered one of his earliest friends, Errama Setti, brother and successor of Nagaya Setti Nāyak, who had died not long after giving Nobili the plot of land for the hermitage. Nobili sent George, his Telugu interpreter, to explain the danger to Errama Setti. George was too afraid to carry out his orders and too ashamed to admit his fear. He told Nobili that he had been badly received by Errama Setti, urged Nobili to leave Madurai at once and finally ran away to Veypar on the Coast. In Nobili's opinion, "It was a good riddance."

"When George had left," writes Nobili, "Father Gonçalo

Fernandez came at night to advise me to go away. He had sent Anthony [one of Fernandez's servants] to speak to that Brahmin, who had replied that if I wished to remain, I must give up this *cavi* dress, wear black, put away the thread and the crucifix which I wear hanging from my neck, and send my Brahmin out of my house because I was a Turk. Unless I did so, they could come to my house and strip me of my dress. All this was beside the point and I did not think it right for me to run away, for it would scandalize my neophytes to whom I preached courage; my accusers would take advantage of my absence to burn my house; my flight would be interpreted as a confession of guilt; on the other hand by remaining here I might compel them to listen to me, and perhaps God would give me an opportunity to speak to the Great Nāyak. After all, the real reason of this persecution was not, as some alleged, that I employed Brahmins to serve me, but that I did not worship their gods, and that I made Christians, which was a clear proof that religion was at stake. Therefore I could not abandon the place with a safe conscience."

Nobili next sent his most fervent convert, Alexis, to Errama Setti, begging him to come to the hermitage. All the following day Nobili waited. Tension was rising: at any moment the Brahmins might arrive to arrest him. The evening closed in. It began to seem that Nobili had asked too much of his friend. According to a Tamil proverb, "The great are not always helpful; the tall palm-tree casts no shade." Poligars were so important, such sticklers about their rank, they usually did not condescend to come to other people's houses. But finally, at midnight, a stir was heard. Nobili opened the hermitage door to find Alexis and beside him, surrounded by a large bodyguard, Errama Setti.

Four months ago, when his brother had died, Errama Setti had found comfort in Nobili's teaching and promised to become his disciple as soon as he had finished the business of his inheritance—to succeed to his brother's estate he had to raise a sum of 70,000 scudi[1] to be paid as investiture fee to the Nāyak. "Every day", wrote Laerzio, "he rises higher in the royal favour because he is a fine looking young man, and so strong that with one hand he can

---

[1] £42,000.

lift a big calf. To preserve that strength he keeps only one wife, which will make his conversion much easier."

Errama Setti now strode into the lamp-lit hermitage. "After the usual salutation," Nobili wrote to Laerzio, "I gave him the pair of spectacles which your Reverence sent me. He then inquired why I was so thin, and I took this occasion to tell him of my ill-treatment by the Brahmins, adding that even those who prepared my food had fled and that I had been obliged to send away my interpreter.

"In his reply he was very hard on George, who, he said, should never have left me in such circumstances, even though I had ordered him to go. My Brahmin servants should be dismissed and replaced by better ones. As for the calumniators, he would deal with them himself, and force them to come to me and beg for pardon; I had nothing to fear, said he, for he was ready to lay down his life for my sake. He comforted me with many other words full of affection. Then I told him in detail all the lies and calumnies brought against me, and refuted each in detail. If he happened to speak about me to the Nāyak, all I asked was that the Nāyak should listen to my reasons, and if he found me guilty he could have me torn to pieces; but if I proved that all the allegations of the Brahmins were false, I asked that no harm should be done to them.

"Errama Setti listened to everything with great attention and told me that the Brahmins would not dare repeat their calumnies to the Nāyak, but if they did he would answer for me. After a long conversation I gave him leave to depart and he went away.

"Calling Alexis he told him to take great care of me because I was very thin, adding that those who had fled were despicable, and that there was nothing to fear. As for himself, he was ready to give his life for my cause. He asked Alexis to come and see him next day when he would call the Brahmin of Chockanātha, and bring him here to ask my pardon. To-day Alexis went to Errama Setti who is to send for that Brahmin. If he comes I shall speak to him in such a way that he will understand me.

"I beg your Reverence, when next you write to me, to slip into your letter a word of praise for my Brahmin [Śivadarma] who conducted himself like a man of honour. Today Errama Setti sent for him and he has just returned. Errama Setti told him not to fear, for he would help him in all his affairs as well as mine, and sent him back in cheerful spirits.

"I do not know how to repay this Nāyak for his kindness to me except by praying God Our Lord to give him light to know Him, the true God. I beg your Reverence to do likewise. He very much wants to study our religion, but is so busy he scarcely has time to take his meals. He asked me for a remedy so that the devil may not hurt him. I told him that the only remedy was to listen to the word of God, but for this a few days would be necessary. He expressed a desire that I should come to his house to instruct him, but to go to him often and at night is a task demanding much thought. I shall see what circumstances permit."

Nobili had given his protector a pair of spectacles. In return Errama Setti showed himself very keen-sighted. Though a soldier, not a philosopher, he perceived that Nobili's rejection of the lingam and contempt for Chockanātha's erotic prowess did not prove him an atheist. He was able to persuade the lame schoolteacher and the eunuch secretary to drop their charges. Despite his monotheism and his complexion, which continued pale as a result of confinement to the hermitage, Nobili was never again accused of being "a malignant and a turban'd Turk".

9. *Mistaken for a Muni*

MADURAI claimed to be Śiva's favourite city. The name was said to be derived from the Tamil *madhurai*, meaning anything sweet, the story being that Śiva was so pleased with the buildings erected round his shrine by the first Pāṇḍya king that he sprinkled the temples, towers, palaces and houses with drops of sweet nectar shaken from his locks. And throughout the years Madurai celebrated events in Chockanātha's life: usually quarrels with his wife Mīnākṣi (the fish-eyed) and visits to his concubines, Madadeial and Piriideial. The god's greatest feast was his annual visit to Mīnākṣi during the month of Chaitr (April-May).

Besides these strictly religious festivals, Madurai observed other agricultural feasts, of which by far the most popular was Pongal. On the first day—*Bhogī-pongal*, Pongal of joy—visits were made to relatives and friends, and presents exchanged. Oh the second day —*Sura-Pongal*, Pongal of the sun—married women bathed with their clothes on and while dripping wet put rice to boil in milk on a fire in the open air. When it began simmering, they cried again and again, "Pongal! Pongal!"—It has boiled! It has boiled!" Friends visited one another and inquired: "Has it boiled?" and the answer was: "It has boiled." That the rice had boiled was a sign of good luck.

On the third day, Pongal of the cows, a vessel of water was filled with saffron powder mixed with seeds of the parati and margosa trees. The mixture was then sprinkled on the cows and oxen. After prostrating themselves before the animals, whose horns were painted and necks garlanded, the feasters drove the cattle out of the town and allowed them to graze where they pleased.

Superstitions were connected with the feast—such as the offering, on the second day, of part of the boiled rice to the idol Vighneś. Already Christians were forbidden to celebrate in honour of Chockanātha; must they be denied the gaiety of every public holiday?

"The Hindus," writes Nobili to Laerzio, of the Pongal in 1609, "are accustomed, at the beginning of each year, to celebrate a very solemn festival, called Pongal, to offer the new rice to the gods. It consists in cooking with great ceremony their rice mixed with milk, before an idol. According to them, it is a disgrace not to be able to celebrate that festival. I allow our Christians to cook their rice and boil their milk at the foot of a Cross which they plant for that purpose and, to their great satisfaction, I myself bless the new rice which is to be used in that ceremony. On that occasion the mother of Visuvasam and Alexis had forgotten to plant the cross, and although she stirred the fire, her rice would not boil, which according to the superstitious ideas of the pagans is a very bad omen. Then, noticing her omission, she was quick to repair it, and immediately, to her great joy, the rice started boiling, for as your Reverence knows very well God adapts Himself to their capacity.

"Our Dadamurti [a recent convert] had never been able, during the last three years, to make the Pongal rice boil, and this year, being a Christian, he had decided not to take part in that feast. But, being informed of this, I told him to plant a cross and do like the others. He obeyed, like the good Christian he is, and his rice did boil. So great was the joy of his children that they ran up to me to announce the news and receive my congratulations. They considered the event as a great favour from God.

"I know very well that your Reverence will tell me that these things are childish, but you ordered me to write everything in detail. I do so the more willingly as these trifles are very big things in the eyes of these neophytes, and of great importance since they serve to attach them to our religion, strengthen their faith and prepare them to bear the persecutions which God will send them, and which perhaps will not be long in coming."

By tolerating such customs and substituting the true God for an idol, Nobili was doing no more than his ancestors had done with regard to the gods of Greece, Rome, Egypt, Syria and other countries of the Empire. As a Roman he doubtless knew how very gradually Christianity had evolved to its present form—how, for instance, no representation of the Crucifixion existed from before the sixth century, since such a manner of death shocked Roman sensibilities—and how much of the pagan past Christianity had preserved. Even the head of the Church prided himself on the title Pontifex Maximus, once the boast of pagan Emperors. And Rome's Renaissance churches were plastered with Cupids: no one in Rome was shocked, for the god of love did not exist, had never existed—only the God of Love. The walls of newly discovered catacombs of Rome had been decorated in the second and third centuries with peacocks as a symbol of immortality—though the peacock was generally known to be an attribute of the goddess Hera. No crucifix had been found in the catacombs, yet Orpheus was depicted there more than once as a prefigure of Christ. So sure of themselves had the early Christians been that they allowed even the pagan past to serve its new Master.

Nobili like the early Christians was obliged to adapt himself: not as regards dogma—he never did that—but as regards Indian customs. Fortunately he was able to preach a suffering Christ and to show the cross, for Indians were accustomed to asceticism and even to death as a mark of love. His difficulty was not that the Indians were insufficiently religious, but almost, rather, that they were too religious. Nearly every living creature, every object, every action, especially among the Brahmins, had been tainted with superstition. Cows, fish, monkeys, grass, coconuts, pearls: there was no end to the things which had either in legend become attributes of a god or were themselves masks of a god.

It would have been easy for Nobili, as his predecessors had done, to see everything as hostile in a world of strange divinities, to throw up his hands in horror and flee to the coast. Nobili, instead, had the courage to conquer his first antipathy and adopt a more magnanimous view, born of the strength of his own faith and his love of the Indians. Brahmā, Viṣṇu, Śiva and the other godlings did not exist any more than did Cupid or Hera. Useless, then, to panic, as Fernandez sometimes did, because so many of the Hindus' daily customs were interwoven with myths concerning the Trimūrti. The thing to do was to purify harmless customs of any superstitious taint and, wherever possible, redirect them towards the true God: to bring Christianity to the Indians, not as a way of life imported by the Parangis from Europe, but as the crown of all that was best in India.

Acting on this principle, Nobili had to decide which customs were not essentially superstitious and could be tolerated. Since he was the only European with knowledge of the Vedas, he had to look for the evidence himself, then submit it to his superiors for their decision. But all the time his own knowledge was steadily growing. As he made new discoveries or as conditions changed, so Nobili adapted his own way of life. Now he grows a beard, now he shaves; on one occasion he rides in a palanquin, on another he makes a hundred-and-fifty-mile journey on foot. One picture shows him with ear-rings, another without them. If he ever did wear ear-rings —as most Tamil men did—it was doubtless during the months when he was known as a Rājā. Sannyāsīs usually renounced these ornaments, though they sometimes wore copper ear-rings as a mark of humility.

One very important change Nobili did make at the end of 1609 or the beginning of 1610. When he found out that sannyāsīs discarded their caste-emblems as a sign that they renounced all worldly honours, Nobili did likewise. He had taken the thread to conform to the customs of the Rājās, whose caste he had adopted: now that he was accepted as a sannyāsī, he had no further use for it, and he never wore the thread again.

As regards the thread of high-caste converts, another step in adaptation had become necessary. At first Nobili made Śivadarma and other Brahmin Christians wear the thread round the neck to suspend from it a crucifix. This angered their Hindu relatives, who considered the new fashion tantamount to discarding the thread. When they threatened to expel the innovators from their caste, Nobili again sought the advice of Archbishop Ros, who replied that the thread should be worn by neophytes in the same way as by their Hindu caste men. Their new faith they could profess by suspending a crucifix or other emblems round their neck, but not from the thread.

A no less important innovation was Nobili's decision to allow converts to continue wearing sandal-paste on their foreheads.

Three sorts of sandal were used in the East: white, red and—the most highly prized—yellow. The white and yellow came from Timor and the surrounding islands, near Java. The red grew on the Coromandel coast and in Pegu, and it was the red which South Indians used, mixing the sandal-wood with water and applying the paste.

Fernandez, like missionaries on the coast, forbade his flock the use of sandal. Sect-signs were worn on the forehead: the Vaiṣṇavite trident marked with clay, the Śaivite bars with ashes. Sandal on the brow, argued the Portuguese, was clearly another of these superstitious signs: probably worn in honour of Śiva's third eye.

Nobili disagreed, and defended his opinion with quotations from Indian books: "Camphor, sandal, musk, saffron, necklaces, bracelets, rings and gold pendants—all must be worn constantly to adorn the body." "The most strongly-scented powders and the most excellent sandal must be recommended for the toilet." "Sandal, perfumes, essence from the roots of the *lanucham*—all must serve to adorn us, to rejoice us and to refresh the body." In the *Bhikṣāṭana*, a mother replied to a girl who complains that she has no ornament: "You have gundendo flowers and sandal, what more do you want? Of all ornaments, flowers and sandal are most beautiful". And in the epic *Rāmāyaṇa* it was said of winter: "In this season one wears neither wet linen nor sandal which is an ornament, despite the habit of using it in the heat of summer to refresh the body."

Furthermore, argued Nobili, custom forbade a man of one sect to wear the emblems of another sect. Yet all wore sandal-paste. Sandal-paste could not be an emblem common to all sects: in India that would be ridiculous, for it would mean that one professed all sects, opposed though they are. Again, during mourning, sect-emblems were not laid aside, yet sandal was not used.

Sandal, continued Nobili, was forbidden to young Brahmins during the somewhat ascetic life they led before marriage, yet they were not forbidden to use ashes and other religious emblems. Sannyāsīs, on the other hand, might sleep in a bed and use sandal: people were even obliged to honour their holiness by offering them

sandal, rose-water and similar gifts. As for the fact that images of
Indian gods were sprinkled with sandal-water: the gods, he replied,
were honoured with what is best: for instance, musk, incense,
flower- and rose-water.

Sandal-ashes were an altogether different matter. They were
used to rub idols, and Śiva, in one of his most distinctive portrayals,
was shown covered in them: an example which his devotees often
followed. Believing them to be distinctly religious, Nobili forbade
his Christians the use of sandal ashes.

Francisco Ros, Archbishop of Cranganore, following the precedent
of the St Thomas Christians, who had used sandal from time im-
memorial, approved the use of sandal-paste as an ornament of the
forehead, composed a special formula for blessing it and issued
instructions as to the manner of applying it. Nobili continued to
wear his rectangular sandal-mark, which he compared to the pom-
pom on the hat sported by teachers in Portugal, and the toga and
gloves worn in Italy. Other Christians wore the *tilakam*, an ornament in shape midway between square and circle, commonly
called the jewel of the forehead. According to the *Kādambarī*, "the
tilakam is an ornamental mark, made of sandal or saffron; it rejoices
and makes the forehead splendid, like a rising sun".

Struggling for such difficult concessions Nobili proved how
well he understood and loved his converts. They on their side
were quick to respond. These first Indians to become Christians
without any temporal motive were as good as the best in Europe.
One impartial visitor said they showed the fervour of novices in
a Jesuit novitiate. Whenever they heard the names of Jesus, of
Mary, of the Blessed Sacrament or the Holy Trinity, they raised
their joined hands before their breasts as a mark of respect. On
their furniture, utensils and walls of their houses they carved the
words "Praise and honour to Jesus Christ". When they met one
another or Portuguese Christians in the street, they hailed them
with the words "*Sesunaderukku Mangalam*—Praised be the Lord
Jesus" or "*Sesuchristunaderukku Mangalam*—Praised be Jesus
Christ". Instead of despising and hating the Parangis, as they did
before baptism, Nobili had taught them to treat the Parangis with
esteem and consideration, as brothers in Christ, through whom

they had received the light of the Gospel. Though he wore a black cassock and shoes, they learned to recognize Laerzio as Nobili's superior, and called him the "Periya Aiyer"—the great master of the house.

In two respects Nobili's neophytes gave, as it were, a new Indian flavour to Christianity. One was their willingness to undertake strict penitence. It was a commonplace of Indian thought that recitation of the Vedas, sacrifice and asceticism wiped out guilt; and the value of confession was also admitted: "If a man who has committed a sin confesses it voluntarily, he is free from it as a snake sloughs off its skin." But the forms of asceticism had had no counterpart in Christendom since the days of St Simon Stylites. Indians hardly turned their head at so common a sight as that of a penitent chained for years to the trunk of a tree; keeping his arms extended for life, so that he had to be fed by someone else; keeping his fists clenched, so that the nails grew into the palm; burying himself except for one small breathing-hole; standing for hours on one leg, gazing at the sun; making long journeys on his back or on his head; swallowing water endlessly, for the sake of its cleansing powers; imitating as far as possible the way of life of a particular animal—a cow or elephant; sometimes even hanging from the branches of a tree in imitation of a bird.

In comparison with these, the penances and discipline—adjudged sufficient for European Christians—which the foreign sannyāsī imposed on his neophytes were no hardship. They had to observe fasting and abstinence on Fridays and Saturdays, which they called *soutta-posana-nal*—days of pure food. But their willingness to suffer more was an encouraging sign, with the possibility of persecution never far distant. Some of them begged Nobili to be allowed to brand the Holy Cross on their shoulders, just as pious Hindus branded themselves with their sect-marks. Nobili could not encourage this, but one little boy without waiting for permission did actually brand himself with a cross.

A second characteristic was the neophytes' love of religious emblems and images. Most men, women and children in South India wore ear-rings, and women loved bangles, necklaces, bracelets and anklets. Moreover, it was the custom to show one's religion by outward signs, not least by the rosary, round which a complicated symbolism had evolved. Most people in Madurai, being Śaivites, used a rosary of thirty-two beads, one or more terminal beads not being counted in with those on the main string. Their favourite bead was the *rūdrākṣa*—eye of the god Rudra (Śiva)—from the *Eleocarpus ganitrus*. These were said to be the tears of Rudra which he let fall in rage and eventually crystallized. Rudrāksa seeds with eleven facets were the privilege of celibate yogīs, while married yogīs had to be content with two-faceted seeds. Rosaries with seeds of five facets were sacred to Hanumān, the monkey-god. Vaiṣṇavites, on the other hand, used a rosary of one hundred and eight beads; and the sect of Jains preferred beads of red coral, crystal and cornelian.

Nobili's Christians were provided with the usual European rosaries of fifty-nine beads. These they loved to display, as well as crucifixes and other pious objects suspended from their necks by a gold thread. Nobili never had enough. Writing to the Duchess of Sora, he asked for "good relics and some more of the small caskets with the wood of the Holy Cross, some copper-plate engravings by a good artist of the Saviour, the Mother of God or of the apostles, also some crucifixes and Agnus Dei from Milan mounted in plain wood with glass, indulgenced medals etc." As it was deemed irreverent to kiss a portrait or relic, because of the impurity of saliva, it is likely that these first Christians observed the Indian custom of "kissing with the eyes": that is, they would place a relic or crucifix they wished to venerate either on their eyes or against their head.

The handbook of their religion was a Tamil Catechism, the work of Enrique Enriquez, the Jesuit who had converted Gonçalo Fernandez. Enrique Enriquez had started by joining the Franciscans, but when after six or seven months it was discovered that he had Jewish blood, he was dismissed, as it was against the Franciscan constitution to admit descendants of Jews or Moors. Ignatius de Loyola obtained from the Pope a dispensation from the impediment of having worn the habit of another order; Enriquez became a Jesuit; and for twenty-five years worked on the Fishery Coast. Despite very bad health he became a master of Tamil and composed a short Tamil Catechism of sixteen pages. This had been printed in Quilon in 1578—Tamil type having been cut by a skilful Spanish lay brother, Juan Gonçalvez—the first book to be printed in an Indian alphabet. This was followed by a fuller Catechism of 112 pages issued in Cochin in 1579.

Nobili, with his wider experience of Indian literature and his insight into the Indian mind, was obliged to replace certain words used by Enriquez in his fuller Catechism by others which he considered more exact. The Catechism contained not only awkward and odd words but sometimes Portuguese words meaningless to Indians. Unable or unwilling to find the Indian correlative for ecclesiastical terms, Enriquez sprinkled his Catechism with such words as *igreja* meaning Church, *gracia* (grace) and *sacramento* (sacrament).

One of Enriquez's slips which had aroused much amusement was the translation of Mass as *misei*. Misei means beard or moustache, and Nobili substituted for it *pugei*—sacrifice, in the form *Christi pugei*—sacrifice instituted by Christ.

Nothing was more important than the term to be chosen for God. Enriquez used *Tambiram*, meaning Lord not subject to a higher lord. But in Madurai Nobili found that all the pandarams, or non-Brahmin Śaivite religious leaders, called one another *Tambiram*. At first Nobili used the word *Śiva*—what causes goodness, but when he discovered that the Śaivites used it to designate God, he replaced it by *Saruuissuren*—master of all things, having power over all things: a term always applied to the real God, never to gods or men.

Nobili was cautious in his use of Tamil. He translated the names of the sacraments and allowed neophytes to make their profession of faith in Tamil. But although so authoritative a theologian as Cajetan permitted the use of the vernacular for baptism—an opinion which Suarez judged speculatively probable—Nobili continued to use the Latin form.

The Catechism presented Nobili with the problem of finding equivalents for certain precise religious terms: but the Gospels made it necessary to explain a whole remote world, with a different social system, different customs, different values. St Peter, being a fisherman, would instinctively fill an Indian with loathing—he belonged to a polluting caste, which took life. Wine, also, was abominated. Every decent person in Madurai shrank from fermented drinks, and one of the castes on the Coast was considered polluting precisely because they drank palm-juice toddy. Again, many of the parables, drawn from an alien agricultural society, were incomprehensible by themselves and had to be carefully explained. The fig-tree, whose leaves were a sign of summer; a single annual crop which ripened in summer—these images would be found odd in Madurai, where each year well-irrigated fields yielded three harvests of millet and two of rice. The familiar animals were not sheep, wolves, foxes and swine but elephants, monkeys, snakes, tigers and vultures.

Did Jerusalem, like Madurai, lie in the Continent of the Rose-apple? And what was that snow which fell on the hills round Bethlehem? Madurai knew only the hot summer and a monsoon season, from October to the end of December, when thirty inches of rain usually fell, filling rivers and tanks on which supplies of water for most of the rest of year depended. The days differed in length by never more than an hour, and as most of the trees were evergreen, nature provided for strangers no obvious clue to the year's cycle. The rainy season in India was known to Europeans as winter, the rest of the year as summer. In Cochin, however, as along all the west coast, the rainy season lasted from April to September, so that winter and summer fell at the same time in a single Jesuit province. The light and shade of traditional Christian imagery required adaptation to this climate, where the summer sun was compared to an unrighteous, cruel king that torments his subjects and, in panegyrics, the people were said to be happy under the protection of their king's open parasol. Where a Western mystic would speak of basking in the sunshine of God's love, a Tamil devotee would speak of reclining under the shadow of His feet.

Another difficulty was posed by dates, which in Madurai, as throughout Hindu India, were reckoned from the subsidence of the Great Flood, when the *Kali yuga*, or Age of Misery, began. Thus, 1606, the year of Nobili's arrival in Madurai, was 4707 of the Age of Misery. This total was divided into cycles of sixty years.

The year itself was reckoned according to two calendars, one civil, the other religious. The civil calendar was solar, so uncompromisingly solar that it did not even specify the number of days to a month. The ecliptic was divided into twelve, and at whatever moment—morning, noon or night—the sun entered a new division, at that moment the new month began.

On the basis of the lunar year savants with the title of *purohitas* issued almanacs called *panchāngam*—the five members, because the almanac contained five leading subjects: the age of the moon in the month; the constellation near which the moon was situated on each particular day; the days of the week; the eclipses; and the positions of the planets. Every court had its own *purohita*, who went every morning to announce to the king, to his state elephants and to his idols, all that was in the almanac for that particular day.

From the Hindu religious calendar it was possible to calculate the Christian calendar, also lunar. Thus, New Year's Day was celebrated on the first day of the March moon—and that gave the date of Easter: the Sunday after the fourteenth day. Then a succession of white, red, green and violet ornaments and vestments proclaimed to Madurai a Christian year with its own unalterable seasons.

Not everyone understood. Since even such outward signs were too new for the mass of the people to grasp, in the Indian way they tried to assess the new religion by its guru. But the stranger guru was rarely seen outside his two small buildings. From scraps of information and irrelevant details some of those who had never talked to Nobili tried to pin him down with an uncommon label (for everyone insisted his religion was "new"), which would also be comfortingly familiar. And so a rumour began to spread in Madurai that Nobili was a Muni.

In a general sense, Muni means a holy sage. According to the *Dhammapada*, one of the Buddhist canonical books: "A man is not a Muni because he observes silence [*mona*], if he is foolish and ignorant; but the wise man who, taking the balance, chooses good and avoids evil, he is a Muni, and is a Muni thereby; he who in this world weighs both sides is called a Muni." The *Sutta Nipāta* was more specific: "A Buddhist is a visionary, and also an ascetic

—a Muni, one that forsakes the world and wanders from the house to the houseless state; because from house-life arises defilement. An ascetic has no prejudiced ideas, he does not enter into disputes, he does not cling to good and evil, he has cut off all passion and all desire, he is free from masks and possessionless. He is still as deep water, he has reached peace."

The word also implied superhuman powers. A late hymn of the *Ṛg Veda* mentions a class of holy men different from the Brahmins: the Munis, or silent ones, who wear the wind as a girdle and, drunk with their own silence, rise on the wind and fly in the paths of the demigods.

This sense was developed by the Buddhists, who had made the word Muni their special property. Now there lingered on among the dozen or so religious sects in Madurai a few Buddhists who, though no longer exercising any influence, kept alive old traditions regarding their founder. Gautama Buddha they called the Muni— by which they meant a being more or less divine. It was in this sense that the name was applied to Nobili.

There were, in fact, some striking points of resemblance between what the Buddha had traditionally done and what Nobili was believed to be doing. Gautama displayed marvellous knowledge as a child: soothsayers predicted that he would be a divine world-emperor. He grew up as a prince of the royal Sakya clan, but left his father's palace to find self-fulfilment by an ascetic life in the forest.

The Buddha had taught a system of practical morality, the key-note of which was universal charity. He attacked the Brahmins' exclusive privileges of teaching and sacrificing; denied the existence of a world-soul and discarded the distinctions of caste within his monastic order—called *Sangha* (Society)—though not as a general classification of mankind. On all these points it was possible for a Buddhist, only vaguely acquainted with Nobili's teaching, to believe that a new Muni had arrived in Madurai.

Nobili himself, in reporting the rumour, specifies that he was believed to have come "to destroy idols and restore religion to its former purity". Now the Buddhists, in their disputes with Brahmins, declared that the Vedas, as they came from the hands of

Brahma, contained perfect truth, but that the Brahmins, in the course of time, had tampered with them. Buddha, they claimed, had restored the Vedas to their primitive purity.

Not only the Buddhists but another minority sect, the Jains, gave the title Muni to their founder. Vardhamāna Mahāvīra, a contemporary of the Buddha and like him of non-Āryan stock, after twelve years of self-mortification achieved the state of *kaivalya*, which implies omniscience and release from earthly bondage. The Jains believed in a succession of "Crossing-makers"—men who, like Mahāvīra, had achieved or would achieve this superhuman state.

Though Christianity had almost nothing in common with Jainism, the Jains might have been able to detect certain parallels between Nobili and their Muni. Mahāvīra was a Rājā by birth; he was not an originator, but the reformer of an old ascetic community; he denied the authority of the Vedas and the orthodox traditions of Hinduism. As opposed to the Brahmins, who advised men to raise a family and only when their hair was turning grey retire to the forests, he taught a total negation of life and the world, and Jaina holy men never married.

So for a time among Buddhists and Jains Nobili was believed to be a new Muni, come to purify the Vedas. When those who knew him well had dispelled the rumour it became convenient to find an accurate and appropriate short name for the stranger guru. He was not a Parangi; he no longer wore the thread of a Rājā. What was he? What did he profess? The point which most struck the people of Madurai was that—in contradistinction to the Brahmin doctrine of a world of illusion—Nobili taught that things are what they seem to be, that what has every appearance of a stone is in fact a stone; that the world, man's body and soul are uniquely and irreplaceably real. So the people of Madurai, who had never taken kindly to idealist philosophies largely Āryan in origin, decided—as a mark of approval—to call Nobili the Teacher of Reality—Tattuva Bodhakar.

The Sanskrit *tatva* (in Tamil, *tattuva*) comes from *tat*, meaning "that". Hence *tatvam* means reality, *haeceitas*, authority, essential quality, the universal soul, etc. Used in the sense of reality, *tatva* is opposed to *māyā*, illusion. To those in Madurai unfamiliar with its technical significance, the title would have conjured up the picture of a learned philosopher, highly respected and admired as a master. Under the name of Tattuva Bodhakar—Teacher of Reality—Nobili continued to be known for the rest of his life.

10. *Creation and Avatārs*

THE Teacher of Reality was accepted in Madurai, at least for the moment. Most Indian teachers believed that the work of redemption by God's grace spread over tens of thousands of lives. They themselves might again be reborn as gurus, to resume their ministry among the same souls, reborn in different bodies. Nobili, on the other hand, believed that he and the people of Madurai had been given only one chance. At sunset the sky-high temple gate-towers cast long shadows over the mud hermitage. In these circumstances, impatience became a virtue.

By Easter 1609, eighteen months after he had started his new way of life dressed as a sannyāsī, Nobili's converts numbered more than fifty. They were very fervent, continually asking him to hear their confession and teach them further. Nobili also gave instruction to catechumens four times a day; continued his Sanskrit studies; and was learning yet another language—Telugu. Telugu was spoken by the comparatively recent intruders from Vijayanagar—Vaiṣṇavites—and also by the inhabitants of the eastern districts of the kingdom of Madurai. Nobili's Sanskrit helped him here, for Telugu literature, written chiefly by Brahmins, contained many Sanskrit words and these had been adopted in common speech. He was now obliged to hold in his head seven languages: Italian, Latin, Portuguese, Tamil, Court Tamil (which differed as much from ordinary speech as the *Aeneid* from the speech of an Italian peasant), Sanskrit and Telugu.

Already, on such a meagre diet, shut up in a mud box in a climate which compelled everyone else to live out of doors, Nobili found his work crushing, yet day and night he was seeking to increase his burden with further conversions. Looking to the future he wrote to Laerzio: "I am well aware of God's special assistance to me, for this fatigue is beyond my strength. It seems to me necessary that your Reverence should send me as soon as possible a good companion endowed with great courage and a desire to suffer for Our Lord's sake. He should be very mortified, so as to adapt himself readily to the ways and customs of this country; this at the beginning is very hard. Nevertheless it is necessary to send him soon so that he may help and encourage me and at the same time learn the language, and the manner of dealing with the people. After my death it may be very difficult to recover the knowledge I have acquired of their secret law, yet on these things entirely depends the conversion of these gentiles, which I have no doubt is bound to make great progress."

Knowing the official temper in Portuguese bases, Nobili hit on a plan for giving urgency to his plea.

"I am thinking of sending to Cochin with this request [for an assistant] two of my Christians, who I am sure will afford your Reverence great consolation. They will be able to inform you better than I can about the progress of this mission. They will move your Reverence to send me some Father such as I asked for in my last letter. Further, the sight of the college, the churches and city of Cochin will confirm them in the holy religion they have embraced. Above all it is important that they should see the Lord Archbishop of the Serra [i.e. Cranganore], arrayed in his pontificals, and pay their respects to him, since this new Christian community is under his jurisdiction and lies within the territory of his Archdiocese."

The neophytes he chose were Alexis's brother, Visuvāsam, aged twenty-five, and a young man of eighteen called Maliappan.

"Don't let your Reverence think they will be scandalized when they see in the college and the city other customs and different ways of eating and dressing, for they are well instructed regarding those matters and are well aware that although our customs are different, we are all serving the same Lord and following the same Christian religion.

"They have a striking illustration of this in Father Gonçalo Fernandez and myself, in my church and his; for although by our manner of living we differ socially, yet in essential things of religion we are alike; we teach the same doctrine, have the same sacraments, etc. So your Reverence need not fear that this contact will be harmful to them. I believe on the contrary that it will be beneficial, specially when they see St Thomas Christians, who though they have customs different from those of the Portuguese follow none the less the same religion.

"It is good they should understand this well so as to be able to explain to others that the same religion may be practised by men of differing social customs, languages and lineage, and that by becoming Christians they do not thereby change their caste, become 'Parangi' as people say."

Cochin lay a difficult fortnight's journey away, across a mountain range called the Ghāṭs. For two young men brought up in the heart of Southern India the journey itself was an adventure, and still more their destination, where they would find things heard of but never seen: the sea, ships like floating palaces, heavy artillery, silk from China, tall stone churches, with gilt altars crowned by crucifixes of silver and ivory.

The two young converts left at the beginning of June 1609, and arrived on the seventeenth, a Wednesday. They were fêted by their guru's black-cassocked Parangi brethren, who lodged and looked after them. Their piety and fervour created a very favourable impression. Those Jesuits hostile to Nobili's experiment, eager to pick holes in their orthodoxy, asked difficult questions about the higher mysteries, such as the Holy Trinity. To every question the converts answered promptly and correctly.

At the end of their twelve days' stay Laerzio wanted to give them fine clothes and other gifts, but they replied that they had not come in search of clothes, and that with such gifts in their hands they would never dare show themselves before the other Christians at Madurai. They would accept only a few rosaries, pictures, medals and other devotional objects so that their master might distribute them, for in Madurai these were rare and highly esteemed.

Accompanied by two Jesuits, the two young men were sent to the Archbishop, who was waiting for them in a village of the St Thomas Christians, on the road back to Madurai. On the feast of SS. Peter and Paul they received the sacrament of

Confirmation. Before giving them the ritual slap, the Archbishop explained that this meant they must be ready to suffer insults and affronts in defence of the faith. "We are ready to give our lives for our faith," they answered. "That would be the highest grace God could grant us."

With an escort of two Christians provided by Archbishop Ros, Visuvāsam and Maliappan recrossed the Ghāts and arrived home a little more than a month after their departure. Nobili heard their news and waited to see whether his embassy would bear fruit.

In fact, Visuvāsam and Maliappan had completely won the hearts of the Cochin priests: they all felt a sudden vocation for the Madurai mission. But the novice-master, Emmanuel Leitao, a highly emotional Portuguese with the gift of tears, was most eager of all to be sent. He could not think of Madurai without crying: and this seems to have determined Laerzio's choice. Leitao was given sannyāsī dress and accompanied up-river as far as Kaduturutti, where Laerzio put him on the road for Madurai.

At Uttamapalyam, on the eastern side of the Ghāts, sixty miles from Madurai, Leitao, exhausted by many sleepless nights, his feet worn by his new wooden sandals, decided to complete his journey in more comfortable style. He obtained an ox, mounted its back and, digging his heels into its flanks, headed for Madurai.

So it was that at seven in the evening on 26th August 1609 Nobili's new assistant, dressed in red-ochre, carrying his staff and gourd, entered Madurai not, as everyone expected of a sannyāsī, on foot, but riding on the back of an ox. He was met, doubtless with much surprise, by Visuvāsam and his brother Alexis, who escorted him to the hermitage, to be welcomed by Nobili as his disciple, according to the custom of gurus.

"On entering," wrote Leitao, "I prostrated myself before him and saluted him with a deep bow, for all this was required by circumstances. He received me with great joy. He then ordered everybody to withdraw, had the doors closed, and having thus recovered his freedom, put aside all the ceremonial prescribed by etiquette, and embraced me with great affection. He was delighted to see my sannyāsī costume and also my complexion, which is not very different from that of the local Brahmins."

Nobili ordered a meal for the weary traveller. "His disciples came to prepare the table, which was soon ready, for a plantain-leaf spread on the floor served as table, table-cloth, dishes and plates. I sat down near the leaf on which the Brahmin cook served the supper, and began to eat; but in spite of my appetite, nature felt such a horror for those new preparations, perhaps also for this new system of eating with the fingers, that I had to force myself to swallow some morsels. This disgust lasted for three days, then I began to get used to it."

Not quite, however. Leitao found it impossible to be content with one meal a day; he therefore dined about mid-day and took a light supper after sunset. On the other hand, Nobili continued to take his one meal in the late afternoon; and so it came about that the two missionaries did not meet at table.

Leitao had not yet mastered Tamil. Until he spoke the language fluently, he could not claim to be a guru. While he continued his studies, he called himself Nobili's disciple, assisting him at the altar and helping him in difficult cases of conscience. From the very beginning he went into rhapsodies about the mission and, having a facile pen, wrote long letters to Cochin about his extra-ordinary graces and how his soul was transported in his new work. He thought the Madurai neophytes were angels.

Now that he had his assistant, Nobili began to plan a new church, for by the end of 1609 his flock had grown to sixty; too many to squeeze into the present mud building. He could not afford to buy land so he turned once again to his benefactor, Errama Setti.

A few weeks earlier Nobili had been able to please the great poligar. The Nāyak of Madurai was preparing for war against his north-eastern neighbour, the Nāyak of Tanjore. Nobili had a goldsmith cast a special gold medal, bearing on one side the image of the Cross with the letters I.N.R.I. and on the other the words IN HOC SIGNO VINCES. On 1st November Errama Setti arrived by night in the hermitage to say that he had received his marching orders. Nobili showed him the medal and explained the meaning of the inscription; then, as gurus were accustomed to do, he tied it on the poligar's right arm, promising him in God's name that if he remained true to his resolve to put himself under instruction after his return, God would give him the victory. Errama Setti in token of his discipleship prostrated himself and kissed his guru's feet.

When, therefore, Errama Setti learned that his guru wanted to build a new church, he willingly provided an additional plot of land. Nobili drew up the plans himself. Since timber was scarce and expensive, much stone and brick would be used. And it was not to be like other missionary churches: a mere replica of Portuguese buildings. The new church was to be in Indian style, with a terraced roof.

As building began, passers-by were doubtless surprised at the simple ground-plan: every portico and shrine of their own temples went to form a complex esoteric diagram, which for the adept became a vision of the deity itself. They were still more surprised that there should be a new temple at all.

The Christian sannyāsī, they complained, was making innumerable disciples. If he were allowed to continue, the Hindu temples would soon be deserted. The chief Brahmin of the great temple of Chockanātha came personally to question Nobili about his intentions. He then launched a campaign of vituperation and slander; the Parangi, he claimed, was building on temple land, which no one had power to alienate, and that his insolence must be punished by the Great Nāyak.

After a week of this, Nobili sent Alexis to bargain with the Brahmin. He offered to pay the price of the land in order to obtain peace. A mutual friend having valued the plot at fifteen scudi,[1] the Brahmin came to the hermitage smiling and affable, even apologizing for his previous conduct. Nobili offered him the silver, which he promptly accepted. The Brahmin then promised his lasting friendship. "I will be a brother and protector to you," he said. "Don't be afraid, make as many disciples as you please. If I am for you, who will dare be against you?"—a claim soon proved unduly optimistic, when a pandaram, believing Nobili responsible for the neglect of his idols, committed suicide so that the odium for his death should fall on the Teacher of Reality.

However, this suicide did not interrupt the new church. Idlers

[1] £9.

gathered to watch the masons, and Nobili's converts made the
most of the opportunity to speak enthusiastically of their guru.
Their words were not to the taste of some of Fernandez's parishioners, who happened to be present. One of them, a Parava,
"moved by some diabolical impulse which I cannot understand,"
writes Laerzio, "told the Aiyer's converts that when he had
baptized them, and put salt in their mouths, he had made them
lose their caste and introduced them into that of the Parangis, in
which all who received baptism were, by that very act, incor-
porated. . . . He dressed up his lies in such plausible words that
they created a great commotion among Fr Robert's converts.
Their Hindu relatives were not slow in exploiting their panic, and
they succeeded so well that fourteen of the neophytes stopped
coming to church.

"Informed of their defection, Fr Robert sent for them in the
hope of disabusing them, but when they reached the outer gate,
they held back without daring to set foot in the church enclosure.
They cried out that they were glad they had embraced the faith of
Our Lord, because they knew very well that it was the only way to
salvation, 'but', they said, 'as to becoming Parangis, we will never
do that; the very thought of it is unbearable to us—we prefer to
die.' "

Submission, resignation and obedience—Indian education
inculcated these. But to one thing an Indian would never willingly submit: the void of castelessness, no longer having set rules to
which to submit.

To avert the imminent defection of almost a quarter of his flock,
Nobili decided on drastic measures. Though a sannyāsī was not
supposed to enter disputes, he would try to silence the charges
with a written manifesto. In the hermitage he had two sets of
writing materials. One, consisting of pen, ink and white parchment paper, he used for letters to Europeans. Nobili doubtless
kept the parchment paper carefully hidden from Indians, for,
being of animal skins, it would have aroused their horror and
anger. The second set consisted of an iron stylus about eight
inches long, the handle ending in a knife; and a heap of young
palm leaves.

The first thing to do in writing Indian fashion was to choose a young tender palm-leaf, with twenty or thirty folds, like a folded fan, then divide the folds by passing the knife-end of the stylus along the ribs. In this way twenty or thirty fairly narrow thin strips were obtained. The leaf—known as *olei*—was supported on the middle finger of the left hand and kept steady by the thumb and forefinger. The stylus did not glide along like a pen; after every word or two, the point was pressed firmly on the last letter so as to push the leaf from right to left until the line was finished. Seven or eight lines could be written on each leaf. At first the words appeared as only a very faint engraving. Later the leaf was smeared with fresh cowdung and wiped clean so that the letters showed up dark. To make a book, a small hole was bored at the end of the leaves, which were fastened together, within two thin binding boards, by small wooden or iron pegs.

Writing in this way, Nobili composed a manifesto, which he later revised and gave to Errama Setti. In its revised form it ran thus:

"The Rājā Sannyāsī who teaches and follows the Sattya-vedam [true religion] wishes to all the sannyāsīs and other men of this city the blessing of Sarveśwara, and spiritual happiness.

"Those who make profession of speaking the truth are accustomed to state in writing certain principles, to be made manifest to everyone and appear as clear as daylight. Since I find myself obliged to affirm certain truths, it seems to me proper, according to the ancient custom of great scholars, to reduce them to writing.

"Some irresponsible persons have spoken calumnies about me before a grave and distinguished man, and as even a good man may innocently believe them, I wish to reply to all the charges in complete sincerity and truth.

"I am not a Parangi, I was not born in the land of the Parangis, nor was I ever connected with their race. God is my witness that I speak the truth and if the contrary is proved against me I am prepared to suffer not only the punishment of hell as a traitor to God, but also to submit to any penalty which may be inflicted upon me by the powers on earth.

"I came from Rome, where my family hold the same rank as

respectable Rājās hold in this country. When I was young I became a sannyāsī and, after studying wisdom and learning the spiritual law, I left my native country as a pilgrim, travelled through many kingdoms and wherever I dwelt, lived and conducted myself as a sannyāsī.

"When I came to Madurai with the intention of going further afield, the Padre who lives here received me in his house, and I decided to remain for some time in this city of Madurai to do penance. With the permission of Nagaya Setti I built a house and, later on, with the help and favour of Errama Setti, I erected a church in brick and with the same material a house, where with the help and favour of the same Setti I have been living to this day.

"With those who come to speak with me I discuss no other questions than those which concern the salvation of their souls. In this matter I treat of the existence of God and His attributes, how He is One and Three, how He created the world and men, and all other things.

"In addition, I teach how that very same God became man to save men. I declare that His name is Jesus Christ which means Saviour, that He is true God and true Man, full of grace and Divine gifts, who delivers us from sin, satisfies for the transgression of all men and offers a remedy against their errors. Moreover I teach that after death God will give each one, according to his merits, and without any regard for birth or transmigration, an eternal reward or punishment. The holy and spiritual law which holds this doctrine of mine does not make anyone lose his caste or pass into another, nor does it induce anyone to do anything detrimental to the honour of his family.

"God is my witness that what I say is true. Just as the Nāyak is the Lord of these lands, and all of us who live in them, whether Brahmins or Rājās or of any other caste, are obliged to obey him in temporal matters, in the same way Sarveśwara being the legitimate Lord of all men, it is fitting that all races should live in conformity with His holy law.

"The law which I preach is the law of the true God, which from ancient times was by His command proclaimed in these countries, by sannyāsīs and saints. Whoever says that it is the law of the Parangis, fit only for low castes, commits a very great sin, for the true God is not the God of one race, but the God of all. We must confess that He deserves to be equally adored by all. Therefore he who wants to attain the glory of Paradise must learn about this God and walk in conformity with His holy will, and do nothing which brings dishonour to his caste, and whoever dares say the contrary deserves the punishment of hell.

"Perhaps some will deem it unbecoming in a sannyāsī like myself to speak in this *olei* of his country and family, but as the lies spread about me are likely to cause greater evils, I am compelled to use that means to make known the law which I profess, the people from whom I came and the land to which I belong, so as to crush a falsehood which might bring disgrace on those I love."

Having written this document in Tamil on a series of *oleis*, Nobili sent for two of the chief discontented Christians. After reading it aloud, he directed them to nail the manifesto to a tree in front of his house, so that all might read it.

The manifesto satisfied most of the malcontents. But some, with surprising inconsistency, applied to Fernandez, the avowed Parangi, for admission into his congregation. Nobili sent a note to Fernandez, warning him against countenancing a step which the neophytes would soon regret, and those who had remained faithful to Nobili informed the malcontents that should they join the Parangis, they would lose caste and so have to be debarred from entering the new church. These two warnings had the desired effect, and Nobili's community was soon reunited.

But now the new wave of Parangiphobia began to be directed against Nobili's Brahmin convert, Śivadarma. Śivadarma had an expert knowledge of *pūjā* or sacrifice, which Brahmins offered daily to their household gods. Śivadarma knew exactly how to welcome the deity with water for washing; a beverage of honey, sugar and milk; clothes and jewels; grains of saffron-stained rice; flowers, incense and a lighted lamp; and finally a dish of rice, fruit, liquefied butter, sugar and betel. Formerly, no important sacrifice had been offered without Śivadarma. Since becoming a Christian, the Brahmin had declined all such invitations. His resentful friends retaliated by labelling him a Parangi; they no longer spoke to him or invited him to their banquets. Śivadarma, feeling the disgrace keenly, asked a friend, one of the most learned Brahmins in Madurai, to examine Nobili in order to be able to give evidence on his behalf.

"The Brahmin accepted the task most willingly," writes Nobili, "and a few days ago he came accompanied by four other learned Brahmins, all graduates in their science. They examined me closely, trying to discover if I was a Parangi or atheist, and see whether they had not to punish Śivadarma for associating with a low-caste man. . . . They entered my house, sat down with characteristic arrogance, and began questioning me on my teaching. They first asked me about God: whether He is self-existent and eternal; then they questioned me regarding His Unity and Trinity (for many of their books and poems teach that God is Triune, but they themselves do not know what to make of this statement)."

This uncertainty as to the nature of God must have proved a dilemma as much to Nobili as to the people of Madurai. The city, in fact, was a melting-pot for three distinct traditions: pure monotheism (long vigorous in South India and fostered perhaps by the influence of St Thomas Christians, Muslims and a group of Jewish traders in the district round Cochin); the belief in the Hindu Trimūrti—Brahmā, Viṣṇu and Śiva—as an inseparable unity, though three in form; and Brahmin monism.

With the monotheists, chiefly Śaivites of Dravidian extraction, Nobili had most in common. As for the Vaiṣṇavites, the Trimūrti they professed could not provide a basis of agreement; Viṣṇu so dwarfed his co-divinities that its form did not correspond to that of the Christian Trinity. But under the influence of the Brahmins, who conducted all courses in Madurai university, monotheistic and trinitarian beliefs alike tended to lapse into an all-embracing monism, far removed from Christian beliefs.

A second danger was that the Brahmins, following Śankara's distinction between a lower and higher truth, would be able to turn Nobili's arguments. A beginner in the spiritual life, they would say, can usefully centre his thought on a God—call him the

Trimūrti, as they did, or Buddha or Jesus Christ. But all such personal Gods are themselves illusion. When the pure, transcendental essence—Brahman—which is beyond all attributes, sinks into the state in which, under a personal mask, it fancies itself to be the Universal God, then the clarity of pure spiritual being is clouded, and this cloud is self-delusion on a cosmic scale: universal consciousness, forgetful of the true state and nature of Brahman.

At the higher level of truth, the Brahmins would say, Christ was merely one aspect of the shades of man's not-knowing-better. He conveyed some truth, yet was himself part and effect of the cosmic play of illusion. The highest truth was "That art Thou": like the butter hidden in milk, beneath the folds of everyday consciousness, God was in every man.

Because European philosophers had concentrated on the multiplicity of existing things, and made only very tentative efforts to apprehend the central unity, Nobili had few classic arguments with which to oppose Śankara's doctrine. A rare instance was Aquinas's reply to Parmenides's claim that apart from one single reality nothing can exist. Aquinas retorted that there are different levels of being or different kinds of beings, which do not belong to one genus and cannot be added together. But this savoured more of assertion than demonstrable argument.

"We next discussed causality," Nobili continues: "the definition and nature of cause; then we passed on to Logic, Knowledge, Science, Methods of Argument, and the various kinds of Certitude. They hold the latter to be of four kinds, i.e. intuitive evidence, knowledge from consequences, knowledge through argumentation, and knowledge through human or divine faith. When I had answered to their satisfaction they began by telling me stories about their idols and asked me if I believed them. I answered I did not, because they contained many contradictions, and asked them if they were willing to listen to the doctrine I was preaching. As they agreed I expounded to them with great zest [con buon gusto], for a full hour, the chief articles of our faith which I divided into four parts: the Unity of God, the Trinity, the Creation and Redemption, and I concluded my discourse, as St Thomas does in his *Summa*, by showing them that a being who not only lacks the divine attributes, but possesses instead the contrary vices, is not worthy of being called God."

Here, again, Nobili was doubtless faced with difficulties. The men to whom he was talking believed that being and non-being are mutually exclusive. Yet between them lay a third—*māyā*—"an appearance of being, without origin, inexpressible in terms of being and non-being": the illusion of the world and the self. The category of *māyā* disappeared when the Ātman merged with Brahman—pure Thought which, however, does not think, even of Itself. This merging was a denial of the principle of identity, as Nobili understood it, and the notion of *māyā* a denial of the principle of contradiction. It is unlikely, then, that St Thomas's arguments from contradiction weighed heavily with Nobili's visitors.

"They raised many objections, asking me in particular why I made use of a church, since God, being a Spirit, is present everywhere, and why I did not adore their idols, whom they hold to be His subordinate helpers in the government of this world. I answered as well as I could, and by God's grace they went away persuaded that I was neither a Parangi nor an atheist, nor a sceptic, for they hold that such people are as ignorant as animals, incapable of understanding science, specially philosophy. After this, our Brahmin [Śivadarma] was free from all trouble."

"But note this conclusion. Before returning home, the Brahmin friend of Śivadarma made a speech to his disciples and a crowd of 200 Brahmins, in which he used very complimentary words about me, and declared that he must tie to the tree in front of his house a pair of sandals and a whip for the castigation of those who were so ready to call me a sceptic or an atheist, for he had thoroughly examined me and found me very learned."

Learned Nobili certainly must have been, even to make intelligible the Christian doctrines of Creation and the Incarnation. He had to make up new technical terms—fortunately Sanskrit lends itself to this—as well as adapt his arguments to an unfamiliar logical system and his imagery to Hindu traditions. But a chief difficulty was that as regards both creation and incarnation Hindus had arrived at conclusions different from his by starting from different premises.

From a basic Hindu assumption that action is less good than inaction and therefore a sign of imperfection, it followed that there can never have been a moment when the Supreme Being willed the world. Again, there is nothing extraneous to God, therefore no matter from which the world could have been created. So Brahman is represented both as efficient and material cause of the world. According to the Upaniṣads. "Just as the spider pours forth its thread from itself and takes it back again; just as herbs grow on the earth and hairs from a living man, even so the universe grows from the Imperishable." "Just as there shoot out from a blazing fire sparks by the thousand, resembling the fire, so do the various beings proceed from that Imperishable; and into it, truly, they return." In short, Nobili's listeners understood "creation" to mean "emanation".

Similarly, they understood "incarnation" to mean "avatār". Viṣṇu's appearances as fish, tortoise or boar showed points of resemblance with Zeus's visit to Leda in the form of a swan. With such beliefs Christian philosophers knew how to deal. But many Indian gods also had human avatārs, such as Viṣṇu as Prince Rāma and as Kṛṣṇa. Like their statues, with four, six or even eighteen arms, these avatārs were continually bursting the seams of humanity.

The god's human body was a mere disguise, his human weakness and emotion assumed; his actions mere sport. Śiva, for instance, is constantly called the Great Deceiver, and his most typical action is the dance. Some Tamil saints, it is true, had taught that their gods endured vicarious suffering for man, but such theories seem to have been never more than marginal in Nobili's day.

Another important difference between the Christian doctrine of the Incarnation and the Hindu doctrine of avatārs arises from a different conception of Time. In Christian thought, time is a straight line, which progresses and cannot come back on itself; in India time is cyclical. Hence, a unique Christian Incarnation, with the resultant importance of history; in India a continual series of incarnations, each expressing the same archetypal truth, but adapted to the needs of the age, superseding one another, with a resultant disinterest in history and historical fact. One biography of the god was never enough. First he must be shown on low, even animal planes of existence, enacting his characteristic part of the magnanimous being, then his gradual progress (with blissful intervals in heaven) until he arrives at that supreme state of embodied spirituality which distinguishes his actual historical biography. In the case of the Buddha, volumes of such earlier biographies had been written.

To accept Nobili's teaching about merely one unrepeatable Incarnation of God's only Son doubtless appeared to his Hindu listeners an impoverishment as well as an inadmissible mixing-up of the contingent and absolute, of time and eternity. In their eyes, too, personality, by imposing determination and form, seemed to be limitation, imperfection.

But the Trinity Nobili taught was a Trinity of Persons. Here once again in a new form he came up against the bedrock of caste. Caste membership restricted and put at a discount the expression of individual personality. Family and caste—these were the tall gate-towers on the Hindu horizon, while the individual person was held to resemble one of the component statues. To caste Indians the idea of God as a Person suggested that God was part of a greater whole.

One of Nobili's chief tasks, therefore, was to convey a new notion of what a person is. If he succeeded, transmigration would no longer be a tenable belief and the Incarnation would no longer appear a limitation. As often elsewhere, he began by opening Indian eyes, for so long shut in contemplation, to the wonders of physical nature. In one passage which doubtless reproduces an actual dialogue, Nobili writes: "When we think of the glands, faculties and limbs necessary even for a small insect to move, walk, eat and scratch, we are struck by the infinite, inexplicable wisdom and workmanship of the Supreme God . . . just as we should be struck by the skill and intelligence of a famous artist who depicts the details of all the rooms of a gigantic palace on a simple metal plate."

"Like the pearl-diver who longs to clutch at all the countless pearls before him but is able to secure only a few," Nobili points out some of the wonders of the human eye: how well it is protected by the eyelids, how the images on two retinas are co-ordinated into one object, and how, like spies, they are placed high in the body, to foresee danger. That they may not be affected by atmospheric changes they are composed "not of flesh but of matter resembling crystal and of fluids like water and wine". He says he would like to be more specific, but the necessary words do not exist in Tamil.

By stressing the wonders of the human body and the inter-action of soul and body (he insists on the fact that the eyes reveal hatred and love, anger and mildness, fear and courage) Nobili taught what Europeans took for granted: the value of the human person. The body did not deserve utter contempt, and the world, far from being illusion, gave precise and beautiful clues to the nature of God. In this way Nobili laid the rose of Christian thought beside the lotus of India. But he could not induce the Indians to prefer the rose. Only grace could do that.

Soon after his thorough cross-examination by five Brahmins, Nobili was again put to the test. "Some Brahmin sannyāsīs," he writes, "who on account of their great learning are held in high esteem in this city, came to my house to have a discussion and find out what kind of man I really was. The two most prominent among them argued well and very earnestly about the following topics. Transmigration, Unity of God, His Will: whether He was free with regard to creation; His providence: how was it that some men were damned and others were saved; man's inclination to evil; since nothing can be done without God's help, does it follow that when man commits sin God co-operates with Him? They asked me whether the help God gives us determines and compels our will, and in what God's help consists. I answered them as well as I could and they showed great astonishment that we should study so much and know so many things."

Nobili says the Brahmins put forward their views on grace. According to the *Śaiva Agamanta*, either the position of the soul with regard to the grace of God is largely helpless, in the attitude of a kitten towards its mother, until grace seizes it and brings it into salvation—known as *mārjārī bhakti*—cat-like faith. Or the soul may co-operate in securing salvation, being in the position of a young monkey grasping its mother—*markaṭamaja bhakti*—or monkey-like faith. Now, under quaint terminology, these two views substantially correspond to the Thomist and Molinist views of grace, at that time so hotly disputed throughout Europe that Cardinal Bellarmine, specially appointed to mediate, had been unable to effect a settlement. Most Jesuits favoured a "monkey-like" conception of grace, and presumably Nobili was no exception. In Madurai, however, "cat-like" faith was considered the more orthodox view.

Evidently, however, Nobili's ready handling of this familiar question evoked respect if not agreement, for he concludes: "They are full of admiration for our terminology in scientific questions, and this gives them such a high opinion of me that they say God enters into this body of mine, and other absurdities which I forgive them, provided they are converted, as I hope they will be if they can overcome their difficulties."

In fact, no one knew better than Nobili how ill-equipped he was to combat, single-handed, school after school of subtle doctrines, never glimpsed before by the Church. Perhaps the Alexandrine Fathers' debates about Plato's *Parmenides* were the nearest historical parallel to Nobili's arguments with the Madurai Brahmins. But the Alexandrine Fathers had debated a Greek text in their own tongue; Nobili was debating in Sanskrit, Telugu and Tamil a system of knowledge couched in Sanskrit and in its most esoteric form not committed to writing.

If he could not study all his opponents' texts, he found it difficult enough to obtain his own. He sent urgent letters to Rome, first for a tract on the eternity of hell or against transmigration as taught by Pythagoras; then for Augustine's *de Gratia, de Libero Arbitrio*, and *contra Manicheos*; and now, in the present year—1610—to Cardinal Bellarmine, asking for a copy of his *de Controversiis*, and pointing out that the volumes he had with him in Madurai were almost entirely useless for arguments against the Brahmins. He was forgetting his Italian, so in a letter to Fabius de Fabiis he asked for an Italian book. He gives a choice of two

titles by Spanish writers, which provide evidence of Nobili's will
to progress even further in ascetic holiness: the letters of John
of Avila or Francisco Arias's book on Mortification.

Meanwhile, among the coconut palms and margosa trees, his
new church took shape. Built of stone and brick, it consisted of
three naves separated by rows of columns in black granite, with
cross-beams also of black granite. It had one main door, and on
both sides two windows with iron bars. Above the porch was a
small terrace. At the east end only a temporary wall was put up,
for Nobili intended to double the church's dimension, when the
size of his flock should demand it.

Above the altar hung a reredos of the Saviour with His Apostles
—not very well painted, for European artists were scarce in
India and Madurai had no tradition of painting corresponding to
its magnificent school of sculpture. At one side hung a small
picture of the Virgin and Child. The antependium, altar ornaments and Mass vestments were exactly the same as in Fernandez's
church, but instead of a wooden bookstand for the missal Nobili
followed the Italian custom and used a cushion. In the sanctuary
hung a curtain of fine Indian cloth, which was drawn during the
preparation and purification of the chalice.

Nobili opened the Church of Jesus, as he called it, on the Feast
of the Annunciation (25th March 1610), for he had a special
devotion to the Virgin Mary, often choosing her feasts for baptism,
and celebrating them, when he could afford it, with a banquet for
the Christians. The church was a fine, graceful building, inspiring
devotion. Though dwarfed by the gopurams of the temple of
Chockanātha and his fish-eyed consort, it was far more imposing
than the mud chapel of the hermitage. It marked the definite
establishment in Madurai of the religion professed by the Teacher
of Reality: a church in Indian style for Indians.

Yet adaptation stopped short at the altar. The first Mass
Nobili celebrated there differed in no way from the first Mass he
had said in Rome. The St Thomas Christians, cut off from
Europe for centuries, had been found consecrating at Mass rice-
cakes and a wine made from raisins soaked in water. This practice
had been discontinued in 1599 by Archbishop de Menezes. Like

all Christian priests in Southern India, a land which grew neither wheat nor grapes, Nobili uttered a Latin formula of consecration over unleavened bread and wine from Europe in his Indian-style church.

Nobili, surveying the church that was meant to expand, and watching the ever-growing body of converts, found it difficult to join wholeheartedly in the celebrations. Three priests would find more than enough to keep them busy, but Nobili was again alone. His assistant, Leitao, had been unable to stand the hard life or master the language. Despite his rhapsodies and genuine eagerness, after only a few months he had to take off his sannyāsī dress and return to Cochin. For Nobili it must have proved a crushing disappointment, which threatened the very existence of the mission. If Leitao had failed, other assistants would doubtless fail also. The Indo-European life was a hybrid, which could not proliferate. It seemed, during the first months of 1610, that he had undertaken a task which was beyond any other European's powers, that the experiment, however much a success during his own lifetime, was so formidable as ultimately to be doomed to failure.

11. *Censured*

IN 1610 the General, Claudio Aquaviva, appointed Nicolau Pimenta Visitor of the Provinces of Goa and Malabar. Pimenta was sixty-four. Born at Santatem, Portugal, he had taught humanities and theology at the universities of Evora and Coimbra before coming out to India in 1596. In a previous term as Visitor he had gained an outstanding success. A man who had visited the Great Mogul at Delhi and the Emperor of Vijayanagar at Chandragiri, who had spoken to the Nāyaks of Gingi and Tanjore and received a turban from the Great Nāyak of Madurai, was understandably inclined to think on the grand scale. When it was suggested that in view of his age the task assigned to him might be divided among several men, he retorted with the Latin adage: *"Pannus brevis est, non patitur duos sartores"*—"The cloth is too small to keep two tailors busy."

Nobili heard of the appointment with considerable misgivings. Not only were the Portuguese strong enough already in India, but "I remember", he writes, "hearing from Dom Martim Afonso de Castro, the late Viceroy of the Indies, who was very intimate with me, that Fr Pimenta seemed to him in his way of governing more like a secular ruler or a general than a religious, and he assured me that he had gathered this impression from two or three conversations he had with him.

"As soon as it was announced in India that Fr Nicolau Pimenta was appointed Visitor of both our Provinces, I wrote to him several times, as was proper, to greet him and inform him briefly of the affairs of this Mission, leaving to Father Provincial Alberto Laerzio the task of going into fuller details, but for reason unknown to me, I received no reply."

Laerzio had already received a letter from the Visitor saying "that the first thing he would do, if he came to the Malabar Province, would be to attend to our affairs [the Madurai Mission] and set them right, for, said he, all expected him to bring this mission back to the right path, from which it had gone astray, as was the talk of Goa."

Gonçalo Fernandez, believing he had at last found a Superior who would take his complaints seriously, sent to Pimenta on 7th May 1610 a letter of four closely written pages, describing, in his own way, Nobili's "innovations". "He does all this," Fernandez concluded, "to make people believe that he belongs to a different nation and that he is of a royal race. According to him, preachers of the Gospel should all be of princely lineage and have no dealings with Parangis."

On receiving this list of grievances, without informing Nobili and without trying to discover whether they were true, Pimenta submitted Fernandez's letter to two Portuguese theologians of Goa. The theologians found Nobili's method superstitious, scandalous and illicit. But, being prudent men, they added the following words: "supposing that the information contained in this letter is true."

Pimenta next referred the matter to the Jesuit consultors at Cochin. Shall the Madurai Mission be suppressed or reformed, he asked. And if it is to be reformed, what are the changes to be made? All the consultors, with the exception of three Portuguese, were of the opinion that the Mission was to continue without any change. However, they desired that Nobili should drop the thread, if he still wore it. Actually, he was not wearing it.

The Rector of Cochin College, Ambrosio Soeiro, added one final point. During the Consult it had been alleged, on evidence which may not have been reliable, that Nobili went about in a palanquin. This, said Soeiro, should be discontinued, to reduce expenses. As for the rest, he had full confidence in Nobili.

Laerzio, deeply relieved, wrote a full account of the Consult to Pimenta and set off to visit Nobili. On the way he picked up a Portuguese priest, André Buccerio, who he thought might make a suitable companion for Nobili. On 18th August they arrived in Madurai.

To save the Madurai Christians from losing caste, Bucceiro in black cassock and shoes stayed in Fernandez's tiled house, while

Laerzio in red-ochre clothes and wooden sandals went to the hermitage. There he announced his good news to Nobili who, in high spirits, wrote a letter to Ambrosio Soeiro, thanking him for his support and hoping he would come in person to fill the people of Madurai with the "ambrosia" of divine love—possibly in company with Pimenta, when the Visitor arrived south. Madurai lay 550 miles from Goa, south by six degrees of latitude. Race and climate, customs and belief, symbolism and ritual differed widely and could not be judged in terms of knowledge available in Goa. Nobili took it for granted that Pimenta was on his way to see the mission for himself.

In this Nobili overestimated the old man's character. At the beginning of September a letter arrived from Pimenta which caused the two Italians shocked surprise. The Visitor had still been in Goa on 26th July 1610, the date of his letter, and gave no indication of leaving. On the contrary, not satisfied with the Cochin Consult, he ordered Laerzio to conduct a special inquiry among the new converts of Madurai regarding Nobili's method.

Laerzio at once obeyed. As his own Tamil was not fluent, he appointed Gonçalo Fernandez and André Buccerio to conduct the inquiry on the following lines. After summoning eight or ten of the oldest Christians, "and administering to them on the Holy Gospels the oath to speak the truth, let your servant Manoel, with the said articles written in Tamil on an *olei* before his eyes, question them and write their depositions in Tamil, while you write them in Portuguese".

A list of ten witnesses was drawn up, comprising three Brahmins, three Badagas (Telugu-speaking northerners), one Itankolli, one Gnani and two Vellalas (the Vellalas, mostly farmers, were the highest caste of Śudras in Madurai). The list was representative both as regards caste and previous religious beliefs. Some knew Sanskrit, others did not even know how to sign their names.

The questionnaire consisted of fifteen searching questions based on the information given by Gonçalo Fernandez. When the answers were written down, the whole ran into tens of thousands of words. The following is a summary of the answers, from which the questions are easily deduced:

(1) (*a*) Following the custom of this country, according to which men call themselves disciples of a particular guru, we called ourselves disciples of the Aiyer. But we were not ordered to do so by our guru who, on the contrary, told us that since we were, like him, disciples of Jesus Christ, we should call ourselves Christians or disciples of Jesus Christ, and so we do, but we do not call ourselves Parangis.

(*b*) We confess the Holy Name of Jesus Christ, by saying "Praise be to Jesus Christ", when we meet one another; we pray in the same words when rising in the morning and before going to sleep, or before beginning our work, etc.

(2) The people of Madurai look upon Fr Robert as a man of great learning and irreproachable habits and hold him in great esteem.

(3) They think that the Spiritual Law (*Jñāna Vedam*) which he teaches is very good, but some who lack judgment, seeing that he does not worship their gods nor admit transmigration, call him an atheist. He never said, or caused to be said, or hinted in any way, that the religion he preaches is different from that of Fr Gonçalo Fernandez, or of the Portuguese; on the contrary, he said it was the same.

(4) The difference between him and Fr Gonçalo is not one of religion or religious ceremonies, but of caste, as the Hindus themselves admit.

(5) The Aiyer never forbade us to attend the Mass or hear the sermons of Fr Gonçalo, nor did he ever forbid us to make our confessions to him, or threaten us with exclusion from the Church of Jesus if we did so.

(6) We know that he goes to the house of Fr Gonçalo to make his confession, and we would do the same if the Aiyer were absent.

(7) We are aware that our Aiyer has changed some words in the Catechism used on the Coast, but we do not, on that account, believe that our religion is different from that of Fr Gonçalo. We know that by making those changes Fr Robert expressed certain things more accurately and elegantly. We call the Holy Trinity: *Pida, Suden, Ispiritu Santu*, three Persons in one God.

(8) Our Aiyer never told us that we were obliged to bathe or

put on sandal-paste. We do not always bathe before Mass; when we do so, it is for the sake of cleanliness, not as a religious ceremony.

(9) No Hindu law prescribes the use of sandal as a religious rite. It is used simply as an ornament for the body. We do not believe there is any religious merit in it. It is not the emblem of any sect. The sandal worn by the Aiyer is the mark of a teacher of the law. No one else is allowed to wear it in the same way.

(10) It is not necessary that missionaries be of princely race, but it is not good that they should associate with low-caste people, not that such association is sinful, or that there is a difference of religion between them and us, but because of the laws of the caste. It is about nine or ten months ago that the Aiyer ceased to wear the thread.

(11) There is no need for the Aiyer or anyone else to say that the law he preaches is different from that of the Parangis, nor did the Aiyer ever say such a thing.

(12) The trouble caused by the Parava was not due to the fact that he told us the Aiyer had made us Christians, but that he had made us Parangis by using arrak [wine] at Mass, and putting salt in our mouth.

(13) The ceremonies used by the Aiyer, either inside or outside the church, and his ways of dealing with the people, are altogether different from those of the Hindus.

(14) In these parts people understand by Parangis vile individuals of low caste whom they hold in horror. After baptism we do not feel the same horror for them because the Aiyer told us that they follow the same law and worship the same God as ourselves. Therefore when we meet them we treat them with greater honour than we did before.

(15) We know who is the Pope and we recognize him as head of the universal Church. We also recognize the Archbishop of the Serra as our Spiritual Head. Some of us went to receive confirmation from him and others intend doing likewise. At baptism we received neither money nor clothes, nor the promise of any temporal advantage; we became Christians because we wanted to save our souls and for no other motive.

This resounding vindication of the Christian guru by his disciples was concluded on 30th September. Fernandez, after listening for two days to sworn witnesses declare that the "facts" he had given Pimenta in his letter were devoid of all foundation, begged to be excused, on the plea of illness, from all further part in the inquiry.

The written testimony was immediately sent to Goa. Pimenta, having ordered the examination of Nobili's neophytes, did not, however, have the patience to wait for the result. In the month of September he held a new meeting, this time of five theologians, who, after examining Fernandez's letter, were to pass judgment on Nobili's method.

The theologians selected four points for comment. The thread worn by Christian Brahmins might, they said, be tolerated in view of the cross attached to it. The baths taken by Nobili and Christian Brahmins were found to be superstitious, and the changes of liturgical names rash and liable to dangerous errors. Finally, the separation from Gonçalo Fernandez was schismatical. Therefore it followed that Nobili's way of acting was a negation of the true faith, that his converts were not true Christians and that the Superiors were bound under pain of mortal sin to suppress the Madurai Mission.

Now at last Pimenta had what he wanted. Whatever the Madurai neophytes might say to the contrary, he could condemn the Italian's method root and branch. He at once sent Nobili a letter to this effect, enclosing the theologians' censures and Gonçalo Fernandez's original list of grievances. They reached Nobili just when it seemed that the Cochin Consult and his own disciples' vindication had removed the threat of suppression once and for all.

Although not a word survives recording his immediate reactions it is difficult to imagine that the first shock of Pimenta's letter did not bring Nobili, for all his self-possession, a few dark moments of doubt. Rashness, superstition, schism—these were no longer enemies' taunts, but the calculated judgment of theologians of his own Order. Had he gone too far? Been swallowed up by India? Had his small brick church, as though by osmosis,

become one more Hindu temple? Were his Indians—Śivadarma,
Visuvāsam, Maliappan and the rest—converts to a new heresy?
Had he, all unknowingly, dedicated his life to the Devil?

One fact is certain. Nothing was so bitter to Nobili personally
as Fernandez's letter, the existence of which he had never even
suspected. He wondered how a man who for the last four years
had heard his weekly confessions and been the confidant of his
most intimate thoughts could accuse him of schism and apostasy.
"If my enemy had reviled me, I could have borne it patiently, but
thou who hadst known my thoughts . . ."

Nobili turned again to Pimenta's letter. There, amid the
denunciations, he saw one small cause for hope. Pimenta pointed
out that if Nobili had anything to plead in his own defence, he
must do so quickly, for the Visitor's report must be sent to the
General by the next post. Nobili consulted his calendar. It was
already the beginning of October. Letters took three weeks to
reach Goa. And the carracks left in November.

Nobili turned for encouragement to his friends. Laerzio was
still in Madurai, as well as André Buccerio, who after his close
study of Nobili's work had become an enthusiastic admirer. However, it soon became clear that Buccerio would never be accepted
by the people of Madurai. Having worked for eighteen years
among the Mukuvars, a fishing caste of Cape Comorin, his habits
and language betrayed him as an out-and-out Parangi. Were he
recognized by Palivedis, a low caste which travelled the interior
selling dried fish, the mission would be compromised. So Buccerio was appointed to help Fernandez, and the post of assistant to
Nobili was filled by an Italian who promised to become an ideal
Christian sannyāsī.

Antonio Vico was now thirty-four. Born in the Marches, he had
studied in Rome with Nobili, who was a year his senior. The two
men had struck up a friendship which had been continued by
letter in India, where Vico held the post of professor of theology
at Cochin. Nobili had repeatedly asked Laerzio to send his friend
to Madurai, but Vico was a valuable man, and also, perhaps, the
Provincial had wanted to avoid any charge that the new method
was an Italian eccentricity. Now that battle had been joined with

Pimenta, it seemed they might as well be sheared for a sheep as a lamb.

Everyone who came fresh to Madurai became an eloquent admirer of Nobili, but Vico surpassed all. He noted that "speculative philosophy and theology and all other sciences are still fresh in his mind". Even Gonçalo Fernandez had to admit that in his fifty years' experience he had never known anyone with such mastery of written and spoken Tamil. Like Archbishop Ros, Vico believed that only "very special gifts from Heaven" could explain Nobili's proficiency, also, in Telugu and Sanskrit.

"Companion of his first labours as a student, I became even then the confidant of his burning desire to work for the salvation of souls, and of his constant zeal for our own personal sanctification. However favourable the opinion I had till now regarding his aptitude for apostolic work I must confess that all I had imagined is nothing compared with the reality. If I did not see it with my own eyes and touch it with my own hands, I would call it the ideal but unattainable perfection of the missionary. Shall I speak to you of that consummate science with which he exposes the most abstruse questions of theology as if they were child's play? Of that subtle talent which, while it enables him to make himself understood by the ignorant, arouses the interest of the most learned and holds them spellbound? Of that matchless eloquence and the richness of expression with which, in spite of the variety and difficulty of the idioms of these people, he astonishes them? Of the gentle art with which he embellishes and renders attractive the most forbidding subjects? Of the ease with which he adopts the ways and manners, however strange, of the people of this country? And finally of that power of persuasion, with which he sways the minds of all?"

Vico was still more impressed by Nobili's humility and modesty, his faith and gentle affability, his piety and love of God, which spread happiness around him. Because of this fidelity to grace, thought Vico, Nobili had been chosen to bear all kinds of sufferings and contradictions.

The latest of these was the imminent threat to the mission's existence. Nobili decided that though time was so short a reply to Fernandez's letter and the censures of the theologians had to be made. Vico, fresh from his theological studies, undertook to write in defence of Nobili. His work—"Method used in the Madurai Mission to convert the Gentiles to Christ"—is a fine though voluminous piece of argumentation, such as none but a professor of theology could write.

Working against time, Nobili himself composed a long, detailed refutation of Fernandez's letter, point by point, and, in answer to the Goa theologians, a series of arguments to prove that the incriminated practices were free from superstition. He drew on such authorities as St Thomas Aquinas, St Ambrose and St Gregory the Wonder-worker to defend the principle of adaptation, on Sanskrit texts to prove that the emblems and customs he retained were civil, not religious. This Latin document of thirty-nine closely written pages he forwarded to Goa, where it would catch the carrack for Lisbon and Rome.

Though Pimenta was the General's representative, with wide powers, he himself could not suppress the Madurai Mission. Only the General could do that. So Nobili and Vico followed up their reasoned defence with letters to Aquaviva to remove any misconception he might have that Nobili's self-defence was inspired by wounded pride, that the zeal for souls of the Goa Fathers was unquestionable, or that the converts adhered to their caste merely from childish obstinacy. And Archbishop Ros, when he learned that the very existence of the mission was threatened, also wrote a strong letter to Aquaviva in its defence.

Two years at least must elapse before decisions could be expected from Rome. Meanwhile, it began to seem that the mission might destroy itself. Fernandez, encouraged by Pimenta's attitude, now came into the open. He told anybody who cared to hear that Christian and Parangi were one and the same thing. In October, eighteen of Nobili's flock gave up coming to church, and catechumens were frightened away.

Fernandez's tactlessness again aroused anti-Parangi feeling. Every such agitation was invariably followed by an investigation of the guru's social orthodoxy by some learned men. On this occasion it was conducted by the Supreme Judge of the Left-

Hand castes: a group comprising leather-workers, traders and artisans. "He wields", writes Vico, "great authority in religious matters, for when the god Chockanātha is troubled, and someone has to die to appease him, it is that Judge who appoints the victim. For you must know that if by chance some insult is offered to the god, or some powerful men appropriate lands or revenue belonging to his temple, the indignation of the god is conveyed to the public in the following way: A group of men is set apart and one of them is selected by the Judge mentioned above as a 'voluntary victim', who usually will throw himself down from the top of a temple tower.

"When it was reported to him that Fr Robert had spoken unfavourably of Chockanātha, this Judge came at once to our house, accompanied by one of those who carry the god on their shoulders when he goes out in procession. However, he conducted himself in a manner quite different from what we and our enemies expected. First of all, he prostrated himself before the Aiyer, and refused to take the seat offered him, but insisted on sitting on the floor. Then speaking with great moderation he said that some people had complained to him that the Aiyer did not worship Chockanātha nor any other gods, and that he had come to inquire into the case.

"The Aiyer answered that he was adoring the true God, and explaining His attributes he said that God could have no wife, and much less concubines, nor be such as Chockanātha was represented."

The Chockanātha myth current in Madurai was this. The river having risen to full flood, the public drum had given the alarm signal and everyone was called upon to reinforce the dyke. For two days volunteers worked in vain: the water carried away all the earth. Finally the man directing the work noticed someone sleeping under a tree. He went up and woke him with blows of a stick, upbraiding him for his laziness. Then he offered him a basket to carry earth and a cake to give him strength. The sleeper rose grumbling, lazily went to fill his basket, then walked to the river and nonchalantly threw into it a few handfuls of earth. At once the level of water fell and the dyke was completed. Witnessing this miracle, all recognized the presence of a divinity. The man was Śiva, incarnate as Chockanātha. He became king of Madurai and then its god.

Without a body and the pleasures of sexual love, it was believed that a god could not be supremely happy. Hence countless stories of Śiva's erotic prowess. As soon as Nobili attacked these, "the visitor began to take interest in the conversation and when the Aiyer touched on certain points he would confirm them by quoting some verses, which he sang (as the Hindu custom is). It was clear that in his heart he did not care for Chockanātha, but out of fear and human respect he worshipped and served him. Thus he went away without contradicting a single statement made by the Aiyer, and promised to return and discuss those matters more at length."

By criticizing the erotic achievements of Śiva, Nobili was doing more than attacking stories evolved by the ignorant. The worship of goddesses was an important feature of Śaivism. Mīnākṣi the fish-eyed was the female counterpart or energy of Śiva. As such her statue, like the statues of Sītā and Sarasvatī, received honour in the Madurai temple. But some devotees went further. By a ritual of spells, diagrams, gestures and dances they accorded Śiva's wife supreme honour, in the belief that the divine nature is essentially feminine, that only a woman perfectly embodies the two great mysteries of human experience: birth and death.

"Next came another learned Brahmin who is very rich and influential. He is a close friend of the Nāyak, with whom he spends many hours daily, and has such a reputation for knowledge that to treat with him is to treat with all the learning of Madurai, as Śivadarma puts it. When the visitor reached our door, and the porter told him that he did not know if the Aiyer was prepared to receive him, he proudly answered that a person of his rank should be received at any time by the Aiyer. He entered the room where Fr Robert receives visitors and sat at once on a red carpet reserved for men of distinction. After remaining a long while without uttering a word, he said that all must leave the room, his men, as well as those of Fr Robert, and then he began to speak.

"He had received, he said, many complaints against the Father and his teaching, and therefore he had come to examine him. To this Fr Robert answered, that in this world there were four good things, but they had four wicked daughters, the first was Science, whose daughter was Pride, the second was Friendship, whose daughter was Contempt, the third was Greatness, whose daughter was Envy, the fourth and last was Truth whose daughter was Hatred. This he had learned at his own cost, for it was because he was teaching the truth that he was hated by many, among whom were those who had complained to his Lordship about himself and his doctrine."

In answer to his visitor's questions, Nobili explained that God was without a body, eternal, and unique on account of His immensity. " 'How can He be everywhere,' asked the Brahmin, 'if He has no body and is incapable of local contacts?' In reply the Father first refuted the opinion that God is everywhere like air in the bodies, or oil in butter and milk, and added that he who had invented this explanation was perhaps a good shepherd, or oilsman, but a poor philosopher. This remark made the Brahmin laugh, and he declared himself satisfied with the explanation of God's immensity, by *essentia*, *potentia*, and *presentia*.

"They next passed to the Incarnation. Was Chockanātha an incarnate God as is believed here? The Father replied that he could not be, because certain sins were ascribed to him which could not be ascribed to God.

"The Brahmin would have liked the Father to go on, but as it was time for him to go to the Nāyak, he decided to adjourn the meeting. He declared himself sufficiently informed as to the Father's doctrine, but before leaving him he wished to test his virtue.

"So he took an insolent and harsh tone, called him 'thou' and began finding fault with him for not showing greater esteem for the Brahmins who are above kings themselves. 'What wilt thou do,' he said, 'if I insult thee and give thee a slap? Shouldst thou bear it patiently and remain quiet like a true sannyāsī?' "

The Brahmin's question had point, for a rumour was circulating that the King of Manamadurai (a petty landowner whose title seems to have been largely honorific) had been slapped on the cheek and, unable to bear the disgrace, had committed suicide.

Nobili had been on terms of friendly correspondence with the King, who had intended one day to visit the hermitage.

"The Father replied, smiling, that he had no reason whatever to act otherwise than he taught others to do. Since he taught mildness and patience to others in words, he should teach the same by his conduct, and he was prepared to do so at all times. After this the Brahmin took leave of the Father, but before doing so, he begged him not to take amiss the advice he had given him and the manner in which he had treated him."

Such interviews as this increased Nobili's good name among the Brahmins, who were coming in still larger numbers to be baptized. One heard a sermon by Nobili and was so impressed that he asked to be instructed. Another came to the hermitage while the Aiyer was being shaved. Nobili could not shave himself, for that would have lowered him to the level of Paraiyans. There were no proper razors in Madurai and it would have been revolting to use soap. So Nobili's beard was cut by a servant with repeated little sweeps of a small hatchet.

The Brahmin visitor noticed that during this painful process one of his disciples read to Nobili out of the Tamil catechism. He was a stranger in Madurai, but he promised on his return to join the disciples of one who, as he said, even while being shaved, was busy with God.

The growing number of Brahmin converts brought Nobili yet another title. He had been accepted as a Rājā by caste and a sannyāsī by profession. But religion could not be taught to Brahmins by a Rājā. The Brahmin converts solved the difficulty by calling Nobili a Brahmin sannyāsī. Evidently there was no idea of giving him a Brahmin pedigree: Brahmin in that title meant religious teacher: a profession, not a caste. Doubtless the arrangement did not meet with universal acceptance, but it satisfied the Brahmin converts. At the end of 1611 Nobili, who believed that "Brahmin" was derived from a Sanskrit root meaning "to know", definitely accepted the new title and from that time Sanskrit-speaking missionaries with Brahmin disciples began to be known as Brahmin sannyāsīs.

Even to provide crucifixes and rosaries for so large a body of converts—towards the end of 1611 they numbered one hundred and fifty—was becoming expensive. The new church, maintenance of a second missionary, payment of the two Brahmin servants and the provision of work for convert Brahmins, many of whom had to give up their former jobs in temples, would not, at the height of Portuguese prosperity, have proved too heavy a demand on provincial funds. But now the Portuguese were in full decline. In 1606 they were unable to prevent the Dutch, who sent out a fleet of twelve large ships annually, from blockading Goa. In 1609 the five annual carracks from Lisbon had sailed not with their complement of 1,500 soldiers, for there were no more soldiers, but with children and youths, some of them only ten years old. In Brazil the Portuguese were fighting single-handed the Dutch and the French; in the East they had to contend with the Dutch and the Malabar pirates, as well as the kings of Arabia, Sumatra, Java, Malacca and Sunda.

The English also, during the years since Nobili's arrival, had established themselves as serious rivals. The East India Company had been formed in London when the Dutch raised the price of pepper from three to six and even eight shillings a pound. The first fleet had sailed in 1601, returning two years later with pepper from Bantam. Like the Dutch, the English saw the advantage of establishing factories on the Indian coast to make cheap cloth for the Indonesian market. This cloth could be bartered for pepper and spices, thus saving the export of bullion. In 1611 the English established such a factory in Masulipatam, chief port of the Golkundā kingdom.

Even in South India Portugal's rivals were gaining ground. In 1608 the Dutch obtained permission from the Nāyak of Gingi to build a fort at Devanapatham. The Portuguese, through their missionary-ambassadors, persuaded the Emperor of Vijayanagar, the Nāyak's suzerain, to dismiss the Dutch, and the Nāyak finally obeyed. But now Pimenta had withdrawn the Italian mission from the Emperor's Court. One of the first consequences was that the Dutch were given the right of trading at Pulicat. The Emperor also agreed to buy Dutch instead of Portuguese guns and ammunition.

This loss of trade meant that the King of Portugal could never afford to pay the annual sum of 300 patacas[1] which he had promised for the upkeep of the two Madurai houses. The province of Malabar shared in the general decline and had recently suffered a sharp loss of income when eighty churches on the rich Fishery Coast had had to be handed over to the Bishop of Cochin. Missionaries who had formerly been supported by parishioners were now an added expense. The college at Cochin was in and out of debt: at one time all its silver had to be pawned. Nobili, after Vico's arrival, wrote to Cardinal Bellarmine that progress now was conditional not on missionaries but on money. He asked for a small grant such as the Cardinal made to Japanese missions, and tactfully mentioned that he had begun to translate Bellarmine's Catechism into Tamil.

The mission derived an income of from seventy to eighty pardaos[2] from two orchards. This sum, divided between Fernandez's house and Nobili's, had lately proved inadequate, and Laerzio, willing to sell anything for the sake of the Madurai Mission, borrowed 360 pardaos[3] from a Portuguese horse-trader to buy a third field and defray mission expenses in the following year.

Shortly after Laerzio's departure from Madurai in October 1610 a thief climbed the garden wall, forced open the cash box and stole the 360 pardaos. Servants and suspects were questioned without yielding any clues. Even Nobili, usually so optimistic, was dashed down by the theft. Unless the money was found, the mission could not continue.

It was the responsibility of Errama Setti, the local poligar, to discover the culprit. He had recently returned from war, where he had led his contingent of 3,000 foot soldiers, two hundred cavalry and fifty elephants with outstanding courage. He had captured a Tanjore fortress, and on his return been received by the Nāyak of Madurai with great honour. He had come to thank Nobili for the gold medal, to which he attributed his victory. However, when Nobili urged him to fulfil his promise and become a Christian, he pleaded that his duties at court just then did not give him sufficient time.

[1] £210.　　　　[2] £47 to £54.　　　　[3] £243.

Hearing of the theft, Errama Setti ordered the arrest of all Christians living in the mission compound and summoned a sorcerer with a view to extorting from them by torture a confession of guilt. But Nobili declined to send his servants to be tortured. This attitude displeased Errama Setti, who had high hopes of his sorcerer's spells. When he was told that the Aiyer placed his trust in God alone, he sneered at the idea.

One day soon afterwards Nobili was resting in one of the two orchards belonging to the mission. During a period of prayer he suddenly thought of the theft and saw clearly in imagination the money hidden away above a door in the hermitage. Returning at once to Madurai, he went straight to the door and above it found the 360 pardaos in a sealed bag.

The mission was saved for another year, but not without cost, for Errama Setti viewed Nobili's independent attitude as a personal affront. He had promised additional land to enlarge the compound, but now he gave it to someone else and ordered a new building to be erected along a large avenue which he had so far left open in front of the church. Finally, he sent Nobili a message saying that as his religion was unorthodox he must send him a written account of its doctrines, to be submitted to the Great Nāyak.

Nobili replied by sending the revised version of his palm-leaf manifesto. This seemed to satisfy Errama Setti, for he continued his patronage, despite criticism at court from other poligars. In August 1611, writes Vico, "at the suggestion of a Durai [poligar], rival of Errama Setti, the Great Nāyak sent for the latter and told him that he was in need of that part of his city *palaiyam*, where the Fathers lived. Errama Setti replied that his elder brother, whom he had succeeded, had given it to a sannyāsī who was now living there, but that His Highness, being the Master, could requisition it if he pleased. The Great Nāyak replied that he would never do a thing so unbecoming as to claim back what had been given to a sannyāsī." So, thanks to the Christian compound, Errama Setti retained possession of his suburb intact. Soon afterwards, the poligar showed a recognized mark of friendship by sending Nobili a basket of fruit.

Nobili did not risk his money a second time. With the 360

pardaos he at once bought a field nine miles from Madurai at a place called Periakulam—the Great Lake. This would yield him and Vico a small income and serve as a place of rest, for Madurai was sultry and still more sultry the hermitage, where day after day the Brahmin sannyāsīs had to remain indoors, lest their fair complexion again elicit the stigma "Parangi". They called the field the *grāmam*, a word meaning village, villa, country house, orchard and ricefield.

Worn out by worries arising from the theft Nobili now fell seriously ill, of asthma and catarrh. For three days he struggled for every breath. He could not sleep, could not even lie down. Vico says "he was brought back to life when a relic of St Ignatius was applied to his chest" and he went to regain his strength in the *grāmam* by the Great Lake.

For long Nobili had wanted to preach in the countryside. As early as 1608 he had written to Ciavarcovadim, poligar of Darapuram, offering to make the week's journey to teach him and his people. War had prevented him then, but now he had his chance. As he convalesced, he became friendly with the stockily built rice and millet farmers around the Great Lake. Their chief objects of worship were the rough stones of the village enclosure: the *Grāma-Devatā*. These represented female deities such as Mariamman, goddess of smallpox, and Kannahai Amman, whose insatiable appetite for blood was allayed by the sacrifice of chickens, pigs, sheep and goats. Before these stones the peasants also laid the flowers of their country: lotus, water-lilies, jasmine, red *gloriosa superba* and tiger-coloured *vengai*. Over and above the stones they recognized a supreme God, somewhat vague in conception, whom they called Aiyanar.

The peasants did not consider the presence of a professional priest necessary at marriages or funerals, hence the Brahmins had had no opportunity for imposing their rites and beliefs. They approached their vague God along the path of devotion as contrasted with the path of works and the path of knowledge. In Madurai Christianity was known as the Spiritual Law, the noun used—*Védam*—also connoting knowledge. But when Nobili began to preach by the Great Lake, the peasants seized on a different salient point. What struck them was its doctrine of loving devotion to a personal God. It actualized all their former vague longings towards Aiyanar. And so they called Christianity *Bhakti-mārga*—the path of devotion *par excellence*.

Nobili's convalescence lasted a month. During that time fifteen of the peasants by the Great Lake chose to follow the new path. Their *pujārī*—the man who sacrificed to the village goddesses—opposed Nobili, so that those who wished had to come to Madurai to receive baptism.

This short experiment raised Nobili's hopes. As soon as Vico had mastered Tamil sufficiently to take permanent charge of the Madurai Christians, he planned to devote himself to the interior, "begging from door to door". According to Vico, it would be easier to make fifty conversions among the country-people than to make one in Madurai, not because it was the fortress of Brahminism, but because its position near the Coast made it the resort of hard-living traders, gun-runners and Indian half-breeds —Parangis of doubtful character. Then the cry went up: "Christianity—made in Portugal—by its fruits you shall know it."

A few months after his return from the Great Lake, early in November 1611, Nobili was unexpectedly summoned to Cochin. Taking his bamboo staff and begging bowl, and accompanied by a few disciples, including a Brahmin named Boniface, he left Madurai by the western gate. After a difficult fortnight's journey across the Ghāts, preaching on the way, he arrived in the Portuguese base.

Scarcely six years ago he had lain ill in the College of the Mãe de Deus expecting to die. From Cochin he had taken ship in a black cassock, speaking not a word of Tamil, expecting to work among the pearl-fishers. Now after five years in Madurai he returned to Portuguese India as a wandering sannyāsī, in red-ochre cotton and wooden clogs, his brow marked with sandal, guru of a hundred and fifty converts in a great university city. Much seemed to have been achieved, but his apparent success would turn out to be worse than failure if the censure of the Goa theologians was enforced by Rome. Only a year had elapsed since the document of censure had been posted to Europe. No decision could be expected from Rome for at least another year, perhaps longer, given the rate at which carracks were being sunk.

Nobili had not been summoned for further censure. The time-lag which so strained the waiting missionaries' nerves had now produced its bitterest irony. General Aquaviva, unaware of the nature of Pimenta's report, then on the high seas, had ordered that Nobili should take his final vows: an honour allowed only to those who had given outstanding proofs of virtue and whose character had never been impugned by their Superiors.

In the College of the Mãe de Deus, on the feast of her Presentation, 21st November, Nobili bound himself by the solemn vows of a professed Father in the Society of Jesus. His vows, which included a declaration of obedience to the Pope, were received by Archbishop Ros in the name of General Aquaviva. It should have been a great day. The Church and the Society set on his work the seal of a double approbation. No dissentient voice was heard now criticizing or disapproving of his method. Every member of the community came to offer congratulations. But the authorities at Goa, the censure, the charge of "schism"—these were in everyone's mind.

Back in Madurai, Nobili began to lay definite plans. He had been well impressed by his reception in the villages to and from Cochin. Here he had no metaphysical structure to contend with, no subtle points in theology or psychology to refute. His appeal could be direct and personal, to men who judged a cow by its milk, a religion by the sort of man who proclaimed it. All Southern India was waiting—an area more extensive than Italy—without proper roads, its hills infested with tigers, leopards and bears. A challenge for one man, but the challenge had been met by countless Hindu sannyāsīs, who had tramped staff in hand in the service of Śiva and Viṣṇu. He too would trace out the path of devotion with his own footsteps across the length and breadth of South India.

For almost a month this optimistic planning continued. Then came important news, quite unexpected, sharp and bitter as the taste of betel. Alberto Laerzio was no longer Nobili's immediate Superior. On 21st December 1611 he had been succeeded as head of the Malabar Province by a certain Pero Francisco. And Pero Francisco was Portuguese.

12. *Nyāya and Nebulae*

NOBILI'S experiment was threatened in two ways: by Portuguese ecclesiastical strength and by Portuguese military weakness. If the first danger appeared more imminent, in the long run the second was more inevitable. Year by year Portugal's hold on India was slipping. History taught the consequences. Where were the ancient Christian communities of Egypt and North Africa? Thrown down and destroyed, for having put their trust in the Greco-Roman culture of a few colonial cities, for never having struck deep roots in the native civilization. Where were the fervent Christian communities of Persia, which had sent missionaries to India centuries before the West? Tied to the apron-strings of the province of Antioch, they had been forced to follow the alien traditions of Byzantium even in matters unrelated to dogma. As a result they had broken adrift into heresy and then into decline. Now the Persian Church was as though it had never even existed. The moral for India was clear: she must have her own clergy, educated as far as possible in her own traditions. Roberto de Nobili was the first to realize this and to take every step within his power to bring it to fulfilment.

The idea of a Brahmin seminary first occurred to him in 1610. Like the ancient colleges of Madurai, which counted forty professors and ten thousand students, it would offer a five-year course in philosophy. The scheme had been delayed first for six months, while Nobili studied the technical terminology in order to be able to deliver his lectures in Sanskrit. At the end of that time a further difficulty remained to be solved. Brahmin pupils in Madurai University were lodged, fed and clothed by their masters with the income endowed for that purpose to the house or temple where they lived. Most endowments were made by the Emperor of Vijayanagar and the Nāyak of Madurai

Nobili had no such income, nor could Laerzio procure it for him.

"The sum required", wrote Vico to the General, "is not a large one; if we had about 350 scudi[1] a year it would cover all expenses and assure a moderate livelihood both for ourselves and for as many boys as we should care to take. And the capital required to bring in such an income in India is not more than 3,000 scudi[2]: even 2,000[3] would be more than enough if we added to that sum the little that we have, which Fr Alberto Laerzio, when he was Provincial, invested for us in certain estates, but, as I said above, we have not enough for half our needs."

Nobili wanted to train seminarists who, having preserved their Indian customs and their castes, would be respected by their Hindu countrymen, to whom they could speak on equal terms. He wanted his future priests to present Christianity to the Indian people in their own languages, not in a jargon in which all religious terms were Portuguese; to be well trained in Christian theology but also experts in the religion of the Hindus around him; to depend for support and protection on their own countrymen, not on foreigners. In the first half of the seventeenth century such a plan was extremely bold and far-sighted.

In Goa, for instance, the fifth Council had ruled: "In order to preserve the dignity of the priesthood, and to assure fitting respect for the clergy, no native of low caste shall receive holy orders or be allowed to exercise the holy ministry." Incidentally, interesting as showing Goa's acceptance of the caste system long before charges came to be made against Nobili, this decree was used chiefly to limit Indian ordinations, for the city already teemed with European priests. Only a handful of Indians had been ordained and they were seldom employed in Indian mission work. For example, a virtuous Brahmin priest named Belchior da Sylva, a sound theologian, was appointed in 1598 as a missionary to—of all places—Ethiopia, at that time an extremely dangerous country, almost impossible to enter. There was no question of Sylva's working in India proper—he had had to renounce his thread and become a Parangi.

[1] £210.   [2] £1,800.   [3] £1,200.

Since his seminary was to follow, so far as possible, Indian traditions, Nobili first had to familiarize himself with the highly complicated and exacting system of Brahmin education. This began when a Brahmin boy was invested with the thread. He then entered on his study of the Vedas, taught by a guru, without books, when necessary writing on loose sand, for lessons were given out-of-doors. Next he studied the "Limbs of the Veda", subsidiary subjects necessary for its proper understanding: *kalpa*, the performance of sacrifice; *śikṣā*, correct pronunciation, or phonetics; *chandas*, metre and prosody; *nirukta*, etymology, the interpretation of obscure words in the Vedas; *vyakāraṇa*, grammar; and *jyotiṣa*, astronomy or science of the calendar.

Having mastered these basic subjects and developed his memory by learning all lessons by heart, the student was free to attend the University. Madurai University was supposed to have been founded in the days of Vaṃśa Śekhara, an ancient Pāṇḍya king, and Śiva himself to have condescended to appear as the forty-ninth professor, teaching the Tamil language. The god also bestowed on the University a sacred bench of solid diamond, on which only a faultless scholar was allowed to sit. According to tradition, between 800 and 1000 A.D., Tiruvalluvar, perhaps the greatest Tamil poet, was refused permission to sit on this diamond bench beside distinguished professors, because he belonged to the Paraiyan caste. Tiruvalluvar meekly acquiesced, but asked if he might lay his poem—the *Sacred Couplets*—on the end of the bench. This was allowed and as soon as the book was laid down the bench at once disappeared, leaving the learned professors afloat in the lotus-pool.

At the University students specialized in one of the six classic systems, or "points of view", which Brahmins regarded as six aspects of a single orthodox tradition. Though overtly contradictory, they were understood to be complementary projections of the one truth on various planes of consciousness. From these Nobili had to choose a starting-point for his own school, since without at least some presuppositions in common he would not be able to make his doctrines understood.

The first of these schools was Mīmāṃsā, of which the nearest

European equivalent is Liturgical Studies, Mīmāṃsā being a kind of priestly science, a clarification of Vedic ritual. The second system was Vedānta, of which the nearest European equivalent is Metaphysics. The third was Sāṅkyha, the European equivalent being Psychology. The word means enumeration, for numbers play a large part in its exposition of human nature and its elements, their manner of co-operation in the state of bondage and of disentanglement in the state of release. Linked to Sāṅkyha was Yoga, which taught the techniques and dynamics of release. The yogī sought to attain a state where he would be merged in himself, oblivious of the everyday world. To attain this state he might adopt such methods as control of breathing or concentration of thought, in order to overcome five hindrances: ignorance of the higher truth that man is unimplicated in the changing world, the sensation of his own existence, sympathy, antipathy, and the will to live. Both Yoga and its sister system, Sāṅkyha, were opposed to Vedānta, for, like Jainism and Buddhism, they accepted the conclusion which follows from the theoretical incompatibility of transmigration and the principle "That art Thou". Renouncing the latter, they set themselves the task of expounding how negation of life and the world can bring to an end the cycle of rebirths.

None of these four systems would have provided a suitable stem on which Nobili could graft his scholastic philosophy, for all taught that the soul is degraded by matter, and must find salvation by turning away from the body, just as a Brahmin must shun the polluting Paraiyan. Now the scholastic doctrine of soul to which Nobili was committed rested on such notions as form and matter, act and potentiality, and—in the last analysis—on the admission that both permanence and change are real. This dualism none of the four systems was prepared to admit. They insisted on considering both terms simultaneously within the unity of a common but more universal principle, to be grasped, at a higher level than common sense, by the intuitive intellect. If Nobili had argued that identification through the intuitive intellect could never be complete, since the lower powers of the soul would not participate, his opponents' retort would have been that what they mean by the soul is precisely the intuitive intellect, nothing else. A closed circle.

With the fifth system, Vaiśeṣika—corresponding to European Cosmology—Indian thought came closer to Western academic tradition. It was realist without being, like Sāṅkyha and Yoga, world- and life-denying. Vaiśeṣika treats of the date of waking consciousness from the point of view of *viśeṣa*—difference, one of the five categories into which the system divides nature. It teaches an atomistic doctrine, according to which atoms have no extension, yet in combination become extensive and visible. The drawback to this school, from Nobili's point of view, was that it pre-supposed cycles of creation and dissolution as well as birth and rebirth of souls. Thus, a desire for creation in the mind of God produces motion and conjunction in the atoms, from which springs a great reservoir of water. In the water appear atoms of earth and fire, from which is produced the cosmic egg, where God produces the new world and its creator Brahmā, to whom He assigns the further work of creation, including that of living beings inhabited by selves conditioned by actions during previous lives.

The sixth system, Nyāya, corresponded to European Logic, but its subject matter was subordinated, as in the other systems, to the final end of all knowledge: salvation. If Nyāya studied logical questions, it was only in order to understand as a reasoned system those truths revealed by the Vedas or discerned by seers. As taught in Madurai, Nyāya followed the *Tattva-Cintāmaṇi* of Gangeśa, a twelfth- or thirteenth-century philosopher. Cintāmaṇi means connection of thoughts, or crown of thinking, and, according to Nobili, who describes it in a letter, the complicated syllabus was in three parts.

"The first part is evidence. It treats of innovation or adoration, whether some God has to be invoked at the beginning of a work; of certitude, of perfect certitude, of certitude by generation and production anew, of what essentially constitutes certitude, of the kinds [*speciebus*] of objects, of local union by contiguity, of the different kinds of union: formal, accidental, etc., of predicate and subject by negation, of the object of sight, of the indivisibility of the will, of the splendour of gold, of the return on itself of the act through which each one knows and understands himself, etc.

"The second part is science. It treats of the 'sign' of inference, of mere consequence, of induction, of fallacy, of the root of fallacy, of its refutation, of the subject, of the discourse, of the causative sign, of all kinds of fallacy, of accidental conjunction, of privation, of the effect by the cause, of all kinds of conjunction, of ultimate certitude or consequence, of cause, of evident demonstration, of certitude from similarity, of error, of doubt, of the change of supposition, of false conclusion from true anecdote, of the god Rudren, of the multiplicity of causes, of natural force and power, of power added anew.

"The third part is authority and treats of hearing, of the corresponding of wo ds, of convenience in general, of union of affection, of desire, of the corruption of sound, of the corruption of the whole world, of the value of the law, whether non-being can be affirmed, of newness, of annihilation, of proper imposition, and finally what a sign should be."

This system of logic and epistemology evidently interested Nobili, since he took the trouble of describing the syllabus in such detail to Laerzio. Nyāya admits four means of reliable knowledge: perception, inference by syllogism, inference by analogy, and the authority of the sacred Scriptures. This was very like scholastic logic; and agreement about perception might have paved the way for Nobili's crucial statement that the human person is a psycho-physical unity.

Nobili reported no lack of gifted young men anxious to attend his lectures. These, delivered in precise but flowery Sanskrit, would have to be of a very high standard, for Nyāya was a maze of subtleties. Its analysis of inference, for example, showed keener observation of human nature than many contemporary schools in Europe: the subject, according to Nyāya, cannot be a thing *per se*: it must be something regarding which there is a desire to establish something else, for only then does it come within the sphere of inference.

On the other hand, as Nobili was quick to point out, the Indians had no adequate conception of cause and effect. As against the Nyāya, which totally ignores the agent, Nobili would have been able to impress an audience by expounding Aristotle's four senses of the word cause, as well as Aristotle's three-membered syllogism, less cumbrous than the five-membered syllogism used in Madurai.

Year after year building of the Christian college was delayed either by lack of money or opposition from Goa, yet Nobili never abandoned his scheme. Among the Brahmin students drawn at least by the novelty of his course in Christian philosophy, he hoped to make converts who would eventually form an Indian clergy. Whether or not he and Vico were allowed to remain as Brahmin sannyāsīs, one day Indians themselves must continue the mission. To foster this plan still further he asked permission from Rome to take Sanskrit instead of Latin as the liturgical language for the new Indian Church.

This was a momentous step. Setting aside a concession to China regarding the use of Mandarin, of which no advantage was taken during Nobili's lifetime, not for over seven hundred years had the vernacular been permitted in the liturgy of the Church, when the two apostles of Moravia, Cyril and Methodius, had obtained the authorization of Pope Adrian II to use *litteras slavonicas* for sung Mass, reading of the Epistle and Gospel and the offices in the Book of Hours.

No less an authority than St Thomas Aquinas had pointed out the great advantage that accrued to the Fathers and early apologists from the fact that they had been pagans. Nobili, despite his mastery of Sanskrit, Tamil and Telugu, despite the fact that he could quote at ease from the Vedas, Purāṇas and most famous Indian poems, was aware that no amount of learning could replace the deepest springs within the soul, fed by blood, tradition and climate, and crystallized in a mother tongue.

Rome's reply to the request for Sanskrit is not known but was probably negative, for during Nobili's lifetime Sanskrit never replaced Latin. This, however, did not prevent his using Sanskrit in another important aspect of his apostolate—some of his literary works. Nobili believed—and acted on his belief—that books conceived and written in the Indian languages (not mere translations) were absolutely indispensable to an Indian Church.

The pioneer in this field was Thomas Stephens, a remarkable Englishman known to everyone under the Portuguese form of his name, Padre Estevão. When Nobili had landed in Goa, Stephens had been missionary in charge of the Christian communities at nearby Salsette. It was the custom to invite new arrivals in Goa to visit Salsette—then the show-piece of Christianity in India—and there is no reason to suppose that Nobili was an exception to the rule. Even if he did not actually meet the Englishman, Nobili certainly knew Stephens's name and was influenced by his literary method.

Thomas Stephens was born in 1549 at Bushton, a village forming part of the parish of Cliffe Pypard, Wiltshire, in the diocese of Salisbury, the son of Thomas Stephens, a well-to-do merchant. Having completed his studies, he attached himself to Thomas Pound, the son of a wealthy country gentleman and nephew of the Earl of Southampton. After aspiring to the place of a favourite in the court of Queen Elizabeth, Pound had fallen from grace. He had then become a lay-apostle and leader of the Catholic gentry in their efforts to preserve their faith. For two years Stephens accompanied Pound, disguised as his servant, in order not to arouse the suspicions of pursuivants.

Pound, like Nobili, was deeply stirred by the letters of Jesuit missionaries in India, and he evolved a plan for drawing to his side youths of promise, taking them to Rome and offering them, along with himself, to the Society of Jesus. Before he could carry out his plan, Pound was arrested, and Stephens crossed to Rome alone. There, at the age of twenty-six, he was received as a novice and in 1579, at the age of thirty, had arrived as a missionary in Goa.

Stephens was not the first Englishman in India. According to the *Anglo-Saxon Chronicle*, King Alfred sent Sighelm of Sherborne as his ambassador in A.D. 883 to the tomb of St Thomas in India and, according to William of Malmesbury's *Chronicle*, Sighelm returned laden with precious stones and spices. More recently, two Englishmen had been among ninety-eight badly wounded survivors from an explosion during the siege of Diu by the Muslims in 1546. In the casualty list their names are given Portuguese style: "Lancarote Barbudo, Englishman, much burnt on his legs" and "Esevam Lopez, Englishman, often wounded and therefore in bad condition".

Stephens, however, had the distinction of being the first English Jesuit in India. On his arrival he was sent to work in the peninsula of Salsette, with a population of 80,000 Indians scattered over fifty-five villages.

The mission there began to prosper, largely through the Englishman's efforts. Stephens was physically strong and energetic: instead of preaching through an interpreter, as many of his predecessors had done—and as was still the general custom in India— he mastered the local tongue, Konkanī, and learned the related language, Marāṭhī, well enough to write in it. He composed a Grammar of the Konkanī language for his fellow-missionaries, and a Konkanī Catechism. At the time of Nobili's visit, he was engaged on something much more ambitious.

The people of Salsette, like other Indians, found one of their chief amusements in listening to long poems called Purāṇas. Purāṇa means "old" and the Purāṇa tells in poetic form the stories of the origin of the world, of the coming of the gods, of the origin of mankind and the exploits of kings and heroes. In Goa an occasional Purāṇa had been seized in raids and scraps ordered to be translated "so that we might form an idea of the aberration and blindness of this people". Stephens decided on quite another approach. Realizing what a hold these verses had on the popular mind, he decided that he would compose a Christian Purāṇa.

Stephen's Purāṇa falls into two parts, the first, of 4,181 strophes, narrating the Old Testament story; the second, of 6,781 strophes, the New Testament. Stephens adapted himself to the form of the Purāṇa and the mind of his audience by including pious but apocryphal stories, including the Nativity of the Mother of Christ and her seclusion till her fourteenth year among the consecrated virgins. Since the people of Salsette enjoyed lurid descriptions, he made the most of the sick and paralysed brought to Jesus. And throughout the long poem the truths of Christianity were skilfully expounded in the form of questions and answers, the questions being put into the mouth now of a Brahmin, now of a Christian.

Stephens used the Ovi metre then in favour: three long lines rhymed together, followed by a short line, which occasionally repeated the rhyme. He wrote in the spoken language of the people: Marāṭhī with a slight admixture of Konkanī.

No one had ever attempted anything like this before. Even more remarkable than the technical feat of composing an epic in a foreign language were the sympathy and imagination required to meet illiterate Indians at their own poetic stage of development, to give them the truth of Christianity under a traditional form which they liked and could easily remember.

The Englishman's lesson was not lost on Nobili. He too decided to convey Christian truths in verse form. But whereas the Salsette peasants, former worshippers of the cobra-goddess, delighted in native woodnotes more than a little wild, Madurai had for two millennia fostered an academic tradition of Tamil poetry, meticulous in detail, exulting in tier upon tier of subordinate clauses. Alongside this the Brahmins had developed their own Sanskrit verse in an even more highly ornate and artificial style, rich in *double entendres*.

Undeterred by such fastidiousness, during his years in Madurai Nobili composed a Life of Our Lady in Sanskrit verse, canticles for marriages and funerals, and a summary of Christian doctrine in a hundred Sanskrit *ślokas*. Besides these verses for Brahmins, Nobili wrote others in Tamil and Telugu (including a *Defence of Religion*), which proved very popular and were sung year after year in the Madurai Mission.

The subtleties involved in philosophic dispute could not be squeezed into verse, but in his prose writings also Nobili displayed that adaptation to the imagery and traditional knowledge of his readers which characterized Stephens's Christian Purāṇa. The *Agnâna Nivâranam*—Dispelling of Ignorance—one of Nobili's three most important Tamil works, treats of God and His attributes in lively dialogues, using the jewelled language a Tamil audience loved.

In one passage the disciple argues that a piece of cloth embroidered and stitched with a number of pearls and rubies is all the more beautiful and better on that account. So, too, the more gods in the world, the better. No, replies the guru, for since omnipotence is a necessary attribute of God, to speak, as some

Hindus did, of millions of gods is an absurdity. Furthermore, it would be impossible to serve such a number. If ten thousand channels are dug from a river, each channel may get scarcely four or five drops of water.

The following passage from the second dialogue—On the Existence of a Supreme Being—shows how Nobili achieved the rich description beloved of Tamils:

"Consider that when you observe this town and temple and the great wonders contained therein you naturally conclude that the man who built them was extraordinarily clever. Now consider the beauty of a temple far more exquisite than this. Imagine its flooring to be set entirely with precious stones of rare value, the walls to be crystal and diamond, the tiles of onyx, the lotus designs of silver, the domes of gold and the steps of precious stones; added to all this ornamentation imagine that the columns are made of polished marble set with priceless rubies, vases of topazes, strings of diamonds, pots of gems, planks and beams of gold, arches of emeralds, silk dolls and serpents of precious stones in green, red and blue hues; imagine the supports to be adorned with pearls and beads, and lanterns hanging everywhere from golden chandeliers; suppose you saw such a glorious temple, you would undoubtedly say that a great king had built this edifice by engaging an excellent artist. But, should you study in detail the handiwork of the Supreme Being, the great king of the universe, should you realize that pearls and marbles are born in ocean beds, gold and silver etc. in the bowels of the earth, and diamonds, emeralds and gems in mountains, should you realize that, not mere lifeless diamonds but live blossoms of variegated colours fill this earth, and that their sweet perfumes diffuse fragrance everywhere, that the sky which is clear as crystal envelops the earth, that the ethereal regions are studded, not like the temple-supports with pearls and gems, but with myriads of wonderful stars, that the moon and the sun illuminate the earth as no diamond lantern can—should you realize all this, you would set a higher store by God's work."

If his style was necessarily imitative, wherever he could Nobili inserted unfamiliar and interesting information. "Though the summits of mountains are neither of mud nor of sand they are gradually eroded by heavy rainfall and by the rays of the sun and moon . . . Hence the earth cannot have existed from all time"— which elicits this reply from the atheist: "Swami, ever since my birth I have not heard such splendid arguments!"

In 1609 Galileo had constructed the first complete astronomical telescope, with which he observed the phases of Venus, the shape of Saturn, the craters on the moon, the numerous stars of the Pleiades and of the Milky Way, the four satellites of Jupiter, and the nebula of Orion. Some of these discoveries were confirmed at the Roman College and news of them reached India by way of Antonio Rubino, a Piedmontese missionary with astronomical interests. Rubino, working at the court of Venkaṭa, was astonished at the interest taken by Brahmins "in the movements and aspects of stars and planets, particularly of those twenty-seven which rule men's lives". He had tried to find out how they predicted "the hour and even the minute of solar and lunar eclipses", but with no success, for the Brahmins guarded these secrets closely.

Nobili, however, had access to Brahmin secrets. Perhaps through Rubino, he also kept himself up to date about Galileo's startling discoveries,—no mean feat considering his isolated position and exacting work. The Indians possessed supplies of crystal but only a rudimentary knowledge of optics. Hence they had no eye-glasses (a lack Nobili was more than once able to fill) and no telescopes.

In the following passage, which continues the dialogue quoted above, Nobili for the first time introduces Galileo's discoveries to India. He also gives distances of planets from the earth. India did not know how to calculate these accurately, for to relate successive transit times to distance, a hypothesis is needed. This Kepler had provided in 1609 with his law of elliptical orbits.

"Note the following: 16 hair-breadths make a scratch, 16 scratches make a finger-breadth, 16 finger-breadths one foot, 5 feet one arm's-length and 3,000 such arms'-lengths make an astronomical *kadham*.[1] The earth measures 7,920 *kadhams* at its greatest circumference. From there down to us it is 1,260 *kadhams* and the sides 2,520 *kadhams*; the remaining outer sides are 19,958,400

[1] A *kadham* is about ten miles.

kadhams. And should the earth be halved latitudinally the upper part is 4,980,100 *kadhams.* Finally, within and without, the earth measures 8,382,528,000 *kadhams.*

"It is possible with the foregoing data to compute in a way the volume of sand on the earth. All this is explained in Geomorphology and is proved by strong arguments. Now, the distance above the earth's equator is 53,160 *kadhams*; and when noon is overhead in this region it travels 522,720 *kadhams* in 60 *naligais*;[1] and the sun 10,000,560 *kadhams.* The distance between the earth and Mercury's surface is 13,693,180 *kadhams*, and when in that position it covers 80,672,510 *kadhams* in 60 *naligais*, which works out at 1,430,576 *kadhams* per *naligai.*

"Venus is 15,277,940 *kadhams* away from the earth. Within a single day and night, while in that position, it moves 102,318,480 *kadhams*, which comes to 1,705,308 *kadhams* in a *naligai.* The planet Mars is 26,460,300 *kadhams* removed from the earth. While in that position within a day it travels 166,359,660 *kadhams* or 2,772,666 *kadhams* for a *naligai.*

"Jupiter is similarly separated from the earth by a distance of 19,810,520 *kadhams.* While in the above position it turns over 376,610,840 *kadhams* in 60 *naligais.* Lastly, Saturn and the earth are 113,595,300 *kadhams* apart and the former covers in 60 *naligais* 714,527,600 *kadhams*, which is 11,900,460 *kadhams* in a single *naligai.*

"Now let us speak of the size of these planets. To begin with, from the phenomenon of the lunar eclipse we know that the moon is smaller than the earth, for it is completely hidden by the earth's shadow during the eclipse. Mercury and Mars are smaller than the earth, but Venus is much larger and can contain 609 earths; whereas Saturn is 884 times larger than the earth.

"Coming up thus in the ascending order to the sun we find its capacity to be 1,728 earths. And apart from the above-mentioned seven planets, you must know that there are others about which the astrologers of this land are ignorant. There is no time to mention all these: we have explained enough already.

[1] *A naligai* is the Tamil hour. There are thirty from sunrise to sunset, and thirty from sunset to sunrise.

"However, about the stars you should know this: the distance between earth and the stellar nebulae is 120,000,060 *kadhams*. At the equinoxes they cover 790,000,024 *kadhams* in 60 *naligais*, or 13,200,000 *kadhams* in one *naligai*. Regarding their number and size it is known that they constitute constellations to the extent of 63 and number 1,400 which can be seen with the naked eye; but the telescope reveals stars whose number arithmetic cannot compute.

"In the giant constellation Orion, we observe only 56 different stars; but through a powerful telescope we can see 10,000 stars. Besides these, from the lower part of the seventh Lunar Constellation northwards through the Milky Way the telescope brings innumerable stars to view.

"Regarding their size it may be generally stated that those stars which can be perceived are undoubtedly larger than the earth; in other words, according to astrologers, if a man were to take his stand in the stellar regions he could not see the earth at all. The larger stars doubtlessly surpass the earth in size and extent. The bright star lying south of the Seventh Constellation is nine times as large as the earth. The other stars may be similarly compared. Those who wish to know more about these wonders are referred to the book *Vulogathuva Sasthiram*.

"From a detailed study of all these things it follows inevitably that the earth was created by a Supreme Being having infinite wisdom, boundless providence and power surpassing thought or word."

Nobili had been the first European to discover the Vedas, which included man's oldest observations about the sun, moon and stars. Now he had made partial return by introducing to India man's newest observations—so new indeed that they were ridiculed by many even in Italy—not for themselves alone, as empirical facts, but to arouse (as in the Vedas) a sense of God.

Given the climate of thought at Madurai, science could play only a marginal role in Nobili's writings. His chief books are philosophical and theological, the most important being the *Gnanopadesam*—Spiritual Teaching—a Tamil work embodying the substance of his religious teaching—begun soon after his

arrival and continually enlarged and improved, until at the end of
his life it would grow into five volumes: a *Summa Theologica* for
Indians.

The *Âttuma Nirunayam*—Disquisition on the Soul—is a highly
technical work, crammed with Sanskrit terms. Of thirty-eight
chapters twelve are concerned with pantheism and transmigration.
Here, as elsewhere, Nobili draws on Hindu scripture to prove his
points. Regarding the unity of the human race, for example,
Nobili cites the *Taittirīya Upaniṣad*: "The generation of men:
two are mentioned, a man and a woman: from these two come
generation and the desire to engender. That is the principle of
generation." He adds a high-Tamil proverb: "The father and the
mother of the world, the first parents . . ." to show that the fable
about the origin of castes is not unanimous even in India. Though
relieved with a few colourful images—such as blind men groping
round an elephant, trying to decide what it is, as a simile of
ignorant men explaining the world—most of the treatise is a
re-statement of Aristotelian psychology in Sanskrit terminology.
One new argument is used against the Brahmin notion of the soul
in the body like a bird in a cage: "When a man lives in a house,
does the house grow with him? When he is not at home, does the
house fall into ruins?"

Other Tamil works by Nobili include the *Tivviya Mādirigai*—
The Divine Model; *Tūshana Tikkāram*—Refutation of Blasphemies; *Punar Jenma Ācheba*—Refutation of Rebirth, also known
as Dialogue on Eternal Life; and *Gnāna Sanchīvi*—Spiritual
Medicine. In these, as in all his books, Nobili taught as far as
possible in parable, a form specially pleasing to Tamils. "Men
distinguish between a piece of mica and a piece of silver, between
a piece of glass and a diamond, between a pearl and the shell; why
do they not distinguish between the true God and idols?" In
another passage Nobili refers to a well-known Puranic swan which
drank only pure milk, not the water mixed with it: "Like the swan
which separates milk from water, man must distinguish truth from
falsehood." "Men who, though endowed with reason, behave like
senseless beasts, resemble the bat. What is the bat? It cannot be a
bird, since it has teeth and gives milk to its young. Then it is a

rat? No, it has wings, it flies. So is the sinner: he has an immortal soul, yet he craves only for earthly things—what shall we call him?" Again, life being considered by the Tamils as a stormy sea, from which the soul is ever striving to escape, Nobili adopts the metaphor to express salvation: "Those who refuse to give up their sins will never succeed in climbing the shore"—"climbing" being the *mot juste*, since the local lakes were surrounded by sheer embankments.

Nobili enjoyed the *reductio ad absurdum*. "If God has a body it must be finite or infinite. Now it cannot be finite, for limitation is repugnant to the divine nature. If it is infinite, see the consequences . . ." Then follows a funny description of an infinite nose, infinite mouth, infinitely distant from one another. And to those who professed pantheism, Nobili replies, "If the world were God, it should be eternal and infinite: having an infinite number of men with an infinite number of hairs on an infinite number of heads."

Nobili used every device of Tamil rhetoric to adorn his books. "One hand stroking, one hand striking, the child must be trained" is his version of "Fortiter et suaviter", but the Tamil gerunds: "oru kei *aneittu* (one hand caressing)" "oru kei *adittu* (one hand chastising)" make the phrase pleasing and memorable. Similarly, Nobili likes balancing the pure assonance of *aleika*—to call or attract, applied to rational beings, and *ilukka*—to drag violently, applied to irrational beings. Another characteristic of his Tamil writings is the wide use of Sanskrit terms and even of Sanskrit grammar, such as his attempt to introduce the Sanskrit superlative ending *tama*. This was perhaps a result of Nobili's Renaissance schooling: to write Italian as much like Latin as possible.

Finally, the *Tūshana Tikkāram*—Reputation of Blasphemies—a Tamil work, the last chapters of which form a handbook on the way to teach the Gospel. Nobili's guiding text is the passage from Exodus: "Thou shalt not speak against the gods". Abuse and ridicule lead only to bitterness and are to be avoided: "if instead of politely offering cool drinks and sweets, one were to throw them in the recipient's face, no sane man would accept them."

The master's task, he believed, was to explain the Gospel and let the disciple draw his own conclusions. Truths deduced were far more personal and binding than those learned by heart. The disciple, after hearing an account of God's attributes, would himself say, "Therefore so and so whom we adore as gods cannot be real gods, since they told lies in this and that circumstance," and later himself decide, "But I cannot go on wearing the trident or lingam," depending on his sect.

Nobili believed that this was St Thomas the Apostle's own method, and cites Metaphrastes, the tenth-century compiler of legends about saints in the Byzantine menology: "When he [St Thomas] saw that they had embraced the false religion of the demons, and cherished it deep in their hearts, he did not refute it at once, nor did he rebuke them or use severity, for he knew that what is deeply rooted in the heart by long habit is not easily removed, and must be changed by persuasion rather than by force."

Here legend and fact join hands, for if (as a constant tradition of the Church has always held) St Thomas the Apostle did visit India, nothing at all is known for certain about his method of evangelizing. Nobili, who modestly believed he followed in the footsteps of another, was himself the pioneer.

13. The General's Letter

PERO FRANCISCO was a schoolmaster, not a missionary. Aged forty-seven, he had lived twenty-two years in India, mostly in Goa, where he had been successively Minister, teacher of philosophy and theology, and Rector of the College of St Paul. A strict disciplinarian, in 1607 he had preached before the Goa Inquisitors a sermon which pleased them so much that when in the following year he was sent to Rome to attend the Congregation of Procurators, they gave him letters of warm recommendation to their Lisbon colleagues.

Pero Francisco was specially appointed by Nicolau Pimenta to reverse Laerzio's Indianizing policy. But no more than Pimenta could he actually suppress the Madurai Mission without express orders from the General. These orders he firmly believed would be issued in response to Pimenta's report and the censure of the Goa theologians. They were not expected to arrive before 1613. Meanwhile, Pero Francisco cancelled Nobili's projected missionary tour in the Madurai kingdom.

He also galvanized Fernandez's mission into action, in the belief that if with the good old approved methods they could achieve the same or even better results than Nobili, the newfangled "dissimulatory" schemes would have no justification. Fernandez and Buccerio (who since joining the "old" mission had reversed his opinion of Nobili's method) were exhorted to become vegetarians. They visited the prisoners in jail and brought them fresh water from the Vaigai river. They treated sick pilgrims who swarmed from all South India to visit the temple of Chockanātha. This social work caught the eyes of certain poligars, who tried to emulate it. The Great Nāyak heard of it with pleasure, and sent alms to have a share in such meritorious deeds.

Feasts were now celebrated at the church of the Mother of God

with flamboyant pomp, sacred dramas were staged, books translated into Tamil and circulated among those Christians who could
read; a poet was engaged to versify the life of Christ and compose
hymns in honour of the Blessed Virgin and the Saints, which the
school-children learned by heart. Large sums of money, provided
by the new Provincial, were spent on displays of pictures, fireworks
and rockets.

In September 1612 Pero Francisco visited Madurai to see the
results. He was welcomed at Fernandez's church by school-children who sang their best canticle, while the parishioners read him
a beautiful address. He was pleased to learn that sick people had
been healed with oil from a lamp which burned before a holy
painting, and that during Lenten sermons many people shed tears
and beat their breasts.

From this edifying picture Pero Francisco turned to Nobili's
parish. It annoyed him that Nobili's house should be called
Madam (*Mutt*) and the church *Koil* instead of *Casa* and *Igregia*,
the terms used by all good Christians. Though admitting that
Nobili and Vico "vie with the greatest penitents in the world", he
could not approve the fact that "they have become thorough
Brahmins as regards diet, dress and ceremonies". For Pero Francisco, like most people who had spent their lives in Goa, had a preconceived idea of what a Brahmin was, based on the special caste
of Brahmins who lived in South Canara, Malabar and Cochin.
This caste—the Nambūdiris—differed essentially from all other
Brahmin castes in the South in that they claimed to be priests.
Many had their own temples. They held entirely aloof from the
world and did not even condescend to teach. They grew their
finger-nails a foot long and their hair into a knot hanging over their
forehead. Among their peculiar customs was succession in the
female line.

Because the Nambūdiri Brahmins based their claim to pre-
eminence not (like the Madurai Brahmins) on birth, but on their
hereditary priestly office, it was usual on the coast to understand
by the word "Brahmin" "Hindu priest". Some Nambūdiris had
even testified in this sense in Goa. In Madurai, on the other hand,
Brahmins, as elsewhere, offered daily sacrifices to their household

gods; as guardians of the Vedas they recited Vedic verses at some weddings and funerals of other castes. But generally they did not offer sacrifices or carry out worship on behalf of other castes. Their function varied: many were teachers at the university, a large number were cooks to high-caste households.

After twenty-two years in Goa, Pero Francisco was so firmly established in his notion of what a Brahmin was that Vico, in the few days that Francisco remained in Madurai, did not attempt to remove it. Instead, he tried to justify his Brahmins' habits in terms Francisco could understand.

Now in Goa and elsewhere on the Coast, where book-learning took precedence over day-by-day association with the Indian people, it was widely held that the Brahmins (and possibly all Indians) were Jews, or at last descendants of Jews.

The belief that the Jewish people were the original race on earth and that Adam spoke Hebrew had been popularized in the writings of Isidore of Seville. Only "at the building of the tower after the flood did diversity of languages arise". At the same time as a result the different races of mankind were constituted. Isidore believed that even in his time—the seventh century—nations could be traced back to the original Hebrew stock by etymologizing on their names. Others, however, had taken new names, "either from kings or countries or customs or other causes", and the genealogy of these he believed to be irretrievably lost.

Isidore's theory had been applied to India by one Guillaume Postel in a book published in Basle in 1553. Postel claimed that the Brahmins were of Jewish origin and possessed some of the original doctrines of Moses not preserved by the Jews.

The grounds for this fantastic assertion were slight. First, a colony of Jewish traders, originally from Baghdad, had been found at Cranganore. When the Portuguese made Cranganore a base, the black Jews had been compelled to settle in the native town of Cochin, and were still there in Nobili's day. Secondly, there were certain vague resemblances between Old Testament laws and Brahmin customs: periods of pollution after birth and death; the Jews covered their heads with ashes in sorrow and penance, so did the Saivites—though with a different motive; the Brahmin sacrifice of Ekiam in which the victim was divided and eaten seemed to resemble the eating of the Paschal Lamb; blessing and curses of gurus carried as much weight as those of parents in Israel; and processions of Hindu deities with their music and shouting were compared to the transference of the ark from the house of Abinadab to that of Obededom, and thence to the city of David: David and all the people were assembled, the ark was placed on a new car made for the purpose, and David and all the house of Israel played before the Lord on all manner of instruments made of firwood, even on harps and psalteries, on timbrels, cornets and cymbals.

A further curious parallel had been noticed by Nobili. During funeral rites, the Brahmins were commanded to wear the thread in an unusual way—hanging from the right shoulder towards the left side. This token of mourning was accompanied by blows on the upper or lower side of the thighs: a custom which recalled to Nobili St Jerome's commentary on the words of Jeremias: "After Thou didst show unto me, I struck my thigh."

Missionaries less knowledgeable than Nobili found further evidence here, there and everywhere. For example, in the name of Brahmā's wife, Sarasvatī. Patroness of literature, music and the fine arts, the goddess was depicted as a beautiful young woman, mounted on a goose, sometimes holding a book or a lute. For those who had never seen a statue of the goddess, Brahmā and Sarasvatī were—quite clearly—their old friends Abraham and his wife Sarah!

Finally, Europeans with some knowledge of Indian myth saw two close resemblances to Genesis. In the Laws of Manu it was written: "When God resolved to draw all things from his own substance, of his own thought he created the waters and put in their breast a productive seed. . . . When the sovereign power divine had finished the work of creation, it was absorbed in the spirit of God, thus changing its time of energy into a time of rest." Secondly, the *Jjala pralayam*—the deluge of water—from which dated the present calendar of the Age of Misery, killed all men except one—Manu or Manouvou—and with him the seven great penitents known as Ṛṣi, ancestors of the different branches of Brahmins. (This division of the Brahmins into branches was compared to the tribal system of Israel.) Now Manouvou is composed of *ma*—

great—and *nouvou*, which the Indians pronounced much as a European pronuonced Noah. Viṣṇu is said to have ordered Manouvou to "take medicinal herbs and seeds of every kind and enter the ark without fear with the seven holy men, with your wives and couples of all the animals." Furthermore, the Indian deluge took place on a date corresponding to 3101 B.C., only a slight difference of 157 years from the Septuagint date of the deluge, 3258 B.C.

Such was the evidence for a theory held as late as the time of the Abbé Dubois, who believed the Indians were descendants of Japheth from the Caucasus region; a theory also extended to China, where some philologists claimed Mandarin to be derived from Hebrew. It was a convenient hypothesis for certain jingoists, since anti-Indian feeling could then be regarded as a logical extension of anti-Semitism, a long-standing disease in the Iberian peninsula. Missionaries, on the other hand, were glad to recognize what seemed a partial bond with the West.

Vico seems to have expounded this theory to Pero Francisco to justify his use of the title "Brahmin." He supported it with additional evidence: the resemblance between the words *Papa* (Pope) and the Tamil *Pāppān* (a name occasionally given to Brahmins). He also made much of a theory according to which Brahmins was a contraction of Abrahmanes—the dispersed descendants of Abraham by Keturah.

Pero Francisco fastened on this would-be-argument, as if it were the mainstay of the whole system and declared that "this proved at most a spiritual, not a blood kinship". Evidently he thought that Nobili and Vico claimed to be Brahmins because of a blood relationship with the Patriarch of Israel, while they accepted that name simply because it was the only one which described adequately their function as "wise men" and teachers of religion. Pero Francisco concluded primly that Vico's arguments "might perhaps suffice to embarrass or convince the Brahmins of Madurai because they were incapable of answering them, but that they would make no impression on the learned men of a European university".

With that, the former schoolmaster left Madurai. Though holding his hand until the General's letter arrived, he could afford to be sharp. Already there were signs that Pimenta's report and the Goa theologians' censure had produced the desired effect in Rome. Fantastic rumours began to circulate about the Count of Civitella who had turned Hindu and was offering incense to idols. The Princess of Besignono, who had been impressed by Nobili's piety when she had met him at Nocera as the guest of her friend the Duchess Anna Carafa, nearly died of grief at the news. She wrote him a most touching letter to win him back to the faith, and offered to pay the expenses of a commission to be sent to India to investigate the case. The Duchess of Sora—mother of Nobili's school friend, Gregorio Boncompagni—formerly one of Nobili's favourite correspondents, stopped writing to him for three years. Cardinal Bellarmine, who loved him like a son, sent him such a stern letter that "he could never read it without shedding tears, though he read it many times". It seemed as though Nobili, who had saved Indian Christians from becoming outcastes, must now pay that penalty himself.

Cardinal Bellarmine evidently thought Nobili was trading on his lineage. "To imitate the pride of the Brahmins seems to me diametrically opposed to the humility of Our Lord"—so he wrote, unaware that Indians expected a precious perfume to be preserved in an ornate phial, and that Western simplicity would, under the circumstances, have appeared worse than vulgarity.

Cardinal Bellarmine's opinion carried weight with the General. On 6th December 1612 Claudio Aquaviva sat down to write to Pero Francisco about the Madurai mission. He was a very old man, with scarcely more than two years to live; the subject under discussion was highly technical, involving the interpretation of alien ceremonies, rites and words; and it seems that his letter—no longer extant—was less clear than it might have been.

The General's letter arrived in Cochin some eight months later. Pero Francisco interpreted the document in terms of his own view that Nobili's method should be condemned. On 11th August 1613 he wrote to Nobili pointing out "the changes which should certainly be made. They are not only those which our Father in his letter orders you to make, but even those which, though not commanded, are suggested by him." It did not matter how strongly

Nobili believed himself to be right. "For to err out of obedience is to act wisely"—twice Francisco repeats what was evidently one of his favourite maxims.

According to Francisco, the General said that Nobili must absolutely change his method; he blamed the use of thread, sandal and baths, as well as the refusal to pass as Parangis before the Indians. All rites and ceremonies borrowed from the pagans and Brahmins must be renounced. "Moreover you must, during the day and in the sight of all, deal freely with the Fathers of the other residence, go to their house and talk with them, and they, in their turn, must be allowed to come to your house without any restriction and not by night only." In conclusion, Pero Francisco forbade Nobili and Vico to administer any baptism unless they accepted his interpretation of the General's letter.

When he received the Provincial's letter, Nobili realized that its implementation would bring about the immediate ruin of the mission. But on turning to the General's letter, a copy of which the Provincial had forwarded, Nobili found a crucial sentence which Pero Francisco had overlooked: "No change should be made which might compromise the existence of the mission". To obey the Provincial was therefore to disobey the General.

Under the circumstances Nobili decided to ask the Provincial's permission to come to Cochin. This, too, was in conformity with another passage in the General's letter overlooked by Pero Francisco: a recommendation that the Archbishop and the Provincial should discuss changes with Nobili.

"After warning him," writes the Provincial, "that his coming was unanimously disapproved by the Consultors I allowed him to come to Cochin or stay at Madurai as he pleased. He then asked my permission to bring with him one of his Brahmins, and I replied he could bring anyone he pleased, but told him that he should, on no account, come with his usual sannyāsī dress, because it was unbecoming in a religious, but in the dress of a Badaga—a long gown reaching to the ankle—or in some other dress, provided it was respectable and modest."

This stipulation placed Nobili in a dilemma. He has taken a vow to wear the sannyāsī dress for life. On the other hand, only by going to Cochin could he save the mission. Fortunately, in his last letter the General had explicitly approved the red-ochre clothes. He decided to go as he was to Cochin and explain his reasons personally.

Nobili arrived in the Portuguese base with two Brahmin converts. It was November 1613, exactly two years since his solemn vows and the decision to travel as a wandering sannyāsī: two years almost totally lost, not in any good cause, but to trivialities and national rivalry. Hearing that he had come dressed as a sannyāsī, Pero Francisco did not even look at Nobili or his clothes and gave orders that he should not be admitted into the college. Then he dashed off a letter to the General, saying that Nobili had arrived in nothing but a loin-cloth.

Nobili, already exhausted by his long journey across the mountains, had to continue a further day's march up-coast to Cranganore, where he received a very different welcome from Archbishop Ros. Though now a prematurely old man of fifty-six, Ros offered to accompany Nobili to Cochin.

In company with so important a person as the Archbishop, Nobili was now allowed to lodge in the college, but for three days Pero Francisco refused to speak to either of them. On the fourth day the Archbishop sent the Provincial a message saying that he had come, as desired by the General, to discuss the Christian community at Madurai, whose administration belonged to him, as Archbishop. The Portuguese Provincial refused to discuss anything with the Spaniard, even to address him a polite word of welcome.

Archbishop Ros had no choice but to return to Cranganore. Thereupon Pero Francisco ordered Nobili to put in writing his interpretation of the General's letter, so that he might send it to Rome along with his own, as proof of Nobili's prevarication. Nobili complied. After a short introduction he wrote:

"Our Father General orders me to reject all dissimulation. This implies that the Christians and the Catechumens have a suspicion that the religion of the Parangis is different from that of Jesus Christ which I am preaching. The way to end this dissimulation is, it seems to me, the one noted by our Father himself, when he says: 'Therefore we indicate here briefly and clearly what appears to us good in the Lord: the first thing to do is to show and declare the truth to the Christians, namely, that the religion of Jesus Christ embraces Princes, Nobles, and people of low condition, that true nobility consists in virtue, and that Princes, if they live badly, go to hell, while the poor, if they live well, go to heaven.' Thus speaks our Father.

"To this I answer that I shall carry out his orders punctually. From his words, quoted above, I gather that he wants me to declare that the religion I preach is the same as that of the Parangis. I shall therefore expressly declare to all the Christians that our religion comprises the Parangis and many other nations, and I shall baptize no one before first explaining to him that the law of Jesus Christ which I preach comprises also the Parangis. I add that if any Hindu asks me if the law I preach includes the Parangis, I shall answer that it does, without the least equivocation. That is what occurs to me on this point. Moreover our Father orders me to teach my Christians that there is but one Church, Catholic, Apostolic and Roman, that in receiving the Sacraments there should be no distinction of persons, and that one does not lose one's nobility by dealing with men of low condition. He says further that all the nobles and the plebeians should keep the places assigned to them in the Church, each one according to his rank. Such is our Father's order.

"It will be obeyed scrupulously. On that occasion I shall explain at length to my converts what concerns the Roman Pontiff, Supreme Vicar of Jesus Christ on earth, and their Ordinary, the Archbishop of Cranganore.

"Our Father orders me to teach them that there should be no difference with regard to the reception of the Sacraments, by which he seems to mean that all must communicate without distinction —*sine distinctione*—that is, not only *formaliter sumpta Ecclesia*, but also *materialiter*, the Christians of my church going to that of Father Gonçalo Fernandez, and those of his church coming to mine. To this I answer that if Father Gonçalo Fernandez assigns in his church distinct place according to our Father General's order, for the high and low castes, as is commonly done among the Christians of St Thomas, where the Pulyas and the Mukuvars remain near the porch while the Brahmins sit in the first rank, the Rājās coming next and the other castes after them, if I say, this is done, I shall inform my Christians that they may go to the church of Father Gonçalo Fernandez, and those of Father Gonçalo that they may come to mine whenever they like, provided they keep to the place assigned to them. I shall also inform my Christians that they may go to the other church for Confession and Communion, and I shall hear the confessions of those who come here from the other church, and give them Communion.

"Our Father says that I should adapt myself to the social customs and observe whatever is a matter of decorum among the nobles. To this I answer that I shall do as he desires, and adapt myself to purely social customs.

"Our Father adds that it seems to be an illusion to refuse to deal with our Fathers and the Portuguese who come here. To comply with his desire in words and in deeds," Nobili continues, "I shall tell all the Christians that we, in this Residence, are Fathers of the Society of Jesus, just as those of the other Residence and the Fathers of Cochin who are dressed in black. I shall also tell them that the Provincial is our Superior in this Province, under the General who is in Rome. I shall also say that I have lived at Cochin wearing the same dress, taking the same food, as the other Fathers who live there, since we belong to the same religious Order, and I am their brother and servant. I shall tell my neophytes that, with the permission of my Superiors, I adopted this kind of dress and food to spread the law of Jesus Christ Our Lord, for it is according to our vocation to adopt the dress and the manner of living which may procure the greater glory to God and contribute more to His service.

"I add that when the Fathers come here, I shall arrange that they go out with my Christians, and when Father Provincial comes I shall declare that he is my Superior. However, Father Provincial (Laerzio) having approved the dress and the manner of taking meals in his house, any Father who wishes to appear before these Christians, will have to put on our dress, and conform to our table manners, because doing otherwise would, it seems to me and saving better judgment, be contrary to the expressed desire of our Father General, and cause a great scandal. I shall also take care that all the Christians show every one of the Fathers the same marks of respects as they show me.

"As to the Portuguese coming to our church, I say that the Brahmins are more considered in that city (Madurai) than in this (Cochin). There, whether in their temples or assemblies, they have precedence even over the king. The Brahmin converts will therefore never consent to yield precedence to others in their church. I shall not even try to persuade them to do so, for I think this would give rise to quarrels and scandals. So much for what concerns us.

"Regarding the Thread, I say first that our Father seems to speak only of mine. Now the question is already settled since I no longer wear any. Whatever be the thread he speaks of, Father General merely says that it is hard to philosophize about *formal, material, primary* and *secondary intention* regarding the thread, the sandal and the baths. To this I say, without claiming to comment or explain our Father's letter, but only to propose what I think, that according to me our Father, while he does not approve of these things, does not condemn them outright. What makes me say this is that, summing up his order to me in these words: 'We shall now say briefly what we think proper to command to your Reverence ... etc.', he does not make the least mention of these various points. Another reason which makes me speak like this is that these things, having been approved by the Ordinary, our Father seems to have been unwilling to forbid them. Whatever it be, I shall state here how I view this affair, and at the end let all I have said be considered as not said.

"Regarding the order given by your Reverence (of not admitting to baptism those who do not remove their thread) I shall first remark, that those who are already Christians, will never remove it whatever I may say to them, for the reasons I shall explain below. As to those who might wish to become Christians, I say that notwithstanding the order (of not minding the thread) given me by the Lord Archbishop, as I am not his subject but the Provincial's, I shall admit none of them against Father Provincial's order, for I do not want to win souls to God through disobedience.

"Another thing I wish to remark concerns the opinion of some

Christian Brahmins who are very learned. When I touched upon that question, as if by accident, without telling them my object, so as not to disturb their conscience and give them scruples, one of them told me several times that there was no Indian law or science which he did not know, and while he showed me passages where it was stated that the thread was not the mark of a sect, he challenged anyone to point out a passage where the contrary was stated. 'When this is done,' said he, 'the matter may be discussed'. He added that though he was bound to suffer all torments for the religion of Christ, he was not obliged, because of *a mere doubt*, to have his eyes plucked out and be driven out of his caste, for it was the least punishment that he could expect if he gave up the thread.

"Moreover I say that these Christians know perfectly well that the Metran [Archbishop] is their Ordinary pastor, and that religious doubts are to be settled by him. Now the Archbishop wrote to me that the thread should give rise to no doubt, that nothing was to be attached to it, either Cross or 'Veronica', and that the Christians were to have no scruple on that point. He added that he had written about it to the Archbishop of Goa, and the Holy Inquisition, and the Lord Archbishop [Dom Alexeio de Menezes] had replied that he would himself willingly wear several threads if he could thereby convert Brahmins, and that he wished that the *slanderers* of this method should rather become its *followers*, and he added other remarks full of piety.

"By order of those who were then my Superiors, I read those letters and others of the same kind, publicly in the church, and everybody knows their contents. That is why I do not see how I can at present say the contrary, specially as our Father General does not disapprove the thread expressly. It seems to me, saving better judgment, that such a step would bring great discredit on the Archbishop, for I should have to say the Ordinary of this church has erred in a grave matter, which would cause great scandal among the Christians. They would think that the same may happen regarding things of faith which I preach to them. For if the Archbishop, whom they consider as their spiritual head next to the Pope, could err so grievously, why not I? I do not think that our Father General wants me to act in this way.

"I add that I have, in Madurai, Christians belonging to the cast of the Rājās and other high castes, who come next to Brahmins and wear the thread, and also Kammālers who, because of their skill in their craft, are also allowed the same privilege. Now none of them, particularly the Rājās who are soldiers, can persuade themselves that their thread is the badge of a religious sect, for they are not so spiritually minded as to have special religious sects as Brahmins have.

"Sandal has always been, and still is, in use among the Christians of St Thomas, as is well known to the Madurai Christians. I do not see therefore how it could be forbidden to the latter without forbidding it also to the former (who live in the same Archdiocese).

"In the matter of *Sandal* I did not introduce anything new, except that, out of courtesy, I had it blessed by the Archbishop. It is a custom in this country never to go out with a bare forehead. The shape we give to the sandal or *pottou* is a square, called *Vidya Bodena*: that is, teaching of knowledge. I add that the Archbishop himself gave sandal to some of these Christians to apply it on their forehead according to the formula prescribed by him. However, should there be any objection to my applying the sandal in the special way that Masters use, I could apply it just like the others.

"As to the ceremonies which accompany the *Baths*, the Fathers here do not observe any. They do as the other Fathers and Christians who bathe when it is necessary. The ceremonies are observed by the Brahmin converts who make a number of signs of the Cross on the water, and recite many prayers, which the Lord Archbishop ordered them to recite, for he did not deem it an imperfection, but a praiseworthy custom, that devout Christians should do for Jesus Christ what they did for their idols when they were pagans. He even deemed it very regrettable that people who, when pagans, thought of their gods while taking their bath, should after becoming Christians never think of Him in performing the same action, specially in view of the words of St Paul: 'Whether you eat or drink, or whatever you do, do all to the glory of God. Be without offence to the Jews, or to the Gentiles, or to God's Church.'

"This is the rule I follow, not for my own satisfaction, but with a view to procuring the salvation of souls, and it seems to me to be in accordance with our Father's letter. My opinion is that this method may be followed in future as it has been in the past, those who work in this Mission persevering in their mode of life, and the Mission going on as before.

"Should another method occur to my Superiors, I am ready to adopt it, even if it were to cost my life and cause the ruin of this Mission."

With this interpretation of the General's letter Archbishop Ros found himself in full agreement. Whereas Pero Francisco knew no Tamil or Sanskrit, Ros, who knew the first language well and had a smattering of the second, put his point of view in a letter to the General: "We are still novices, we have no experience, we do not know the languages of these people as we should, we are unable to read their books, and we calumniate what we cannot imitate."

Pero Francisco, however, saw in Nobili's statement further proof of rebellious obstinacy. Realizing that if he could end the Archbishop's support, Nobili would be at his mercy, he now began to intercept Ros's letters to Madurai and Nobili's letters to Ros. He also decreed a number of petty regulations which he knew would prove irritating. He forbade Brahmin Christians to be employed in Nobili's house or to use glass rosaries. Clothes belonging to Nobili and Vico must be washed by low-caste men. This, in Brahmin eyes, would have polluted the clothes and necessitated a re-washing. He also ordered a big cross to be erected in front of Nobili's church. Nobili had purposely omitted this, for he knew from experience that to display holy images to the masses who were ignorant of their significance was merely to encourage sins of sacrilege.

Already, in December 1612, the Provincial had forbidden Nobili and Vico to baptize those who wore the thread or tuft of hair. Since the General had expressed the desire that the Mission should continue, he could not recall Nobili and Vico from Madurai. But in August 1613 he did the next best thing: he forbade them to baptize anybody at all.

14. The Two Briefs

MADURAI enjoyed a period of peace and prosperity. Pilgrims flocked to the temple of Śiva, countless as the statues on the twenty-tiered gate-towers, and students crowded the porticoes to receive instruction in the Vedānta. While no one was allowed to be baptized in the name of the Christian God, devotees of Śiva and Viṣṇu thronged to the festal processions which made the streets and houses of Madurai seem merely outlying sanctuaries of one vast Hindu temple.

In Nobili's own words, "Today the Perumal's[1] idol was placed in a tastefully decorated car and carried on the shoulders of Nambūdiris, Brahmins and others. Streets were festooned and the dust laid with water; walls painted with broad white and red stripes; sandal-paste, saffron, perfumes and rose-water sprinkled; bouquets of flowers strewn all over the streets; and cymbals, clarinets, trumpets and drums were played. Amid this pomp and grandeur the colossal car of the god was prepared, fitted with huge wheels and marvellous wooden dolls representing serpents, lions, bears, tigers, stags and other animals, arched under peculiar carvings, the altar throne tastefully and artistically finished and well decorated with muslins of gold and silver thread, brown, red and black, as well as with silk robes and ribbons bearing golden letters. Chains of white and red pearls and jasmine decorated the entrance. Choruses of temple girls danced and sang and offered incense; elephants and horses paraded to the pounding of giant drums on their backs. Kings and nobles, merchants, Vadukars and Vellalas advanced two abreast in rows; the Brahmins chanted verses; over all fluttered a rain of flower-petals."

And at night, when to the wailing of conches and thudding of drums pilgrims in their thousands chanted to Śiva, and the tart

[1] An epithet of Viṣṇu.

198

smell of camphor burning in Śiva's sanctuary drifted into the near-by hermitage, it is not difficult to imagine Nobili's moral loneliness and, in view of the Provincial's ban, his sense of frustration.

But Nobili's blood was the blood of soldiers who had won glory against heretic and Turk. If he could not baptize, at least he could still teach. Then teach he would. Since his apostolate now lay chiefly among the Brahmins, those convinced of the truth of Christianity would have to wait for the day—if it ever came—when Nobili could baptize them without destroying them as social creatures. Men of other castes must go to Fernandez's church for baptism.

This existence in a strait-jacket continued for a year. It seemed to Nobili and Vico as though nothing worse could possibly happen, but they were mistaken. Incited by these repressive measures against the Brahmin sannyāsīs, some of Nobili's dearest converts, for whom he had sacrificed so much, even the right to baptize, now turned against him.

Alexis Nāyak was the second Indian to have been baptized by Nobili—at the end of 1607. He was then aged eighteen, of very strong character and absolutely fearless: one day he even challenged a sorcerer to try all his tricks on him, saying that with a sign of the Cross he would put him to flight. On another occasion when some of his jewels were stolen, he not only had a suspect arrested and tortured, but consulted a magician to discover the thief. As a punishment for this scandal, Nobili forbade Alexis to enter the church until he had made public reparation. After a sleepless night, Alexis threw himself at his guru's feet, sobbing in contrition, and begging to be allowed to give all he possessed to the church and spend his life serving Nobili in the meanest offices.

Nobili cautioned him, waited, imposed tests and finally concluded that Alexis did indeed have a vocation. He was allowed to lay his jewels and finery at the foot of the altar, put on a coarse gown and read a solemn formula which he himself had composed. He vowed to God that he gave Him all his possessions, and that he would live in celibacy and chastity till his death. To this he added, at Nobili's suggestion, a vow of obedience to his guru.

For a little more than a year all had gone well. Alexis spent an hour in meditation every day and took the discipline several times a week. During Mass he wept with devotion; this had greatly impressed Emmanuel Leitao. His Hindu friends were edified to see one who had been known for pride and vanity living so humble a life. He was called Alexis Swami, and Nobili hoped that one day he would become a priest.

One or two Brahmin converts resented Alexis's position of trust in the community. They found it intolerable that a young man of inferior caste should order them about. They complained to Laerzio on one of his visits, and Laerzio removed Alexis from his special position. This was a humiliation Alexis could not bear. Neglecting his vow of poverty, he began to steal.

One day a captain with a troop of soldiers under the command of an officer came with an order from Errama Setti to Nobili. Alexis was to be handed over at once on a charge of theft. To save his dearest convert, Nobili took a very strong line. "Errama Setti," he retorted, "will first have to cut off my head, then he can take the young man and whatever else he finds in this house." The officer, who belonged to the Rājā caste, was deeply impressed by Nobili's attitude. "This man is truly a Rājā," he said, "for that is the way true Rājās speak." After a few ineffectual protests, the captain led his soldiers back to barracks, and Nobili was able to smuggle Alexis away to Quilon on the Coast. He had arranged for Alexis to attend Cochin College, with a view to preparing him for the priesthood.

Alexis did not come up to expectations. For a time he wandered about on the Coast. Finally, after five years' absence, he returned to Madurai in May 1615, restless and discontented.

On his arrival Alexis was not only refused admission to the Mutt but released from his vows, unfrocked and secularized. His proud spirit could not brook such a humiliation; his love for his guru was turned into hatred; and he began to seek a means of revenge.

It was then that he met the Brahmin convert, Boniface, who had accompanied Nobili to Cochin for his final vows. Boniface on that occasion pestered Archbishop Ros for money, and on his return celebrated his marriage with certain ceremonies which Nobili had forbidden as superstitious. As a result, he had been excluded for a time from the church.

Boniface went for consolation to André Buccerio who, perhaps because he had not been considered a fit companion for Nobili, had come to share his colleague Fernandez's view of the Italian's experiment. Buccerio received Boniface well and listened sympathetically to all his complaints. He hinted that Nobili's influence was coming to an end. Boniface was promised money and temporal advantages if he spoke what Buccerio called the truth. Boniface agreed. His calumnies were written down and sent to the Provincial in Cochin.

Alexis now joined with Boniface to exploit to the utmost the state of demoralization and uncertainty to which Pero Francisco had reduced the Madurai community. By coaxing and bullying they recruited half a dozen discontented neophytes, whom they induced to collect and report to Buccerio any incident which could bear a scandalous interpretation.

Alexis was greatly stimulated by some imprudent words of Buccerio. Being quite sure Nobili would be expelled from Madurai, Buccerio had inquired whether in such circumstances Alexis would have sufficient authority over the other converts to take charge of the Mutt. These words, reported to Alexis, so spurred his ambition that, to hasten his own accession as "Abbot of the Monastery", he accumulated the most outrageous calumnies against Nobili. These were all forwarded to Pero Francisco.

Nobili watched in silence, without a word of reproach or self-pity. Even to his family he never wrote of his own trials. Yet because of his sensitive nature he must have suffered more than most men would have done from this double betrayal. He had always counted on the Indians—to the extent of his own total sacrifice for their sake. For them he was exposed to censure by his family in Rome, to taunts and strictures by his colleagues, to abusive pamphlets throughout Europe. And now the Indians too had turned against him.

Yet partly he was prepared. In Rome as a boy—so remote now it must have seemed almost a previous birth—he had flinched while his aunt's spiritual adviser, the ascetic Jean de la Barrière, was condemned and deposed by his own Cistercian monks—for political reasons. Cardinal Bellarmine, it was true, had finally caused Barrière to be reinstated, but the Cardinal's stern letter to Nobili showed no likelihood of a second reprieve.

Eagerly the conspirators awaited decisive news from Cochin and the fruits of their plotting: status and silver. In August 1615 news did indeed arrive: not, as the conspirators hoped, the expulsion of Nobili, but the death of Pero Francisco. The effect was like that of a thunder-clap on a flock of sheep. Conscience-stricken and terrified, they ran one after another to throw themselves at Nobili's feet and ask forgiveness. Some were too ashamed to face him and asked Vico to intercede on their behalf.

Readily, without any recrimination, Nobili forgave and gladly gathered around him the Indian community. This reunion proved lasting. Nobili had the satisfaction of seeing Alexis make amends by a life of exceptional fervour, and Boniface—two years later, on the death of Buccerio—read a sworn retraction of all his calumnies in the presence of Archbishop Ros.

Slowly the pain of the last few months began to lift. After the reconciliation with Alexis came news of the appointment of a new Provincial: Gaspar Fernandez, no friend to Nobili but at least not an enemy, as he proved by summoning the Italian to Cochin to discuss his mission.

Nobili this time chose a longer route through the plains via Shenkotta and Quilon, which offered a chance of preaching in villages which had never heard the Gospel. For, as he wrote to Cardinal Bellarmine, he "longed with a great longing to tramp staff in hand those vast spaces to win souls to Jesus Christ". Fifteen days after leaving Madurai he arrived at Quilon, and on 30th October he sailed into Cochin harbour.

His brethren in the College were prepared, on the strength of calumnies and rumours from Madurai, to shun him. But they had reckoned without Nobili's presence. Nobili was now thirty-eight, but his emaciated, lined face made him seem much older. His physical stature, his obvious holiness, his learning, made the small men who had prattled against him shrink back. He returned like a scarred veteran from ten years at the front to reserves comfortably established with familiar books in their colleges, who fought the battle of the missions across the mangoes and pine-apples of refectory tables. What could they show against the heroic silence and modesty of the great pioneer, his perpetual fast and unremitting work? They began to wonder if they had not been persecuting a saint.

Soon friends gathered round Nobili: Francisco Ros and a number of Italians, as well as the Portuguese Estevão de Britto, future Archbishop of Cranganore, and Ambrosio Soeiro, former Rector of Cochin. They made no secret of their admiration for Nobili, nor of their anger at the cruel treatment he had endured.

Laerzio headed the reaction. Writing to the General, he said, "There is no doubt that we are dumbfounded seeing what passions can do, especially among those neophytes so young in faith, when they find encouragement. They are wonderful in adapting them-selves to the mind of those who govern and in speaking accord-ingly. Father Provincial and Father de Nobili will write to you about this." But once again Nobili did not write to justify himself or whine.

Meanwhile, true reports of the Madurai Mission were beginning to reach Rome, and brought about a reaction there also. Cardinal Bellarmine wrote to say how great was his relief to learn that all was well with dear Padre Roberto. The General—it was his last letter about the Madurai Mission, for he died on 31st January 1615—showed that he still trusted Nobili: he did away with many restrictions, though as the dispute about the tuft of hair and thread was now *sub judice* in the Roman Curia, he could not allow Nobili to baptize the catechumens who wore those insignia.

Despite this reaction in his favour at Rome and Cochin, Nobili could not resume work in Madurai. He could not even return there at once, for he now had to face a new enemy, more formid-able even than Nicolau Pimenta or Pero Francisco: the Arch-bishop of Goa himself, Primate of the Indies.

Dom Frei Cristovão de Sa e Lisboa of the Congregation of St Jerome had succeeded Archbishop Alexeio de Menezes in 1610. While Menezes had personal experience of the St Thomas Christians, the new Archbishop was a comparative stranger to

India, having been formerly Bishop of Malacca. On his way to take up the new appointment he had passed through Cochin, where he had stayed with his friend the Bishop, arch-enemy of the Jesuits and of Nobili. Here some bargaining was done. The Primate designate gave the Bishop of Cochin a certificate declaring that the Bishop did not favour the Nestorian Archdeacon of the St Thomas Christians who was giving such trouble to Francisco Ros: a declaration contrary to the most notorious facts. In return, the Bishop of Cochin wrote an attestation that the Primate designate was entirely fit for his new dignity. As a parting gift, the Primate designate offered the Bishop of Cochin a precious ring. Laerzio, despite repeated pleas to be allowed to speak to the new Archbishop, had not been allowed even a quarter of an hour in defence of the Madurai Mission.

On taking possession of his See, Archbishop de Sa decided that the keeping of the laws made for the Christians of Goa must be insisted upon all over India as a condition for receiving baptism. One of these laws was that no Christian should wear sandal-paste, the tuft of hair peculiar to the three highest castes, or—most important of all—the thread.

The laws dated back to 1567 when the first Synod of Goa, under the presidency of its archbishop, had forbidden the wearing of the Brahmin thread by Christians and non-Christians alike. No reason was given, but it seems likely that this distinctive sign of the supreme caste was viewed as a direct challenge to Portuguese political supremacy. The prohibition was renewed by the second Synod in 1575, and again by the third Synod in 1585. This time the thread was condemned as a token of a false religion, like ashes on the body, and because it was tainted by superstitious ceremonies. "What is worse," the decree continued, "those who wear the thread are reported to have to recite daily prayers to their idols for the triumph of the Brahmin religion and the destruction of Christianity in India." In conclusion, it was laid down that if the rule could not be enforced, the thread should be allowed to be worn under the clothes so as not to be seen.

These Synods had been held at a time when knowledge of Indian customs was slight. Moreover, their decrees had not been binding on Nobili. Archbishop de Menezes himself had dispensed Nobili from them and even encouraged him to allow high castes to retain their thread.

But in Goa opinion was now hardening against the Indians. It was feared that if concessions were made in Madurai to the Brahmins, the Christian Brahmins of Goa would demand back their ancient privileges and replace the Portuguese as leaders of the people. Moreover, Archbishop de Sa was not well disposed to Brahmins. On one occasion a well-qualified Brahmin named Matthew de Castro was presented to him for ordination by the Provincial of the Carmelites. Cristovão de Sa replied that he refused on principle to ordain Brahmins, and nothing could shake him from this decision. It is not surprising that the new Archbishop invoked the Synods' decrees and applied to Rome for permission to take severe measures against Nobili for infringing them.

The atmosphere in Rome, already becoming favourable to Nobili, was now still further improved by news from China, the country where missionary adaptation had proved so successful. Ricci was dead and had been succeeded by the Sicilian Longobardi. Later he was to change his opinion, but at this stage Longobardi allowed converts to pay homage to Confucius and their ancestors, provided that superstitious Buddhist and Taoist accretions to these rites were eliminated. The rites themselves were believed to be purely social, not religious. When the Jesuits of China asked permission to translate the Bible, the missal, ritual and breviary into Mandarin; for Chinese clergy to use Mandarin in the liturgy and administration of the sacraments; and that the head might be covered during Mass, Cardinal Bellarmine favoured the concessions, with the result that in 1615 Pope Paul V issued a brief granting them all.

When Archbishop de Sa's petition arrived in Rome, to offset its effect Nicolau Godinho, professor of theology at the Roman College, composed a masterly thesis based on Nobili's letters defending the method used in Madurai. This thesis was then made the subject of public disputation which his students held before the most influential men of Rome. The students concluded that there was nothing reprehensible in Nobili's method.

Such, too, was Cardinal Bellarmine's reconsidered opinion, which carried great weight with the Pope, so that when Paul V replied to the Archbishop's petition in a brief dated 4th January 1616—*Cum sicut Fraternitas*—he showed great consideration for Nobili's method by endorsing his desire that conversions be made easier. Instead of rejecting *a priori* the thread and other disputed tokens, he ordered Archbishop de Sa and Archbishop Ros to examine them carefully to see whether they could not be stripped of the accidental superstitions connected with them, and allowed to the neophytes.

The brief took almost two years to reach India. However, long before then, Nobili's friends in Rome informed him of its likely terms. Nobili was relieved, but his relief was doubtless tinged with disappointment, for it meant that he still could not resume his important apostolate among the Brahmins. However, he returned to Madurai, where in April 1616—after nearly three years during which they had been forbidden to baptize—he and Vico again began their ministry among Hindus of the Śūdra caste. But all the time they were thinking of the still-delayed decision about caste-signs. For them it was not merely a question whether they could dress in this or that way, or whether they could follow this or that custom, but whether the Indians as a nation should be given all legitimate facilities to enter the Christian fold. And so they continued to inform their superiors about Indian habits, and especially about the thread.

Vico explained to the new General, Vitelleschi, that for most Brahmins "not to sweep one's house is a sin; not to cleanse one's body of dirt is a sin, to go about naked is a sin, to sleep in one's clothes at night is a sin, to wear patched clothes is a sin, to wear dirty clothes is a sin, to eat without cleanliness and decency is a sin, not to clean one's teeth or not to ease nature cleanly is a sin, to eat or drink what is unwholesome or filthy is a sin, and so of the rest. But to do these things, natural and conventional though they be, with the addition of various ceremonies and prayers, is to merit a reward either in this life or in the next. . . . If we consider only this circumstance of ceremonial, in this sect it is common to all other things, especially those pertaining to civil life; so that if nothing that is purely natural or civil, not even a toothpick, can be without its rites and tutelary gods, it is clear that the thread cannot avoid having them either, since it is a thing of such importance that it distinguishes and makes the castes."

Nobili and Vico devoted themselves to defending the thread, tuft, sandal-paste and baths, for Rome showed no interest in the other charges arising from Gonçalo Fernandez's original list of grievances. The two most important—that Nobili refused to minister to Portuguese travellers in Madurai and his separate high-caste church—had been refuted, curiously enough, by Buccerio in an early letter to the General in 1610, a letter which carried all the more weight in view of Buccerio's later hostility. Buccerio noted that Nobili heard the confession of a Portuguese captain called Affonso Alvares de Caceres, who was ill. On the same occasion one of the Captain's Portuguese companions went to the Mutt, made a general confession and received Communion in his church. This Portuguese was greatly impressed by the mission; he told Buccerio that were it not for his wife in Goa he would have willingly remained to serve Nobili.

As regards caste, Buccerio explained that the St Thomas Christians of Purukad did not allow the Christian Mukuvars to enter their church to attend Mass; they had to do so from outside until a church was built for them. In the same place, while the St Thomas Christians could go upstairs to see the missionary in his house, the Mukuvars could see him only on the ground floor. In South Travancore the St Thomas Christians objected to their parish priest visiting Buccerio because he was in charge of the Mukuvars of Colachel. The fact that Portuguese officials deemed it an honour to visit him did nothing to raise him in the caste hierarchy. If, concluded Buccerio, it was necessary to put up with such discrimination in old parishes, to humour non-Christians, it was even more necessary in Madurai, until the Hindus learned to distinguish between caste and religion.

This view had been accepted in Rome, and Pope Paul's brief *Cum sicut Fraternitas* did not even discuss the question of high-caste church, or Nobili's titles: Aiyer, sannyāsī, Rājā and so on.

In the first week of December 1617 the long-awaited brief

arrived by carrack in Goa. To Archbishop de Sa it proved a bitter disappointment. What he wanted from Rome was not an order to hold a round-table conference with a fellow Archbishop and some theologians, but a statement that Nobili's case concerned the Faith of the Holy and Apostolic Church, and so came under the authority of the Holy Office of the Inquisition. What he wanted was to sit on his primatial throne, flanked by his two Inquisitors, and pass sentence on a wretched priest who had lapsed into idolatry. The brief was intolerable and derogatory to the Primatial dignity. Archbishop de Sa would not accept it. He ordered his Inquisitors to write at once to the Grand Inquisitor of Portugal insisting that Nobili be judged by the Inquisition, and by the Inquisition only.

The office of Grand Inquisitor of Portugal and the East Indies was held by Fernão Martins de Mascarenhas. For eight years he had been rector of Coimbra University. Though one of the most eminent theologians of his day he was no dry scholar and during an epidemic of plague had personally cared for the sick and dying in the province of Algarve. He had been offered the archbishopric of Lisbon at the age of thirty-seven, an honour he declined. Now aged seventy, he was known to be a friend of the Jesuits for whom he had founded a college in Villa Nova de Portimão.

The letter of the Goa Inquisitors set Mascarenhas a dilemma. The Goa Inquisition had already ruled that the thread, tuft and other signs were superstitious; therefore, it was claimed, all they had to do now was pass sentence on Nobili. On the other hand, there was the Pope's recent brief. Did it overrule the bull of the Holy Inquisition? Mascarenhas decided it did, and wrote to Goa ordering the brief *Cum sicut Fraternitas* to be observed.

Along with Mascarenhas's letter arrived a second brief from the Pope, dated 18th February 1618 and addressed to Archbishop Ros. This second brief granted a request by Ros, who had been ill and felt himself unfit to travel, excusing him from undertaking the journey to Goa. The Pope directed him to hear from Nobili what he had to say about the rites in dispute, to put his vote in writing and send it, through Nobili, to the Archbishop of Goa.

At the same time the Archbishop of Goa and the first and second

Inquisitors were instructed to read and consider the opinions of the Archbishop Ros, of Nobili, and of other priests of the Society of Jesus and to send a full report of the whole affair to the Apostolic See. This second brief was still more favourable than the first to Nobili's cause. According to the first brief neither he nor his fellow-Jesuits were to take part in the conference, while according to the second their presence was specially insisted upon and Nobili had the right of vote, which was never given to an accused. Through his delay caused by invoking the Inquisition, Archbishop de Sa had brought on himself what he most wished to avoid: a direct clash on equal terms with Roberto de Nobili.

15. *The Goa Conference*

AT Goa the salvation of India would, as it were, be hanging by a thread. No one realized this better than Archbishop Ros. Though still very weak, despite his exemption he insisted on accompanying Nobili to the conference. The two men embarked at Cochin in December 1618 and after a stormy voyage of thirty days, instead of the usual ten, sailed up past the anchored warships and stepped ashore at Goa.

The conference was set for 4th February, so Nobili had a few weeks in which to assess the atmosphere of this other India which, since his departure thirteen years before, had shown itself consistently hostile. He found the old swagger was still kept up. On New Year's Day elephants painted with the arms and crosses of Portugal and mounted by trumpeters paraded through the streets to the palaces of the Viceroy and Archbishop, bowing their heads when they passed church doors, and again when the Viceroy and Archbishop offered gifts to their keepers. The four thousand Portuguese and half-breed soldiers on the island still blustered and strutted, taking advantage of the fact that in Goa the title of soldier was the most honourable of all. Though many had been sent to India in exile for crimes, even the poorest assumed titles of nobility, to make the Indians believe they were all of illustrious parentage. Inter-marriage was already weakening the stock, and the title "Portuguese of Portugal" or "*homo blanco*"—always esteemed—was now more prized than ever before.

It was becoming increasingly difficult to pay these soldiers, let alone provide for the missions. Every year the King issued more and more urgent calls to fortify and to charge captains for corruption and failure to carry out their duties. 1614, perhaps, marked the beginning of the end. For in that year the King, in order to provide for administrative expenses, had ordered all lucrative commands and high appointments no longer to go to those who had earned them by loyal service, but to be knocked down to the highest bidder.

Nobili could expect less and less support from this new mercantile officialdom. Portuguese Asia—the title was already a caricature. The day might even come when a Protestant power would control the sub-continent. In 1616 the Danes had established themselves at Tranquebar, the Dutch had several bases, and the English, by 1619, had regular factories at Surat, Agra, Ahmadabad and Broach. These events would hang over the forthcoming conference. Though specifically concerned with certain Indian customs, it was being held, as the Pope pointed out in his brief, "to find a solution that would facilitate conversions". Implicit in its findings would be the answer to the larger question: "Was Christianity in India to be linked in future to Portuguese forms, to forms in danger of extinction?"

Before the conference, Nobili submitted to the Archbishop of Goa and others a short memoir setting out his case, and Archbishop Ros also circulated a treatise dealing with the thread, tuft and baths. Archbishop de Sa, hearing that these documents had produced a favourable impression, called to the conference a number of friars and secular priests who were neither directly concerned nor prepared to enter into serious discussion. Nobili deprecated this attempt to pack the conference, but his protest was disregarded.

On the morning of 4th February 1619 secretaries brought paper and ink to the great hall of the Archbishop's palace—with the Viceroy's palace and the black-stone office of the Inquisition one of the most magnificent buildings in Goa—and prepared to usher in the members of the conference. Five Canarese priests in black cassocks—recruited from Portuguese islands and bases in or around Goa; three Portuguese seculars; two Franciscan friars in brown habits and sandals; two Dominicans in black and white cowled habits; two Augustinian friars; three Portuguese and one Italian Jesuit—they entered in groups and took their seats flanking the scarlet episcopal throne. Then came the two Inquisitors, whom Nobili was meeting not as Judges but as fellow-theologians.

They were followed by Archbishop Ros, still not fully recovered, worn by a lifetime's work among the St Thomas Christians—now almost totally blind, so that he had to be led to his seat.

Then came Nobili, his red-ochre Indian clothes falling in folds around his tall, thin body, wooden sandals clamped to his feet. As he looked round the members of the commission, he had every reason for dismay. Six of the eight outsiders called in by the Primate had no preliminary notion of the controversy; they had never even thought about the questions involved. None of them had ever been in provinces ruled by Hindus, nor heard about the customs and rites of Madurai. Vedas and Upaniṣads, Purāṇas and *Bhagavad Gītā*—to the Primate's claque these would merely be wicked words.

Last of all, Dom Cristovão de Sa appeared, majestic in scarlet, episcopal amethyst gleaming on his right hand. He doubtless saw to it that every possible detail was added to show off his rank, for Dom Cristovão had a high opinion of his office as Primate of the Indies: a few years back he had entered the town of Baçaim on horseback under a pallium, with a fidalgo holding the reins of his horse. Such show-off was strictly forbidden and had drawn a sharp reprimand from the King himself.

As soon as the Archbishop had called the meeting to order, Nobili rose to speak. He asked his Grace whether he might bring as witnesses certain Brahmins knowing Sanskrit. His case was largely based on such texts as *The Laws of Manu* and the *Taittirīya Saṁhitā*, and with the aid of Sanskrit-speaking Brahmins he promised to prove it. The Archbishop refused. Nobili then asked that at least Brahmins should be heard explaining the meaning of the emblems under dispute. Without waiting to hear the opinion of the members of the conference, Archbishop de Sa replied angrily that only those present in the great hall should be heard, and the whole question decided by their vote.

"In my opinion," added the Primate, "the thread and tuft ought not to be tolerated. Even if they are caste-signs and have no religious significance, to tolerate them will cause scandal in the diocese of Goa." This verdict was supported with confused and noisy cries by the five Canarese priests, sitting together in a corner.

The Archbishop then repeated that the matter was clear beyond the least doubt. "All the same," he said, "in order not to lay myself open to complaints or accusations, I invite the Jesuits to express their opinion."

The leading Jesuit theologian present was André Palmeiro. After teaching theology at Coimbra, he had embarked for India only two years previously and now held the post of Visitor of the Malabar province, in succession to Pimenta. He had recently received a copy of Nobili's memoir. He now rose to his feet and faced the Archbishop.

"At Coimbra," he said, "I publicly taught the opinion contrary to Nobili's. I detested the Brahmin thread with a more than Vatinian hatred. When I was appointed Visitor of the province of Malabar, my first decision was to end the Madurai Mission—to root out every last trace of it.

"But now I have weighed the arguments of Father Robert, I have revised my opinion and my plans. Conscience forced me to change them. Furthermore, I declare that we are all bound, not only by the Pope's brief but also by our duty as Christians and religious, to facilitate the conversion of these people, to imitate the tolerance and tenderness of our Holy Mother the Church, by throwing wide open to all men the door of salvation instead of driving them into hell. Far from being settled, the important question of caste-marks demands a solution. In my opinion the emblems signify not religion but caste and social rank: that is established by arguments so solid as to be—in a moral question such as this—absolutely decisive."

Now Palmeiro's opinion carried weight. He had been described by Suarez, the most distinguished living theologian, as "a very learned man, without equal in Portugal". His sudden volte-face was all the more spectacular because he was known to have promised the Archbishop that he would make Nobili come and apologize on bended knee.

When the murmured comments had died down, Baltasar Garcia, a Portuguese Jesuit, for nineteen years professor of theology at Goa, rose to speak. He also endorsed Palmeiro's view. So did two professors at the theological seminary of Goa: Jerónimo

Cotta, a Portuguese, and Antonio Albertino, an Italian. They had all taught orally and in writing the opinion contrary to Nobili, but after examining the arguments in his favour, especially the treatise by Archbishop Ros, they could no longer, in good conscience and without fear of serious sin, oppose it. They ended by saying that they were moved not by prejudice but by pure love of the truth.

The Archbishop then called upon the Augustinian and Franciscan friars of Goa to give their opinion. Some seemed undecided but by his expression and tone the Primate intimidated those who raised arguments against his own viewpoint; he seemed to want to overwhelm and crush them rather than ask their opinion. Though some confessed they did not know what the dispute was about, all four sided with the Archbishop.

Next, three Canarese priests gave their opinion. Two boasted of having learned some Church law—but they had to admit they had forgotten most of it. As for theology, Nobili says "they had just waved their hand at it from a distance". But, in order not to provoke a scandal in Goa, they cast their vote for the Archbishop.

The next witness to be called was the Second Inquisitor—Dom João Ferdinando de Almeida—a secular priest, a nobleman and a scholar with doctorates in canon and civil law and theology. He was one of the most zealous and holy religious in Goa, and in Nobili's opinion he should have been held up as a model to the clergy of India. Like Palmeiro, he was known to have been hostile to Nobili, and could not even bear to hear his name pronounced.

"In the past," he said, "I was violently opposed to the opinion of Father Robert de Nobili. But now I have changed my mind. The arguments brought forward and the voice of conscience have dictated this change. I have come to the conclusion that the emblems under discussion, being stripped of all superstitious ceremonies and rites, not only may, but should, be allowed to the neophytes of Madurai.

"It seems to me difficult—I go further and say, morally impossible—that subjects of Hindu princes should give up those caste-emblems to embrace the faith of Christ. As for you, Reverend Fathers," he said, turning to the Canarese priests and friars, "I am not surprised that you can neither answer our arguments nor cast away your doubts, since you have not read, as I have done, the excellent treatise written on that subject. All the same, I am sorry that the Pope's instructions regarding the conversion of pagans should be utterly disregarded, and the door that had been thrown open to the preaching of the Gospel should again be closed as if with iron bars, by your decision.

"I do not believe any scandal or offence is to be feared in this town, if those emblems are permitted in Madurai. Is there any scandal because in China or Japan marriages between Christians and infidels are allowed with the Pope's sanction? Because the vernacular is used in the Holy Sacrifice, and the priest keeps his head covered during Mass? Was there any scandal in the diocese of Goa, when in 1582, with the sanction of the Roman Pontiff and the approbation of the assembled Synod, certain Abyssinians were for political reasons circumcised—though of course without the rites of the Mosaic law?

"As for me, I know it has always been the ancient and venerable practice of the Catholic Church to let converted infidels keep customs they were unwilling to give up, even if the customs bore marks of certain superstitions, provided they were pursued with pious intent, and the evil intention purified by her blessing, and sanctified by her holy mysteries and sacred ceremonies."

With the Second Inquisitor, five out of twelve speakers had now supported Nobili. Then the First Inquisitor rose, a Portuguese secular. In a short speech he claimed that toleration of the emblem would cause scandal in Goa, and cast his vote for the Archbishop.

All eyes were now turned on Archbishop Ros. The speech of one with thirty-five years' experience of Indian customs might win over hesitant opponents and turn the scales in Nobili's favour. But the old man explained that the long debates had tired him. Like Nobili, he was fasting; it was now two o'clock in the afternoon; he could continue no longer without a little food. But he promised to speak on the following day.

The Archbishop of Goa replied coldly that the question must be terminated there and then. So many priests could not be convoked a second time. "Why delay?" he asked. "What further arguments and difficulties are we looking for, which the day and hour do not suggest? For my part, I can defer my verdict no longer. I proclaim it openly: I cannot on any account tolerate such a scandal in this city." Becoming heated, he added, "Is my episcopate going to be ruined, to crumble into nothing, all because of the extravagant opinions of a single man?"

Nobili rose to interrupt. "It is not a question of my own person, but of the salvation of souls and the cause of Christ. These dictate my way and my method."

The Archbishop replied with still greater vehemence, blaming Nobili in the most severe terms for introducing a false, absurd method of evangelization which would ruin his diocese.

"It is the cross of Christ," he continued, shouting so loud that Archbiship Ros thought the Primate would burst his head, "not the emblem of pagan castes which ought to be exhibited. It is by witnessing with our blood, not by wearing a thread that the Catholic faith must be preached. Jesus Crucified must be brought into full light, not hidden away by underhand methods." With these words, the Archbishop rose and stormed out of the hall. Slowly the conference dispersed. Nobili returned to his room in the Jesuit house. No one seemed to know what would happen next.

Months ago the Primate had confided to Palmeiro that he intended to condemn Nobili at a trial which would take place only for form's sake. Instead, at a conference of equals Palmeiro had deserted him, and a Castilian archbishop whose diocese had not even existed fifteen years ago had disregarded the wishes of Dom Cristovão de Sa, Primate of Portuguese Asia, occupant of the oldest see in India. He had a good mind not to give the Castilian any hearing at all. But next day, when his Portuguese priests reminded him of the terms of the second brief, the Archbishop changed his mind. This caused no surprise, for he was known to veer round suddenly.

The conference reassembled. Again Nobili's red-ochre cotton confronted the Archbishop's scarlet silk, the spokesman for Asia the man who believed he was a turncoat. Between them rose the stooping figure of Nobili's staunchest supporter.

Francisco Ros opened by saying that Nobili's method was neither new nor absurd, but borrowed from apostolic times; that the Church in the past had allowed even abhorrent rites and ceremonies after stripping them of their perverse and impious significance, and substituting another in keeping with Christianity.

"There is no scandal to be feared in the archdiocese of Goa," he continued, "especially as the Sovereign Pontiff after seeing many texts taken from Hindu books has declared by an authentic rescript, duly certified by a public notary, that the thread in question is not a religious but a caste emblem and has covered it with his own authority. On the other hand, we acknowledge that we are bound to explain to the people of Goa our way of acting. If they are satisfied, as they surely will be, all scandal is removed. If they are not satisfied, the scandal will be passive and pharisaical. Now, to avoid giving that sort of scandal, one may refrain from doing certain good works, but one is not bound to risk such calamities as exile, social ostracism, loss of honour and worldly goods, as well as injury to the soul."

Taking the Gospels in his hand, Ros concluded with a declaration on oath that the emblems were in no way superstitious, and that once Christian ceremonies had been substituted for superstitious rites, they not only could but ought to be permitted.

Archbishop de Sa then asked whether the members of the conference had anything to add in Nobili's favour.

Only one man rose—Antonio Albertino, the Italian theologian. He thought he could help Nobili by invoking the system of Probabilism, first expounded in 1577 by the Dominican Bartholomeo de Medina and in the first half of the seventeenth century accepted by all moral theologians. Probabilism held that when there are divergent views as to the lawfulness of an action, for each of which solid arguments may be advanced, then, provided the lawfulness be alone in question, we are under no obligation to follow the more probable of the two views, but are equally free to adopt either course.

"No one," said Albertino, "can deny that the opinion supported by the Archbishop of Cranganore is at least probable. Now as long as it remains within the limits of probability, it is permissible, and according to the Pope's rescript, it ought to be permitted. It would be unjust to forbid the use of those emblems to the Madurai neophytes, since they are favoured by a probable opinion. According to the theologians, we must abandon our own opinion and follow the probable opinion of the penitent. Now, in order that the opinion of the Madurai neophytes can be called probable, it is not necessary that the Archbishop of Goa or any other opponent should judge it probable, as long as the Archbishop knows it is based on a probable reason and on the authority of competent persons. It is enough for the opinion to have such authority in order to become probable in itself, by its own nature. Since therefore, according to the teaching of the theologians, one is free to follow a probable opinion, and cannot be obliged to follow the contrary opinion, it seems impossible to refuse this concession."

The case for Nobili was now closed, and his opponents took the floor. "In a flood of confused words," runs Nobili's account, "not so much with arguments as with sarcastic mockery, they poured out their hatred." Nobili, they cried, was the shame—the ineffaceable shame—of the missions; he complicated the simplicity of Christian truth, he deformed the method bequeathed by the apostles, mixing with it pagan rites and ceremonies; he was destroying the old traditions of the diocese of Goa; he was polluting the Gospel with specious emblems of caste; then, by frauds and deceits, insinuating this into the depths of men's hearts. Instead of giving them salutary and profitable advice, with his superstitious inventions he led the credulous minds of the Hindus into error and deception; he mixed together things profane and holy, earthly and heavenly, vile and excellent.

Unless the thread were permitted, Nobili had contended, it would be impossible to convert a single Indian. Seizing on the words, one of his opponents cried,

"If the Hindus damn themselves, that's their look-out. All we have to do is prove the truth of Christianity. If they don't listen, so much the worse for them!"

"So much the worse for us too," retorted Nobili. "Since it is we who will have to give account of their souls. And even if they do damn themselves, is that enough to console and reassure an apostle's heart—when, by making certain concessions, he can save them?"

At this a friar, in brown habit and sandals, rose and pointed to Nobili's red-ochre rags. "Did Our Lord wear clothes like those?" he cried.

"No," replied Nobili quietly. "Nor did he wear clothes like yours."

But still they continued to mock.

"All you have to do now," they cried, pointing accusing fingers at Nobili, "is to put the Brahmin thread on Christ crucified!"

"A Father of the Society of Jesus," shouted the Archbishop of Goa, "has passed to paganism, and he asks us to connive in his apostasy!"

All reports emphasize the uproar in the hall. One can imagine the heavy beams of the high timbered roof reverberating; the hall showing all the disorder of a carrack in a monsoon storm, as wave after wave of abuse continued to crash on the thin figure of Nobili. The Archbishop of Goa was always first to voice the most outrageous charges, and praised those who gave a particularly smart turn to their raillery.

When Nobili was able to make himself heard, he made a final speech of defence. "It is not my personal honour but that of the Society which is under attack. It is superfluous, most reverend Prelate, to overwhelm me with insults. It will suffice if my arguments are examined and the contrary opinion put forward. In that way, by a comparison of ideas and a friendly discussion, we may throw some light on the dispute.

"I left Rome for Madurai only to preach Jesus Christ. I have not lost all religious sense; my only wish is to be useful to souls. Without any fault on my part, without any shadow of proof, you accuse me of inventing a false and absurd method of spreading the Gospel. That is totally unjust. I preach Christ openly, without fraud or disguise.

"If this assembly refuses to listen to me and despises me to that extent, elsewhere perhaps I shall find more friendly and attentive ears. Elsewhere perhaps I shall find men to defend my cause. If

my arguments carry any weight, I have no doubt that the Holy
Father, Vicar of Christ Our Lord, will see that truth triumphs.

"If I continue to work for my cause, it is not to win honour or
personal advantage. By the grace of God the thirst for honours
does not torment me, and I feel no ambition for the vain applause
of men. I work for my Master, Jesus Christ; for Him alone I lead
a life full of hardships. Let others struggle for the good things in
life: let others enjoy them. As for me, I have decided to spend my
days unknown in some obscure corner to sacrifice my wretched
life for the salvation of souls."

So spoke Nobili in his own defence. He had no intention of
offending the Archbishop of Goa. But in Nobili's reference to the
struggle for advancement the Archbishop suspected a personal
attack. He flared up and cried that Nobili had insulted him in the
coarsest and most disgraceful way.

The Archbishop then commanded the final vote to be recorded.
It would seem that only Archbishop Ros, the four theologians and
the Second Inquisitor sided with Nobili. The authority of the
Primate of the Indies had emerged triumphant. Archbishop de Sa
had done what he intended to do, and on the following Sunday
gave public vent to his victory by preaching in his Cathedral on the
temptation of Christ and dragging in Nobili's name to accuse
him of favouring idolatry and diabolical practices.

Pleased with his success in the conference-hall and the pulpit,
the Archbishop forwarded a transcript of the proceedings to the
Grand Inquisitor of Portugal. The Grand Inquisitor, in his turn,
would record his opinion and transmit the documents to Rome.
It seemed now only a question of time before final sentence was
passed on Nobili. As Goa went, so would go India.

16. The Pope's Decision

EVEN Nobili's closest relatives began to wonder whether the struggle had not better be given up. To advance the kingdom of God in the East he had left his family, his country, the prospects of a distinguished career, and what had been the result? His plans had been thwarted, his orthodoxy questioned and the family reputation tarnished. Why should he continue in that hopeless adventure? Pressing invitations began to arrive, urging him to return home.

Exhaustion, physical and moral, had weakened Nobili. He suffered from a continual pain in his chest. Vowed to a pittance of rice and herbs, he could never regain full health. In Goa, when he was not openly ridiculed, he was shunned. He had come to India to work among Indians, to help Indians of all castes—and that precisely was what he was now forbidden to do. He weighed the invitations and sent this reply to his brother, Marquis Vincenzo:

"If my going to Rome were like returning there from Frascati it would be easy, but I do not believe that you or anyone else would think it proper if, after taking so much trouble in learning the languages of this country, instead of using them to cull the fruit of my labours, I were to abandon the task I have undertaken.... As for our relatives, I beg you to offer my excuses if I do not write to them. One reason is that my occupations hardly leave me any time to rest even during the night, but the chief one is that having practically forgotten Italian I am obliged to seek the help of another to write: that is why I do not write with my own hand though I should like to do so; and in future, if I have no one to help me, I shall be obliged to write in Latin."

However, he did find time to appeal to his brother Sforza, asking him to use his influence with the Pope and Cardinal Borghese in defence of the Nobili name, and to his married sister

Clarice, asking for money—"At times I cannot even afford to buy rice, though it is very cheap."

When it became known that the Archbishop had sent one of his relatives, Mateus Godinho—a canon at Goa—post-haste by the overland route to influence opinion in Rome, Archbishop Ros countered by sending letters in favour of Nobili's method from the Bishop of Japan and the Brahmin King of Cochin, Vira Kerala Varmā. Nobili, too, continued his defence in writing—with a long appeal to Pope Paul V, recommending his mission. He had done all he could, short of going himself to Rome. It was time to return to Madurai.

Nobili went to say good-bye to the Primate. He was received coldly, and asked what he hoped with his appearance of zeal and piety. Did he hope to carve a way to a bishopric?

"Your Grace," replied Nobili, "my chief motive for entering the Society of Jesus was to escape honours and dignities a little more distinguished than the bishoprics of India." These were the last words he exchanged with Archbishop Cristovão de Sa.

As Nobili returned South, interest in his case began to grow not only in India, Portugal and Rome but throughout the world. Educated men with no special interest in theology began to discuss it. New authorities were invoked, new views expressed. Pietro della Valle, the Roman traveller, met Canon Mateus Godinho in Isfahan and eagerly asked for the latest news. In his *Travels* he notes one of the Jesuit arguments: that since the thread is some-times even granted to Muslims, it cannot be a religious sign. In Pietro's opinion, that is no more than granting to a Jew (Jews in Rome had to wear yellow hats) the privilege of wearing a black hat without becoming a Christian. It can be done by way of dispensation, yet no one would deny that wearing a black hat or a yellow hat is, besides being a mark of status, also a mark of the religion or sect which a man professes. As for the Jesuit argument that sannyāsīs renounce the thread, Pietro della Valle thought that proved nothing, for if a knight of the noble Spanish order of Calatrava decides to enter religion as a friar or monk, he lays aside the cross; the cross being part of the insignia of his knighthood, but even more the paramount symbol of his religion.

Another argument invoked against Nobili was that the Italian Jesuit Maffei, in his *History of India*—at that time the classic work on the subject—had written that Brahmins were priests and *curatores rerum sacrarum*, and the triple thread worn by the King of Calicut was a sign of the Brahmin superstition. To which it was retorted that Maffei, who wrote about 1557, only fifteen years after Jesuit missionary work began, had never been to India. He culled reports secondhand and shared current prejudices against the Indians, whom he referred to in his book as "the barbarians"

Amid high feeling caused by these and other less relevant arguments Archbishop de Sa's transcript of the conference reached the Grand Inquisitor. Dom Martins de Mascarenhas convoked the tribunal of the Inquisition to examine the documents. Lisbon, Portugal, all Portuguese Asia were counting on the loyal decision of a Portuguese in favour of a Portuguese archbishop. But Mascarenhas was no jingoist. Nor was he impressed by the voting three to one against Nobili. He preferred to weigh the quality of the arguments on each side. Having done so, the Grand Inquisitor concluded that Nobili, not the Archbishop, had the stronger case. His decision was accepted by the King of Portugal, despite the fact that Archbishop de Sa had appealed directly to him by letter, asking him to intervene and condemn Nobili before Rome should have time to see the transcript.

When the documents reached Rome from Lisbon in 1621, Pope Paul V was dead and had been succeeded by Gregory XV. Pope Gregory appointed a pontifical commission to examine them and submit a *Votum*, which would form the basis of the final Papal decision. The commission included Cardinal Bellarmine—now aged seventy-nine—Cardinals Benzil, Ara Coeli and Sforza, Nobili's cousin. These great names provided status but the essential work was to be done by three theologians: Dom Michael, a Neapolitan Benedictine of Monte Casino, a Carmelite named Campanella and—as president—Peter Lombard, Archbishop of Armagh and Primate of Ireland. Since Peter Lombard was one of the most distinguished theologians in Rome, it was understood that his opinion would carry greatest weight.

Peter Lombard was then nearly seventy. Born in Waterford, he studied at Westminster School, then at Oxford under the historian Camden. After a brilliant career at Louvain he received his doctorate and was ordained. From a professorship at Louvain in 1594 he was appointed provost of Cambrai cathedral, and in 1601 Archbishop of Armagh. Since he could never take possession of his see, he lived at Rome, where he had acquired a reputation for distinguishing, in new discoveries or techniques, what was compatible, what incompatible, with the teaching of the Church.

In 1616 Peter Lombard became famous when he headed the list of eleven theological consultors appointed to give their opinion on the two following propositions extracted from Galileo's work on sunspots: (1) The sun is the centre of the world and altogether devoid of local motion, (2) The earth is not the centre of the world nor immovable, but moves as a whole, and also with a diurnal motion.

Lombard had led the way by signing his name to a unanimous decision that the first proposition was foolish and absurd philosophically, and formally heretical; as for the second, it merited the same censure in philosophy and, from a theological standpoint, was at least erroneous in faith.

After Galileo's private interpretation of the Scriptures, Nobili's —for it was Nobili's claim that in Madurai he had been applying the method practised by the apostles and chiefly by St Paul, whereas his opponents contended that his method, by departing from tradition, was heretical. Fortunately Lombard, if no astronomer, knew his theology. In fact, he was an excellent choice to settle so thorny a problem—who could be more impartial in a dispute relating to Portuguese, Italians and Indians than an exiled Irishman?

The most scholarly document in the whole case, indeed almost the only one to draw directly on Indian views of the customs in dispute, was Nobili's *Answer to the objections raised against the method used in the new Madurai Mission to convert pagans to Christ*. Nobili had originally written it in reply to Gonçalo Fernandez's accusations. Running to thirty-nine pages of Latin, studded with Tamil and Sanskrit quotations from the most diverse sources, invoking the authority of the Fathers, St Thomas

Aquinas and ecclesiastical tradition, it was more than a treatise on the thread, tuft, sandal-paste and baths—it was a classic defence of the principle of adaptation: of the right of an alien civilization to receive the Word of God on fair terms.

The substance of Nobili's defence was embodied in the second of four chapters, running to fourteen pages. First, he establishes the principles of adaptation. In the first Council of the Church, argues Nobili, on the question of Jewish rites, the apostles adopted the most lenient resolution, and the one most favourable to freedom. They did not enter into details about the customs and habits of the pagans in order to modify them. They even used indulgence, recommending the Gentiles to observe certain Jewish rites, the infringement of which would have most revolted the Jews. The time had not yet come to abolish them.

A host of customs, Nobili continues, which still exist to-day in Christianity came from former pagan customs: novenas, for instance, substituted for the *novendialia sacra* of the Romans, celebrated with lights, decorations and garlands of leaves. Some Councils wanted to abolish the *novendialia* but their prohibitions had no effect. The feast of the Kalends of January, in honour of the god Janus, was prohibited by the Council of Auxerre; but when this prohibition proved ineffective, the Church sanctified the Kalends by hallowing it with the blood of the circumcised Saviour. Pope Gregory did the same as regards the *lupercalia* or *saturnales*, celebrated at the beginning of February with candles and torches: the outward ceremonies were kept as Candlemas in honour of the purification of the Blessed Virgin.

Nobili quotes the reply of Gregory the Great to St Augustine, apostle of England. "Tell Bishop Augustine that after pondering the question of the English a long time, I have adopted the following decision: do not destroy their temples, but only the idols inside: so that this act of grace may induce these people to renounce their errors, to know the true God and to come to adore Him in places familiar to them." The English were even to be allowed to continue sacrifices of oxen—no longer to demons, but to the glory of God.

Nobili then turns to usages and customs. No action or emblem is in itself good or bad except as an expression of will, and should not be condemned without knowledge of its purpose and essential circumstances. Its purpose, however, can only be discovered in Brahmin books, such as codes of law. With extensive quotations from the most authoritative Indian texts he shows that the thread, hair-tuft, sandal-paste and baths can lawfully be tolerated.

The evidence in Nobili's *Answer* had impressed everyone who read it. Already the *Answer* had produced the first reaction in his favour in Rome, of which the mildness of the first papal brief was so far the most important sign. An erudite piece of theological argument, it was well calculated to impress such a man as Peter Lombard. Any queries Lombard may have had were doubtless satisfied by Alberto Laerzio, who visited Rome from 1620 to 1622, when Lombard was examining documents for and against Nobili.

At the end of 1622 the Archbishop of Armagh took up his pen to write the report on which the future of Christian India depended. Being an old man, he drew it out to twenty-nine pages, and being exceptionally learned he could not resist contributing a quiet word to the great debate: "Are Indians Jews?" Lombard prefaces his opinion with new evidence for the theory that the Brahmins are indeed descendants of Abraham: Marco Polo, he says, heard tell of certain Abrayamin (with power to charm sharks away from pearl-divers); in testimony of Brahmin descent, he cites St Jerome's letter to Paulinus: one Apollonius Thyanaeus went to the rich kingdoms of India, crossed the broad river Phison and came to the *Brachmanae*, where he heard Hiarca (sitting on a golden throne) teaching about nature and the courses of the stars and days.

His preamble finished, Lombard states the question in these words. Are the thread, tuft, sandal-paste and baths primarily and essentially social or religious? After summarizing clearly the two conflicting opinions, he reproduces a text from St Augustine's *City of God*, cited by Nobili in his own defence: "It is a matter of no moment in the city of God whether he who adopts the faith that brings men to God, adopts it in one dress and manner of life or another, so long as he lives in conformity with the command-ments of God, and hence, when philosophers themselves become

Christians, they are compelled indeed to abandon their erroneous doctrines, but not their dress and mode of life, which are no obstacle to religion."

The implication was clear. Nobili, following the instructions of a Father of the Church, could not be charged with being a disloyal son. Lombard then lists fourteen reasons for allowing the emblems in question:

(1) When the thread is put on a Brahmin for the first time, the officiating Brahmin says, "I make thee glorious and famous with the thread."

(2) All castes adore the same gods, but only Brahmins have special signs such as the thread and tuft.

(3) Brahmins and other castes have certain other signs in common for worshipping gods. Yet the mass of Indians do not claim distinctively Brahmin signs.

(4) Brahmins and other castes can worship the same god, and put his sign on their brow.

(5) Atheist Brahmins, such as Buddhists, wear the thread, etc.

(6) Members of monotheistic sects, such as the Jains, repudiate religious signs, but keep the thread, etc.

(7) Sannyāsīs, who renounce all worldly pomp, keep religious signs, but give up the thread and tuft.

(8) Certain other castes—architects, goldsmiths, silversmiths, ironworkers, woodworkers, potters—who have excelled in their profession, are allowed to wear the thread. But in religious offices, they cannot sacrifice or celebrate with Brahmins.

(9) When Brahmins are converted to Christianity they keep only caste-signs (i.e. they renounce such marks as the *nāmam* on their brow).

(10) A group of learned Brahmins testified that these signs are caste-signs. So did other experienced men, notably Dom Jerónimo de Azevedo, Viceroy of India from 1612 to 1617.

(11) Gaspar, first bishop of Goa, baptized the King of Tanor, who was wearing the thread and tuft. Later the king, to conform to Portuguese usage, put aside these signs. This action brought on him the scorn of his chieftains and the hatred of his people: to reconcile them, he left the Church. Moreover, Archbishop

Alexeio de Menezes allowed the baptism of the nephew of the king of Calicut, who was wearing these signs, and later confirmed him at Goa, still wearing the signs.

(12) In China converted mandarins are not made to renounce their peculiar dress, hair style and long finger-nails.

(13) Brahmins among the St Thomas Christians wear the thread.

(14) The Grand Inquisitor, Martins de Mascarenhas, supported by three other bishops, three members of the Council General of the Holy Office and three other Inquisitors—all say the signs are civil, not religious.

Peter Lombard rejects the opposite opinion because its up-holders have no experience of missions in the interior. As for its endorsement by Brahmin witnesses, these men are ignorant of their own scriptures. What they say about the invention and first institution of the thread is a myth: namely, that the wife of Brahmā wore it, and Brahmā handed it on to the Brahmins. Lombard compares the Greek and Latin poets celebrating Bacchus, god of wine and Ceres, goddess of crops.

Peter Lombard then sums up: "From all I have said I conclude by stating what can, and should be, decided by the Holy See about those badges, and by adding my vote and approbation which I briefly condense in four propositions.

"1. The Thread, the Kudumi, the Sandal and the Baths in use among the Brahmins and other noblemen of those regions of the East Indies subject to Hindu kings are from their nature badges and insignia of social rank. Yet because of the error of the gentiles, they are mixed up with certain superstitions which refer them to the worship of idols. Therefore to facilitate the conversion of those Indian Brahmins, and other nobles to the Christian faith, it is expedient that when they wish to become Christians, those signs should be stripped of all the superstitions associated with them and used as badges and insignia of their nobility, provided they protest that they ask for them for no superstitious use or purpose.

"2. Among those Hindus, both nobles and plebeians, various other badges are in use which by their nature pertain to the worship of idols or false gods. Therefore when some of those Indians wish to become Christians, they must reject all those signs, with a similar protestation that they will never use them in future.

"3. The laws of those Indians forbid the Brahmins and other nobles to converse with the plebeians. According to this prohibition the Brahmins and other nobles who become Christians remain separated from the Christian plebeians even in religious matters. Now those Christians, whether Brahmins or nobles, must protest, when required to do so, that they do not separate from the others for religious reasons, but on account of other causes which are necessary and must be temporarily tolerated.

"4. When some of those gentiles, whether Brahmins or not, who exercised in Hinduism any religious ministry or priesthood, wish to become Christians, they must protest that they give up such priesthood or ministry. And if they are entitled to the above badges, they must also protest that they will not use them in virtue of the priesthood or ministry which they have renounced, but only as badges of their nobility.

"This being said, we may add that the exhortations of Saint Paul in the first epistle to the Corinthians (I Cor. c. 7, v. 20) applied also to the Brahmins and other Indian converts: 'Let each one persevere in the vocation to which he has been called'.

"Petrus Lombardus Archi-episcopus Armacanus, Primas Hiberniae."

To this opinion were added those of the other two theologians. Since the Benedictine voted for Nobili, and the Carmelite against, Lombard's vote proved decisive. It could therefore be confidently expected that the Pope would in due time pronounce in Nobili's favour. At the end of 1622 the General of the Society wrote to Madurai to give Nobili the good news.

It was not until 31st January 1623 that Pope Gregory XV issued the Apostolic Constitution *Romanae Sedis Antistites*.

"Taking pity on human weakness, till further deliberation by us and the Apostolic See, we grant by the present letters, in virtue of the Apostolic authority, to the Brahmins and other gentiles who have been and will be converted to the Faith permission to take and wear the thread and [grow] the kudumi as distinctive signs of their social status, nobility and of other offices; we allow them to use sandal as an ornament, and ablutions for the cleanliness of the body; provided however that, to remove all superstition and all alleged causes for scandal, they observe the following regulations and conditions:

"They must not receive the thread and the kudumi in the temples of idols, nor, as it is alleged to have been done from a minister of idols, whom they call *yogī* or by some other name, nor from a preacher of their law or priest whom they call *bottou* or otherwise, nor from any other infidel whoever he may be, but let them receive these insignia from a Catholic priest, who will bless them, reciting pious prayers approved by the Ordinary for the whole diocese; and before receiving the above insignia let them make a profession of faith in the hands of the same priest. However, when giving the thread, the priest, to remove all secret idolatrous significance which might be attached to that ceremony, will avoid holding the upper end of the thread with the thumb of the right hand, and the lower end with the left hand and raising the right hand, as we are told is the custom. Moreover those who are to receive the thread will no longer go to the priest of the pagoda, if that custom existed, to be initiated there."

The thread, of three strands, was to serve solely to recall the Holy Trinity; it was not to be held in the hand during prayer; threads already received during the initiation ceremony were to be destroyed and replaced with new ones blessed in honour of the Trinity. All prayers or mantras associated with the thread and tuft were forbidden. There was no insinuation that Nobili had tolerated such superstitious practices; the cautionary phrases were merely included as a safeguard.

So, after thirteen years, the quarrel was finally settled. One or two cynical enemies might sneer that Rome had justified Nobili the Roman, that the Pope had protected a blood-relation of Popes. But Nobili and even many who had disagreed with him accepted the Constitution in no such petty spirit. For them it marked the beginning of a new epoch. Following Nobili's example the Church had stepped out at last from the snug and safe Noah's ark of Europe to encounter on fair terms and to win not only the Brahmins of Madurai but all Indians, all the civilized nations of the world.

17. *Imprisoned*

In the years before the Constitution reached Madurai, the King-dom of Pearls was torn by war. Ever since Nobili had first arrived in India Nāyaks of Madurai had been trying to throw off the suzerainty of Vijayanagar. They would refuse to pay the annual tribute amounting to a third of the revenue; whereupon the Em-peror would send an army south to loot and if possible enforce payment. This was such a recognized pattern that a pandaram of authority could claim that "just as the arrival of the Emperor of Vijayanagar at Madurai means the ruin of the Great Nāyak, so Nobili's presence here is the ruin of the pandarams", meaning that the people lost faith in the idols, and the pandarams lost the income derived from their worship.

In 1614 the Emperor of Vijayanagar died and a war of succes-sion broke out between his nephew Śriranga II and his putative son Jaggā Rāya. Tanjore supported Śriranga, and Madurai, Tanjore's enemy, joined with Gingi to champion Jaggā, on the understanding that when he became Emperor, Jaggā would not enforce payment of tribute. It was more than a petty local feud. The Nāyak of Madurai alone could muster 100,000 troops.

In 1616 the Nāyak had to move his capital from Madurai to Tiruchirāpalli. The northern city, even richer but a little smaller than Madurai, was dominated by a rock rising sheer from a plain to almost three hundred feet above street-level. This impreg-nable natural fortress, two walls guarded by one hundred and thirty crenellated towers, the never-failing Kāverī river, a healthy climate and the fact that the city lay near the scene of operations made Tiruchirāpalli a more suitable base. However, it did not pre-vent Jaggā Rāya and the Nāyak of Madurai suffering a crushing defeat at the battle of Topur and the Nāyak being taken prisoner. Although he was soon released, and a marriage arranged between his daughter and the new Emperor of Vijayanagar, hostilities with Tanjore dragged on and Tiruchirāpalli remained the capital.

In 1617 Nobili, still cramped by the ban on new baptisms, paid two visits to Tiruchirāpalli, where many of his converts, members of the court or soldiers, had gone to live. He covered the seventy-odd miles on foot, staff in hand, as a beggar. In Tiruchirāpalli he found himself in a city proud of its Dravidian traditions and without the university which made Madurai a stronghold of Vedānta. Among the peasants at the Great Lake and non-Brahmins in Madurai he had already encountered *bhakti*. In Tiruchirāpalli devotion to a personal God was still more prevalent and developed. Only loving devotion could liberate the soul from its round of rebirths: in the phrase of Tirumalar, a famous Tamil poet: "*Anbe Śiva*"—"Śiva is Love". "You are gold, you are jewel, you are pearl", "My hill of coral! in love of you . . . I have journeyed far to see the bright flower of your feet"—so ran the Tamil hymns, using imagery which St John of the Cross might have envied. Clearly this lay not far removed from the spirit of Christianity.

Nobili would have liked to start breaking new ground in and around Tiruchirāpalli, but the still impending quarrel about adaptation had forced him to delay. In 1618 he had been obliged to leave the mission altogether and spend some months at Cranganore, waiting for the Goa conference. Vico was placed in charge—for the first period of any length. War had impoverished the country, and left Vico almost destitute. Errama Setti, junior Captain of the Madurai cavalry, having fled the battlefield of Topur, was now back in Madurai. He pestered Vico for a coat of Portuguese crimson velvet; Vico was in no position to provide it, whereupon Errama Setti imprisoned one of the Christian community. Vico wrote in desperation to Nobili for the crimson velvet coat and concluded his letter with the pious wish that the church and the house might soon collapse; then he would be free to go and settle in a quieter place.

This incident revealed how essential was Nobili's authority to the very existence of the mission. By May 1619, the Goa conference finished, he was able to return and check the spell of petty persecution. The work of preaching continued, still hampered by war and, in 1622, by famine so severe that the dead were no longer buried and the dying carried to the riverside so that they might be washed away when heavy rains flooded the Vaigai.

In 1623, learning that no trouble was to be apprehended from Rome, Nobili decided to carry out his long-cherished plan of spreading the Gospel elsewhere in South India. He had a base among his converts in Tiruchirāpalli; from there he hoped to create centres whence the faith would spread to neighbouring villages. These would also provide useful rallying points in case of local persecution.

Taking the seven-knotted bamboo staff of a wandering sannyāsī, Nobili set out in June, escorted by a few Brahmin disciples. From Tiruchirāpalli he walked north-west to Salem. This town, lying on the Tirumanimuttar river, surrounded by high ranges, in exceptionally green and fertile country, was the capital of Sellappa Nāyak, a powerful poligar tributary of Madurai. As soon as he arrived, Nobili sought the shelter usually accorded to wandering sannyāsīs, but he was turned away by rich and poor alike.

"What do we want with your law?" they jeered. "We have enough gurus and gods without adding more."

The people of Salem meant what they said: the number of Hindu gods was usually put at 330,000,000. Finally Nobili was obliged to take shelter outside the town in a *chatram*—a sort of inn—with a roof supported by four columns and open to all winds. He spent forty days and nights in the *chatram* and contracted a very painful illness.

Moved by pity, one of the influential men of Salem offered Nobili lodging in his own house. Here he recovered his health and began to receive inquirers. Chief among them was the former ruler of the neighbouring state of Sandamangalam, Tirumangalam by name, who had been dethroned by his younger brother. Tirumangalam soon expressed the desire of becoming a Christian. As a result, Nobili's reputation spread; more and more visitors came, chiefly noblemen and theologians. To his catechumens Nobili would distribute palm-leaves or thin gold plates inscribed with sentences from Scripture. These, it was soon found, had the power of curing the sick and possessed.

Sudden cures had always been a feature of the Madurai Mission. On one occasion Visuvāsam's uncle fell dangerously ill. Nobili, suffering himself from fever, had been unable to go, but he sent Visuvāsam with some holy water in which powder of bezoar stone had been mixed. "This combination of natural and supernatural remedies and the faith of the patient brought about a speedy recovery, but made it difficult to say whether it was due to the holy water or to the bezoar. However, as the cure had been very sudden, it was agreed that the bezoar could not have done it, so all the credit went to the holy water. Visuvāsam tried to improve the occasion by preaching to his Hindu friends, but they assigned the old man's cure to a third cause: it had so happened because it had been written all along on the sutures of his skull."

Nobili, in reporting such cures, was careful to avoid any suggestion that he thought them miraculous. But not so the people of Salem. A nobleman attached to the court had been suddenly stricken with total paralysis. For two years he had followed the doctor's prescriptions and magic devices of the Brahmins. Now he was carried to Nobili, whom he asked for a "miraculous gold plate". Nobili told the courtier that if he wanted to get well he must strip himself of all superstitious and idolatrous emblems, and put his faith in Christ. The courtier returned home, where he smashed or burned his idols. In less than two weeks he was able to walk, and the first thing he did was to throw himself at Nobili's feet and ask for instruction.

The cure reached the ears of the poligar of Salem, who asked Nobili to heal his wife and brother, also crippled with paralysis. In short time they too were able to walk, and the poligar sent for Nobili to thank him. Nobili accepted the invitation.

The protocol for visiting a petty king was strict. Nobili could not go alone. He must be escorted by Brahmin converts, one carrying his breviary, another his parasol, a third a tiger-skin, another a vase containing holy water, a fifth perfumed water. This suite was welcomed at the palace gate and ushered in to the throne-room thronged with Brahmins and courtiers. The king was not yet present; by coming in later he would specially honour the sannyāsī, who would then be considered as receiving the visit.

Holy water was offered to Nobili, who sprinked some drops on that part of the floor where he would sit; perfumed water was sprinkled on ceiling and walls; four men spread the tiger-skin with much ceremony. Finally Nobili sat down, cross-legged, on the tiger-skin.

Sellappa Nāyak now entered, in rich robes and turban. He paid Nobili his respects and took a seat on a simple platform two feet above the level of the floor, with his back to the wall. A discussion then followed on the destiny of the soul. Against the Vedānta doctrine that beatitude lies in the identity of the Ātman and Brahman, Nobili argued that either these words were meaningless or they meant that man's beatitude consisted in nothingness, "for to become· God is to cease to be oneself, and to cease to be oneself is to cease altogether to be".

Here Nobili used the outspoken language of one who eyes an enemy, dangerous because its masquerade was so complete. Christianity professed to give that final peace which must satisfy the give and take in human nature. Man recognized his dependence in and by the act of loving God: the soul itself is both lover and beloved. But Śankara's Vedānta also professed to satisfy the active and passive principles in man. The traditional Hindu way of doing this was to shape personal gods to human needs—as, for example, in certain two-in-one statues which, on one side, represent Śiva and on the reverse, instead of showing Śiva's back, represent his wife Parvāti, the female principle: herself of dual aspect, both smiling and cruel. The Vedānta, however, went further: it made knowledge of God itself a matter of give and take. The soul stripped away pleasure and pain, then went into the dark to be lost. But the dark waves, instead of sucking down, at the last moment rose up in a water-spout. The moment of self-obliteration was also the moment of awareness that "Thou art God". Man himself, like the statue, was both passive and triumphant.

At the end of the debate Sellappa, who clearly favoured a religion of *bhakti*, concluded that Nobili had had the better of the argument. He then led his guests to a private apartment, questioned him for two hours and ended by telling him to ask for anything he wished. Nobili replied that all he wanted was the Nāyak's friendship. The Nāyak was so moved at this that he at once assigned Nobili a house in the Brahmin quarter of Salem.

From his new house Nobili was shortly summoned to the palace to advise the Nāyak on important business. Two strangers had arrived in Salem and promised, at a price, to change iron into silver and copper into gold. Was it prudent to trust them?

Nobili was led in to meet the alchemists. He had a knack of summing people up quickly.

"Are you sannyāsīs or married men?" he asked.

"We are married and have children," replied the alchemists.

"So you are in need of money to support your families?"

"Of course."

"Then, since you have the secret of transforming base metal into silver and gold, why don't you make use of it for your own benefit?"

The alchemists, reports Nobili, did not know what to answer. They may have been shocked. Alchemy was a recognized way of leading to liberation from rebirth, in that it taught transubstantiation. One school believed that quaffing gold would produce a profound change in the body and preserve it from all decay. The alchemists may have couched their offer in figurative terms, and been misunderstood.

Sellappa Nāyak, however, believed the men were charlatans. He was disappointed, for he had been counting on inexhaustible treasures, and led Nobili to his private apartments to discuss the matter further. There he learned of another alchemy, which transforms wretched creatures into children of God. During four hours he listened appreciatively to the strange guru who expounded to him the mysteries of God, "Who, having created human nature wonderfully, transformed it more wonderfully still."

Sellappa's growing favour now drew on Nobili the hostility of the Brahmins and of Sellappa's chief guru. They feared the Nāyak would follow the example of the exiled king, Tirumangalam, and ask to receive instruction in "the path of devotion". After failing to poison the new friendship, the Nāyak's guru decided the next best thing would be to remove Tirumangalam, Nobili's leading catechumen. He instigated Sellappa to declare war on the usurper of

Sandamangalam under the pretext of restoring the throne to its rightful king. Knowing that Tirumangalam would take part in the campaign, the Nāyak's guru planned an unfortunate accident, in which the catechumen would lose his life. But Tirumangalam heard of the plot and leaping on his horse escaped into the neighbouring state of Moramangalam.

Here Nobili joined him. With the arrival of Gregory XV's Constitution at the end of 1624, he was free to resume the baptism of high-caste Indians and on Christmas Day 1625 he baptized the most influential of all his Indian converts. Though in exile, Tirumangalam Nāyak was still a rightful king and his authority would ensure protection for the new converts in the north of Madurai kingdom, who together with those in Madurai city now numbered over three hundred. When Tirumangalam's brother offered to associate him in the government of Sandamangalam if he lent help in a local war, Nobili wrote post-haste to the Provincial asking for a rich war-standard with the Cross on one side and on the other, in Sanskrit, the words; "This sign will bring you victory." Who could tell, but with this labarum Tirumangalam might become an Indian Constantine?

With Tirumangalam were christened his mother, wife and daughters. These conversions did not point beyond themselves as they would have done in Europe. Nobili could not expect an Indian counterpart to the Countess Sforza, who had built a convent and the great round church of St Bernard in Rome. But the Christian women proved dutiful and pious. Though they did not observe purdah, as in Northern India, noble women seldom ventured into public alone. In the Madurai church one nave was reserved for women and separated by a curtain so as to be invisible to the men. Outside the house women had no life of their own. The Tamil phrase for "marry" was "buy a wife", and according to the *Padma Purāṇa* "if her husband happens to be old, sick, coarse-mannered, violent, debauched or vicious, blind, deaf, dumb or deformed, a wife must still devote herself to him, for he is her god on earth". The only women educated to read, sing or dance were courtesans attached to the temple, and fathers, not mothers, gave children their religious instruction.

Partly because of their subordinate status, women were often subject to possession. One of the things that most struck Nobili about the hinterland of India was the frequency of this phenomenon. Complicated mantrams were chanted to make an evil spirit take possession of a woman; exorcism was accomplished by the use of a stronger mantram. Women queued at the temple of Chockanātha, waiting for darkness, when professional exorcists would throw them into a frenzy, question the spirit and sometimes dispel it, if necessary with whips of margosa twigs. Nobili more than once had to recite the Christian formula of exorcism over a possessed woman, and he even allowed his first convert, Albert, who had been well-known as an exorcist, to drive out devils with holy water and the sign of the cross.

For the next few years Nobili spent much of his time outside Madurai, travelling between Tiruchirāpalli, Salem and Moramangalam. In 1625 he was joined by a second assistant, a young Portuguese named Emmanuel Martins who gave every promise of becoming a suitable Brahmin sannyāsī missionary. The mission had now entered a new phase. In Madurai Nobili's efforts had been directed primarily towards the Brahmins, with their undisputed influence over all castes. But from 1612 to 1624, when the Constitution arrived, he was strictly forbidden to have anything to do with them. And after that date when he was working in towns where Brahmin influence was less strong, he did not give special attention to the highest caste. For now Nobili aimed at nothing less than winning the whole country to Christ.

A starting-point was provided by a chance encounter, as momentous in its way as the arrival of the Telugu Brahmin, Śivadarma. On 31st July 1626 a strange individual came to Nobili's house in Moramangalam. His face was covered with ashes and his body loaded with amulets and religious emblems, including the lingam. He told Nobili that he was a pandaram of the sect of Śiva and he belonged to the lowest of the low—the untouchable Paraiyans. He lived in Tiruchirāpalli, where he held the rank of priest among the Paraiyans.

Nobili's visitor, however, was no ordinary Paraiyan. He belonged to the ancient race of Valluvans, and like some other Valluvans claimed at least a spiritual descent from Tiruvalluvar, "the divine poet", whose *Tirukkural* (Sacred Couplets) was the most important Tamil religious book, composed about A.D. 800–1000 and expounding the same sort of eclectic thought as the *Bhagavad Gītā*. Even high-caste scholars bowed to the Paraiyan's learning and the Great Nāyak himself had granted him the honour of riding a horse and using a parasol, as well as a rice-field for his living expenses.

The Paraiyan explained that he had come across a little Tamil book called *Signs of the True Religion* by Tatva Bodhakar. He had been so impressed by reading it that he wished to become a disciple of its author.

The stranger's arrival proved somewhat embarrassing to Nobili, whose high-caste friends in Moramangalam would have considered themselves polluted by the Paraiyan's presence. However, he was impressed by the man's manner and learning, and the fact that he claimed two thousand disciples, including many Śudras. He told him to remove the lingam, ashes and other religious emblems, then began a course of instruction. After a few months, when the time came to choose a Christian name, Nobili could find none better than *Muttiudeyan*: "He who possesses happiness"—a name which the other missionaries translated as Hilary. And so Nobili, who had baptized Śivadarma, the first Brahmin of the Madurai Mission, now baptized the first Paraiyan: a natural complement, for he had never intended to found a sect composed exclusively of an élite.

Hilary, not content with his own conversion, at once set about bringing his two thousand former disciples into the way of salvation. Soon he had gathered several hundred round him and they built a chapel in Tiruchirāpalli to pray daily and preach among other Paraiyans.

Hilary's former colleagues were not like the Brahmins, discreet and subtle in their methods. They were low-caste roughs. Exasperated by the loss of many disciples, the Paraiyan pandarams retaliated by demolishing the chapel and arresting Hilary and the chief catechumens. Nobili intervened for their release, but soon a second attack broke out. Jeering at him and asking why he had abandoned the lingam, the pandarams set upon Hilary. The

Paraiyan who had smeared himself with ashes in honour of Śiva was now thrown headlong in the dust for a higher cause. His back was lacerated with blows from bamboos—wielded with such fury that one was shattered in splinters. This ill omen made such an impression on the watching crowd that they prevented further violence. But the persecution was noted in the mission annals as the first when Christian blood was shed.

As the mission increased, so the missionaries' strength diminished. Vico was reduced, in the words of one witness, to "mere skin and bones". Nobili was racked by constant attacks of fever and catarrh. Before he was fifty, his eyesight had grown very dim, and he was writing to Europe for glasses. Travelling, he was more alone than ever and his old friends were being taken from him. Archbishop Ros had died at the age of sixty-seven, just before Gregory XV's Constitution arrived in India. Laerzio, appointed Provincial for the second time in 1627, had arranged a last reunion with Nobili: in Tuticorin, the town from which they had first set out to start the Madurai Mission. At the end of the year, while sailing north from Quilon, the Provincial was captured by pirates, bound with chains, exposed half-naked to the burning sun, flogged and threatened with death. He was lucky to escape but he never recovered, and died at Cochin in 1630 at the age of seventy-three. Laerzio's loss was a severe blow to Nobili. By his courage, patience, tact, breadth of vision and unconquerable zeal he had seconded the daring method of adaptation from its first tentative beginnings to its final triumph and wide establishment.

For by 1630 the mission consisted of no less than three self-contained centres. Moramangalam in the north with Salem, Sendamangalam and some neighbouring villages were served by Vico. In Tiruchirāpalli Nobili was preaching to the high castes and, through Hilary and others, shepherding the low castes into the fold. In Madurai Emmanuel Martins was ministering to high-caste converts and looking after the Christians of the old Portuguese mission, which in those years since Fernandez's departure and death, was without a priest.

Nobili, even by travelling fast and often, could not protect all three centres with his own commanding presence. Only one man

could do that—Tirumala, Lord of the Holy Mountain, Nāyak of
Madurai, the most powerful king in South India. Francis Xavier
and the daimyos of Japan, Matteo Ricci and the Emperor of China,
Rodolfo Aquaviva and Akbar, the Great Mogul—many attempts
had been made to find an Oriental Constantine; all had ended in
failure. But this did not discourage Nobili. As a sannyāsī, he
stood far removed from politics and court intrigue. Opportunities
might be few and indirect, but he would make the most of them.

Tirumala had succeeded his rather insignificant elder brother,
Muttu Virappa, in 1623, at the age of thirty-nine. Highly intelligent, even cunning, with a taste for power, he dreamed of making
Madurai the leading kingdom of the South. His predecessors had
annually paid a third of their revenue—1,200,000 patacas[1]—to the
Emperor of Vijayanagar as tribute, in return for no obvious advantages. Tirumala stopped paying the tribute and on inscriptions
referred to himself as an independent king.

The tribute saved was used to indulge Tirumala's expensive
tastes: women, of whom he kept more than two hundred in his
palace, and elephants. Elephants were a most important part of an
Indian king's household. Their resemblance to rainclouds magi-
cally entailed the country's fertility and welfare. In time of war,
clad in steel plates, with large scythes attached to their trunks and
tusks, they carried a dozen soldiers in a reinforced howdah. In
peacetime, they were essential to every procession. Tirumala had
more than three hundred and paid high prices for new ones. They
were caught around Cochin in large covered pits. Little by little
the pit was filled until the hunter could attach the elephant's legs
with chains and finally mount his capture.

Tirumala spent on some of his elephants five patacas[2] a day,
pampering them with chickens, eggs and butter, a food said to
make them strong as towers, and tending them when they fell
ill, according to the *Hasti Ayurveda*—"Sacred Wisdom on the
Longevity of Elephants", a veterinary manual couched in 7,600
stanzas of verse and forty-six chapters of prose.

Almost every day Tirumala appeared on his palace terrace,
surrounded by courtiers, while in front of him his elephants were

[1] £840,000.   [2] £3 10s. 0d.

drawn up in two rows, the space between being occupied by a bodyguard of three hundred Muslims. On religious feasts he would appear in a gold-embroidered robe and turban, with ear-rings of eight large pearls and a necklace of diamonds matched by diamond bracelets, and mount his biggest elephant, caparisoned in velvet spangled with pearls and tusks sheathed in thin layers of gold. To guide the elephant he used an *aṅkuśa* or hook, the handle of which was encrusted with jewels and pearls. Generally the first of his queens sat on the same elephant and handed him betel pre-pared by royal pages. While Tirumala, chewing betel-leaf, guided his elephant to the temple, dancing girls accompanied him on foot singing his praises to the tapping of tambourines.

His boundless greed astonished even Tirumala himself. He was often heard saying, "When shall I be satisfied with money?" No one was admitted to his presence unless he brought money, and the favour he bought was retained only till somebody else came with a bigger present. His officials took a lesson from Tiru-mala's rapacity, among other measures imposing customs duties on foreigners not only at the frontiers but in all villages of importance.

The first Jesuit to have dealing with Tirumala was Antonio Rubino, rector of Tuticorin, who in 1627 went as missionary-ambassador to the court at Tiruchirāpalli on behalf of the Paravas. To escape the customs officials he was provided with a special passport: a very fine white cloth thirty-nine yards long on which Tirumala's hand was imprinted with musk.

Tirumala listened gloomily as Rubino pleaded for his Paravas: prevented by political circumstances from fishing pearls, they could not find the money to pay their annual tax of eight hundred patacas.[1] Tirumala had been only four years on the throne and still felt nervous that the Emperor of Vijayanagar would claim his arrears of tribute. It would be prudent to consolidate Portuguese friendship with a generous gesture. He granted Rubino's request, waived all taxes from the Paravas for three years and ordered that afterwards they should only pay five hundred patacas[2] and fifty head of cattle instead of the traditional two hundred.

Nobili's relations with Tirumala began three years later, in 1630.

[1] £560.   [2] £350.

He arrived at the elephant-guarded palace with all the display of a famous sannyāsī and offered Tirumala presents with an address in Sanskrit. Tirumala seems to have taken a liking to Nobili and was highly impressed with his learning. On the spot he granted him an official licence to preach and build churches wherever he pleased in the territory of Madurai.

This was a useful beginning. But it proved difficult to follow it up and speak directly to Tirumala about Christianity. All his palace servants were women, and the Nāyak spent most of his spare time at private plays, exhibitions of dancing and concerts of songs: entertainments which no sannyāsī could attend.

Nobili's next approach had to be less direct. Back in Madurai a pandaram convert was put in charge of Tirumala's favourite herd of cattle. In this post he often met a boy of twelve, the Nāyak's son by his favourite queen. The herdsman spoke so impressively of his new religion that the young prince arrived one day in state at the hermitage. He was courteously received by Nobili, who answered his questions on this or that point of religion and gave him a copy of his *Principles of Catechism* in Tamil, probably an abridgement of the *Gnanopadesam*.

The prince had the book read and explained to him in the palace. He was quick for his age, understood the teaching and was favourably impressed. He paid a second state visit to the hermitage. This time one of his pages brought a box of sandal-powder which, in accordance with custom, he distributed to Nobili and all those present.

It was a problem for Nobili what gift to offer the prince. Even the best object in the hermitage would seem paltry when carried back to so rich a palace. At the same time Nobili wanted, if possible, to recall Christian teaching to the prince's mind. He finally decided to offer a silver bottle filled with holy water. The prince would easily understand its Christian symbolism, for Indians showed special reverence for water and even had their own holy water. Brahmins filled a copper vessel whitened with lime and in a ceremony involving rice, mango-leaves, sugar, betel, sandalwood and akṣatas gave the vessel's contents the sacred character of Ganges water.

The prince gracefully accepted the silver bottle of holy water and prepared to leave. Before mounting his horse he bowed to it, as to a god, and rubbed it with sandal. Nobili pointed out that an animal was not to be adored as a god. The prince seemed to understand and replied that he had bowed because he had been taught to do so, but he would never do it again. He added that the hermitage, with its simple furniture, was too poor for so excellent a guru, and he would tell his mother and his uncle to provide better.

This hope of an ally within the palace was suddenly frustrated by political events, which forced Nobili to leave Madurai for Tiruchirāpalli, and the Nāyak to hurry to the coast. Once again the pearl-fishers were the apple of discord. In 1631 Tirumala had requested the Viceroy of India to replace the Portuguese commander in Tuticorin with a man who would treat his subjects the pearl-fishers fairly. If his request were refused, Tirumala threatened to hand over the port to the Dutch. To offset the danger, the Viceroy sent a fleet of ten ships to lie off Tuticorin and a Portuguese ambassador to improve trade relations. The ambassador offered to buy all Madurai's saltpetre in exchange for highly-prized Ceylon elephants. The elephants tempted Tirumala, but he hid his interest and said that the Dutch wanted his saltpetre too. Finally he concluded a good bargain, whereby he would receive elephants, gold and silk worth 40,000 seraphims.[1]

The Nāyak soon thought better of his agreement. The Dutch were strongly established in Pulicat and anxious to obtain an ally further south. Perhaps they made Tirumala a better offer. At any rate, after the Viceroy had delivered a number of elephants to Tuticorin, Tirumala failed to deliver the saltpetre. Instead, on his way to pilgrimage at Trichendur, he arrested Antonio de Menellese, the Portuguese commander at Tuticorin, along with his suite, and threw him into stocks, demanding a ransom of 10,000 seraphims.[2] Tirumala also insulted and roughly treated the Portuguese ambassador at Tuticorin, who was waiting to weigh the saltpetre.

The Viceroy replied by declaring war on Tirumala. Thirteen ships bombarded Tuticorin; and in case of reprisals the Christian pearl-fishers were warned to be ready to take ship and settle in

[1] £9,000. [2] £2,250.

Ceylon. At the same time the Portuguese out-manœuvered Tirumala by concluding an agreement with the Emperor of Vijayanagar
for a joint attack by land and sea on Pulicat. After many delays,
the attack was launched and Pulicat taken. But the Dutch were
now so rich that they bought back the town a few days later from
the Emperor for more than 29,000 pardaos.[1]

In the years immediately following the outbreak of war between
Portugal and Tirumala, the position of Nobili and his companions
was doubly awkward. Martins was Portuguese; Nobili and Vico—
at least in the Viceroy's opinion—owed allegiance to the King of
Portugal. The fact that the Italians observed political neutrality
angered His Excellency. He detested the Jesuits anyway and,
anxious to find a scapegoat for the recent series of disasters, he
denounced Vico to Rome as the cause of the Nāyak's refusal
to sell saltpetre. This was not all. The missionaries had already
run very short of money, for in 1630 the Viceroy withdrew State
assistance from the Church and now war, by making communi-
cation with Cochin difficult, still further impoverished the mission.

Moreover, in the eyes of all who suspected them of being crypto-
Parangis, Nobili and his fellow-workers were from 1635 onwards
considered enemy aliens. Few of their letters reached Cochin—
hence the difficulty of reconstructing events in this period. Other
difficulties plagued the mission. Antonio Vico died in 1638, after
fourteen years' devoted service. During the last seven years of
his life, too sick for strenuous work, he had relieved Nobili from
administrative worries by assuming the post of superior. He was
replaced by Sebastião de Maya, a Portuguese aged thirty-nine.

While Nobili continued to work chiefly in Madurai, suffering
from attacks of illness which recurred almost every month, Martins
played a dual role at Tiruchirāpalli, converting high castes by day
and—in co-operation with Hilary—Paraiyans by night. More than
once the Nāyak, as Nobili's personal friend, protected the missionaries from anti-Parangi riots. As long as war lasted, the mission
ran a constant danger of extinction.

The Portuguese, for their part, could not afford a long war.
Tanjore and Ramnad had concluded an alliance with the Dutch;

[1] £13,500.

if Tirumala joined also, the Dutch would be only fifty miles from Ceylon, one of their prize objectives. The Portuguese could not risk losing the cinnamon and elephants of Ceylon: they contented themselves with a token bombardment of Tuticorin. Soon they found a chance of patching up peace, when Tirumala, profiting from the presence of an army on the Coast, decided to annexe Travancore, formerly one of his loyal vassals. The Portuguese offered to help, and Tirumala accepted, with the result that war between Madurai and Portugal was formally brought to an end.

In 1639 a treaty was signed. Tirumala undertook to give the Portuguese a fortress in Pampa, called Uthear, or wherever the Viceroy might desire one, to be manned by a Portuguese captain, fifty Portuguese soldiers and a hundred Lascars. Tirumala also allowed a church to be built at Ramanacor and seven churches between Pamban and Tondi; gave his subjects permission to become Christians, promised men and supplies to help the Portuguese in Ceylon; and gave his word to refrain from trading with the Dutch.

This treaty—typical in its suggestion that missionary work was an extension of foreign policy—had been drawn up by the Portuguese in order to strengthen their hold over the Paravas of the Coast. It gave Nobili no further advantages than those Tirumala had already granted him, and did little to quieten Indian feelings of hostility roused by an unnecessary war.

These feelings flared up violently in 1640: an ominous year in the Indian calendar, for it marked the end of a sixty-year cycle. At such a juncture any catastrophe might come to birth, and therefore any preventive action was justified. The explosion was touched off in July when a rich Paraiyan of Tiruchirāpalli belonging to the Lingāyat sect asked a neophyte of his own caste to give him his daughter in marriage. The Christian answered that he would never give her to a man who wore a lingam round his neck. At this the Paraiyan joined with the pandarams of Tiruchirāpalli to ruin Martins and his disciples. They took their complaints to Venkaṭarāya Pillai, a man of low birth whom Tirumala allowed to do pretty much as he liked, for he was in love with Venkaṭarāya's sister, a dancing girl raised to the rank of royal concubine.

This was the opportunity Venkaṭarāya had long been waiting for. To his intense annoyance, some of his own relatives had recently become Christians. Furthermore, he needed money, and Christian gurus—on the strength of their gold chalices—were rumoured to possess untold wealth. With the Nāyak away on the coast, he was free to act. He had Martins arrested and imprisoned, then taken across the Kāverī river and forbidden ever to return to Tiruchirāpalli.

On 22nd July, the same day as Martins's arrest, Venkaṭarāya Pillai sent a messenger with a letter to one of his relatives in Madurai instructing him to throw Nobili and Sebastião de Maya into prison. In Maya's own words, "A young Tiruchy neophyte having heard of this joined the messenger on his way and travelled with him as far as Madurai, where he left his companion and hurried to our house to tell us of our danger. We took advantage of that charitable warning and put in a safe place what we held most precious: the sacred vessels and church vestments. But our persecutors were too quick for us, and nothing escaped their rapacity. They caught us in the very act of hiding our things, and our embarrassment increased their suspicions and stimulated their greed as well as their cruelty towards our Christians.

"Father Robert presented himself quietly before the soldiers, who put him under arrest and posted a soldier before his door.

"As for me, foreseeing what was going to happen, I had tried to say vespers and compline, but I was soon interrupted by the soldiers' shouts and dragged by them to my companion's room without being allowed to snatch up my crucifix and breviary or anything else. We remained exposed to the curiosity of the mob who crowded around us, while three hundred soldiers, not one less, were plundering our church and presbytery. Some time later Sivandi Pillai, who was commissioned with the execution of the orders from Tiruchirāpalli, came on the scene.

"Followed by an escort of guards, servants, and a crowd of inquisitive idlers he advanced slowly, leaning on the arm of a young man. His feet rested on wooden clogs with silver knobs, his arms were encircled with large golden bracelets and a gold chain of exquisite workmanship was hanging from his neck; his clothes were extremely fine and costly. He sat majestically on a rich carpet, which had been spread for that purpose in front of our house, and proceeded to give orders, while he chewed betel with great solemnity. The fruit of the plunder was laid at his feet: Mass vestments, church ornaments, missal, breviary, crucifix, pictures of Our Lady, two inkstands, two small boxes, the registers of baptism, etc. But neither the chalice nor the other precious objects were to be seen; they had probably been kept by the plunderers. Seeing these holy things thus profaned I was stricken with grief, and informed Father Robert. Being almost blind, he could not see the sacrilege. Then in that imposing tone of voice which is particular to him and commands the respect of all, he rebuked the raiders severely and threatened them with God's anger.

"The effect was immediate. Quaking with fear, the soldiers dared not touch those sacred objects except with the greatest show of respect, and they allowed us to take our breviaries. Since noon we had been exposed to the rays of a tropical sun and the sarcasms of our enemies; only at nightfall were we taken to prison with three Brahmins, of whom two were our servants. We have been here for seventeen days surrounded by soldiers who keep a strict watch on us day and night without allowing us the least relief. We do not know what is happening outside our prison, we are told that all our neophytes, specially those who have shown us special devotion, have been cast into irons and tortured: in this way our persecutors hope to discover the immense treasures we are supposed to have. This thirst for gold is always the most powerful incentive our enemies have recourse to when they want to turn against us the courtiers or magistrates, who live by such plunder. Although in their repeated searches in the past they found nothing in our house but extreme poverty, they still persevere in the hope of discovering hidden treasures, hence those tortures.

"For the last seventeen days we have been living in utter destitution, without change of linen, without water to wash, without any other food than a handful of rice, though we are thankful we have some of our Brahmins with us. But what pains me most is to see the plight of Father Robert de Nobili, a venerable old man [sixty-three] loaded with infirmities, deprived of all necessary help and maintaining himself only through the force and energy of his soul. Yet, thanks to God, we are not in chains, like Father Martins in Tiruchirāpalli. The gentiles, who come from morning to night to visit us, far from insulting us show us compassion and even certain affection. Father Robert is constantly preaching the Gospel to them; and all go away pleased with his instructions and charmed by his polished courtesy. The impression he makes on our visitors is such that it is generally believed he has the art of bewitching and binding to himself all those who come to speak with him. In consequence some who at first showed us great esteem and affection have cooled a little because they fear his magical influence.

"We are strictly forbidden to correspond with our neophytes, so that we do not know how we stand. The most sinister rumours are being spread regarding the fate that awaits us. Some say that the Great Nāyak who is expected any day [from the war] wishes to have the pleasure of killing us with his own hands, and this is the reason why we are kept in prison so long. Others say something else. In reality everything is uncertain, even whether the Nāyak is aware of our sufferings. It is just possible that Venkaṭarāya Pillai is the only one responsible for this persecution. We can therefore give you no positive information either on the present state of affairs nor on the hopes and fears which may be entertained with regard to the future."

Why had they been imprisoned? Not because they preached an unorthodox doctrine. For a Hindu, every way to the Truth was good. Not because they were Parangis. Against Nobili that charge was now seldom made. Chiefly because the unjustifiable war waged by the Portuguese had changed the attitude towards foreigners from tolerance to suspicion and ill-will. Subjects of the Nāyak had been killed, one of his towns bombarded: Madurai had suffered because of rivalry between two nations which did not even appear on Indian maps. The missionaries might not be Parangis, but they were undoubtedly white men, foreigners in touch with the Portuguese, and therefore potentially dangerous. Most suspicious of all, they were colleagues of Martins, who by

ministering now to Brahmins, now to Paraiyans, had in an ominous
year infringed the inviolable rules of caste. This mixing up of
high and low was regarded as the most certain way of causing
political revolution.

At the end of 1640 Tirumala returned from a campaign in the
Marava and learned of his favourite Venkaṭarāya's high-handed
action. The missionaries' imprisonment contravened the spirit if
not the letter of his new treaty with the Portuguese. He knew
Nobili personally, he remembered his Sanskrit address and his
strict observance of Indian customs. No danger was to be feared
from him. Tirumala gave immediate orders for the release of the
two Brahmin sannyāsīs.

Hardly had Nobili and Sebastião de Maya recovered their
health and begun to reorganize the mission, when Tirumala,
uneasy about the political situation in the north, left Madurai for
Tiruchirāpalli. Again Sivandi Pillai threw Nobili and Maya into
prison and continued to harass the Christians in the hope that they
would reveal their master's treasure.

For about a year, it seems, Nobili and Maya languished in a
narrow, stifling cell. They suffered hunger and thirst, lack of
privacy and loss of property—in particular, some of Nobili's
manuscript writings, including his Sanskrit poetry. But they could
not hope for martyrdom—except under extreme provocation, it
was not the Indian practice to take a man's life in a religious cause.
And so, to physical pain was added the mental anguish that time
was being lost, that their sufferings in no way advanced the growth
of the mission.

18. The Door left Open

TOWARDS the end of 1641, Tirumala returned from Tiruchirāpalli and again released the missionaries. Neither the church nor the house was restored to them, but Nobili thought it an unsuitable moment to trouble the Nāyak with recriminations. He went quietly to live in the old palm-thatched *retiro*, where his apostolate had begun twenty-five years before.

The heroic behaviour of Nobili's Paraiyan convert, Hilary, and his success in bringing other Paraiyans into the Christian community had raised a serious problem in missionary method. Repeated persecution in Tiruchirāpalli showed that it was no longer feasible for Martins, a Brahmin sannyāsī, to minister to high castes by day and to untouchables by night. However discreetly he acted, he only alienated both groups and provoked official disapproval by his infringement of caste rules.

Nobili began to look for a better arrangement within the framework of accepted Indian conventions. Among the Vellalas were a group of pandarams, respected by the high castes yet with many low-caste disciples. These pandarams belonged to the Śūdra caste: as such they could speak to Brahmins, Rājās and Vaiśyas (but not eat or lodge with them) and at the same time associate with polluting castes. Nobili decided to introduce a corresponding order of sannyāsīs into the mission.

They were to be known as pandaraswamis—religious teachers. They need not be Sanskrit scholars nor strict vegetarians, but, as Nobili intended them to associate closely with himself and other Brahmin sannyāsīs, they must abstain from meat. They could not engage Brahmins as their servants, nor lodge or eat with Brahmins, nor bear the title and insignia of gurus. They were to refer Sanskrit scholars to Nobili, Sebastião de Maya or Manuel Martins, from whom they would not be separated by any impassable barrier.

The pandaraswamis would work hand in hand with a group of Indian lay-catechists, whom Nobili himself had been training over the years. The catechists varied widely in rank: Peter Xavier (Savari Rayan) was related to the ruling dynasty and a close friend of Tirumala; Constantine (Dairiam) was formerly a wandering yogī. A high-caste catechist was called "Ubadesiar", one of low caste "Pandaram". They were divided into "Stala" catechists, attached to a particular church, and travelling catechists, each with a special gift: one a fine speaker, another a poet, another a singer. These talents were used to assemble a crowd in a strange village and prepare the way for the travelling pandaraswamis.

As his first pandaraswami Nobili chose Baltazar da Costa, an energetic and scholarly Portuguese who arrived in the Madurai Mission in 1640, aged twenty-seven. After having his ears bored, he put on gilt earrings, swathed his body in a loose yellowish tunic slightly redder than Nobili's and set off to begin his work at Karur, four days' journey from Madurai. From there he travelled the kingdom, remaining less than two months in each place. He was accompanied by Peter Xavier or another Indian catechist, and very often Hilary went ahead to prepare his way. The new method met with instant success. From July 1640, when he set foot in the mission, to July 1643, Baltazar da Costa baptized in the kingdoms of Madurai, Tanjore and Sathiyamangalam no fewer than two thousand five hundred adults: mostly Paraiyans and other polluting castes, but also some Śūdras, including army officers.

Nobili was delighted. Just as he had hoped, the seed sown among the higher castes had now borne fruit in every caste. Baltazar da Costa's mission was not a new one, but the continuation and development of the old one: the working from higher to lower castes which Nobili had inaugurated by baptizing Hilary. For, as Costa himself admitted, if low castes now flocked to the pandaraswami, it was because the high castes had come to respect the Brahmin sannyāsīs. Christianity had been given standing in the kingdom: all could profess it without fear.

But quick success bred its own defeat—in recklessness. During 1644 Baltazar da Costa began to mix up his high and low caste converts. Though Nobili cautioned him against it, he wanted to put an end to such odious distinctions, with the result that a pandaram who called himself "the guru of Lanka [Ceylon]" posted up proclamations in Tiruchirāpalli warning the people against certain foreign swamis who aimed at nothing less than the destruction of the civil power. Martins and six Christian Brahmins were arrested in church, thrown into irons along with Fr Alvarez, a visiting Portuguese missionary, and finally expelled, their church being handed over to a Muslim army officer.

Martins and Alvarez crawled back to Madurai exhausted, lucky to have escaped with their lives. Nobili listened as they poured out their troubles in his old palm-thatched *retiro*. He decided there was only one possible remedy—go to Tirumala himself and ask him to extend to his brethren Nobili's own licence to preach throughout the kingdom. Only then would all the missionaries be safe from persecution. But to petition the Lord of the Mountain without a present would be waste of time. As Nobili had no possessions at all, Baltazar da Costa said that he would choose and procure a suitable gift.

About the choice of presents for Oriental monarchs there were several schools of thought. A striking clock had delighted the Emperor of China. Paintings had been tried with success at the imperial court of Chandragiri. Illuminated books had so captivated Jahāngīr, the Great Mogul, that he had the illustrations copied on to his palace walls and ceilings. White elephants had their advocates too, but Tirumala had the fastidiousness of an expert: he would probably look the most expensive gift elephant in the mouth.

Others sang the praises of music. As early as 1517 the Portuguese Governor in India had sent a certain Cristovão de Figueiredo to the Emperor of Vijayanagar with musical instruments, and in 1520 an embassy led by Dom Roderigo de Lima offered organs and a clavichord, with a musician to play them, to Prester John. With a clavichord, too, Matteo Ricci had delighted the court of Peking. Never had the gift of a musical instrument been known to fail in its purpose of concord.

None was considered more efficacious than the organ, since its choice by Queen Elizabeth of England as a present for the Sultan of Turkey. Her Majesty's combined organ and striking 24-hour clock, sixteen feet high, in the form of a baroque façade, had been built by Thomas Dallam, a Lancashire man, at a cost of £550. At the top stood a holly bush full of blackbirds and thrushes, which sang and shook their wings, and a statuette of Queen Elizabeth set with forty-five jewels, to whom eight figures bowed the knee in obeisance. The organ, capable of playing automatically for one hour, had been presented to Mohammed III at Constantinople in 1599, with highly gratifying results.

Would an organ please the Nāyak?

Tirumala liked music and already had some Western tastes—a chef from the Fishery Coast prepared his food in Portuguese style: he could be expected to show an open mind. Perhaps, also, Costa thought such a present appropriate to the occasion: the organ, which had originated in Byzantium, now linking East and West, yet from its use in church and cathedral as unmistakably Christian as stained glass. At any rate, he set about procuring an inexpensive organ from the coast.

Tirumala, then at the height of his power, had found a new way of spending the tribute he saved annually. He had started to build on the grand scale. Outside the main entrance of the temple of Chockanātha, in axial alignment with the east gopuram, he built a huge subsidiary hall, a hundred yards long by thirty wide, divided longitudinally into a nave and two aisles by four rows of elaborately carved pillars: Chockanātha's temporary residence during the festival season. Tirumala also built himself a new palace, consisting of an arcaded courtyard eighty yards long and fifty wide, and a high hall. The pillars were of stone, forty feet high, joined by foliated brick arches and ornamented in shell-lime stucco.

On one side of the courtyard stood a throne-room, an arcaded octagon covered by a dome (another sign of Tirumala's Western tastes), and it was here, towards the middle of 1644, that Tirumala received a group of holy men: two pandaraswamis and two Brahmin sannyāsīs. He wore a robe embroidered with gold thread, matching turban, necklace and bracelets of diamonds and ear-rings of eight large pearls. Nobili, who had consented to lead the deputation, stepped forward and bowed to the Nāyak. Nobili was then sixty-seven and Tirumala fifty-nine. After formal greetings, Nobili began to speak in that authoritative voice which remained with him to the end. Not content with Telugu, the Nāyak's mother tongue, he used Tamil and Sanskrit, describing the plight of his brethren and urging the Nāyak to grant a generous licence.

Tirumala seemed impressed by Nobili's erudite speech, but hinted that requests for such favours were usually accompanied by a present. Tirumala had become notoriously stingy: "when he received a present of a thousand patacas,[1] as a return he would give a gold-embroidered shawl worth only four".[2] He would pay visits to strangers simply for the sake of the present they were bound to offer. Nobili and his brethren knew that unless theirs met with his approval, the licence would not be issued.

Baltazar da Costa signalled to his attendants to bring in the presents, specially sent from Cochin. First they laid in front of the throne an assortment of European musical instruments. These Tirumala politely admired, but with no great enthusiasm. His palace was filled with similar instruments: bow-harps and lutes, conches and pipes.

Finally the attendants carried in the jewel of the collection: a small organ, complete with pipes, keyboard, stops and bellows. Tirumala began to show interest. What was it? He had never seen anything like it before. Nobili explained, and an organist from Cochin, who had accompanied the deputation, sat down and began to play the little organ.

As its notes pealed through the octagonal throne-room, Tirumala listened in pleased astonishment. The idea of pressing keys to admit wind into a series of pipes was unknown in India. No wind instrument so loud or capable of being played for so long had ever been heard in Madurai. Tirumala decided it was exactly the grand ornament for his new palace. He thanked the deputation profusely and showed himself much more friendly. He asked Nobili to give him the names of their persecutors in Tiruchirā-palli, so that he might punish them. When Nobili excused himself on the grounds that his religion taught forgiveness, Tirumala

[1] £700. [2] £2 16s. 0d.

showed suitable edification. There and then he not only gave Nobili's brethren licence to preach freely throughout his kingdom, but, his avarice subdued by the organ's warm notes, he decreed that every article of property stolen from the missionaries should be immediately restored.

As Costa later observed, "In every part of the world the word and signature of a king are a sure guarantee, but here it confers no more stability than a weathercock." It is a measure of the organ's success that Tirumala never retracted this licence.

Tirumala had only a few months to enjoy his gift before being faced with a new enemy to the north. Unlike his predecessor—a weak dawdler—Śriranga III, Emperor of Vijayanagar, showed no intention of acquiescing in Tirumala's bid for hegemony. The Emperor would prove that he was still "Husband of Good Fortune, God of great provinces, King of the greatest kings, Lord of all horse-forces, Taker of the spoils and riches of Ceylon, who cut off the head of the invincible Viravalalan, Lord of the east, south, north, west and of the sea, Hunter of elephants, who lives and glories in military power".

Śriranga ordered Tirumala to pay almost twenty years' arrears of tribute. When Tirumala hedged, Śriranga assembled an army and sent a letter saying he would flay Tirumala alive and make out of his skin a drum to be beaten during processions, as a warning to other treacherously minded vassals.

Tirumala's first retort was to assemble Brahmin sorcerers, and order them to kill the Hunter of elephants by black magic. Such attempts were fairly common, and even Nobili had once been their object. On that occasion the magician, a pandaram, began by tracing figures in the sand and circles in the air, gradually working himself up into a frenzy. Eyes bloodshot, face distorted, grinding his teeth, he shrieked, stamped and beat the ground with his hands and brow in front of Nobili, who was seated. Nobili calmly asked what kind of joke he was playing. When the magician retorted with incantations, Nobili simply smiled. "Spare your throat and lungs," he said. Exasperated by his victim's coolness the magician, frothing at the mouth, opened a box of black powder. Throwing the black powder on Nobili he shouted, "You have laughed—well, now die!" Apparently he expected Nobili to fall dead: when nothing happened, he had to retreat amid the jeers of a crowd.

Tirumala's experiment in black magic proved scarcely more successful. The Brahmins multiplied their sacrifices and incantations; they even caught and killed a hooded cobra, but they did not succeed in killing the Emperor, though they claimed they had made him sick.

Tirumala's next step was to meet the Nāyaks of Tanjore and Gingi, whom he tried to persuade to wage war on Śriranga, as the means to full independence. They agreed, somewhat half-heartedly, but soon the Nāyak of Tanjore grew frightened and betrayed the confederate plans. Śriranga at once marched south.

Now of all the unwritten laws in Southern India none was more binding than the unity of the Hindu South against the Muslim kingdoms of the Deccan. For almost three centuries Islam, in the person of the Great Mogul, had been prevented from engulfing all India by alliances of Hindu states in the much weaker South. Tirumala, however, had no strong sense of religious loyalty. Already he employed a Muslim bodyguard and had Muslim favourites. Now, fearing for his own kingdom, even for his throne, he took action which horrified every Tamil: he made an agreement with the Muslim Sultan of Golkuṇḍā—a tributary of the Great Mogul—whereby Golkuṇḍā was to invade Vijayanagar from the north.

Tirumala's treacherous plan succeeded. Śriranga had to retrace his steps, was defeated by the Sultan of Golkuṇḍā and obliged to take refuge with his one remaining loyal vassal: the ruler of Mysore.

Disturbances in his own kingdom, including a *coup d'état* in the city of Madurai which was only narrowly foiled, now inclined Tirumala to make peace with Śriranga. All the time he had acted with cunning, feigning to be as frightened of Golkuṇḍā as the other Nāyaks, and arranging things in such a way that if he failed in his intrigues with the Muslims he could, as a last resort, come to an agreement with Śriranga.

This he now did. Peace was concluded, but it was to save neither party from the Muslim. Already most of Vijayanagar was overrun, and Tirulama's treason had destroyed all confidence between the southern Hindu kingdoms. Bījāpur and Golkuṇḍā, quiet for the moment, were merely waiting their chance to pounce.

India was poised like an inverted pyramid, with the weight of Islam at the top. It was obvious that before long Madurai would fall to the Muslim alliance. But Nobili, undaunted, continued his mission to the Hindus under the lengthening shadows of an aged civilization. "Almost blind," says Baltazar da Costa, "he works like a young missionary, making up by his zeal and energy for his lack of bodily strength." Much of his time now was spent building up a Christian literature in prose and verse, to which he encouraged his converts to add. Of these Indian Christian versifiers the most gifted was a very important figure in Madurai— one whose conversion had taken place in curious circumstances— a dancing-master.

The highly developed and expressive character of the Indian dance—it was sometimes known as the fifth Veda—had struck nearly all Nobili's contemporaries who wrote about India. In the words of the Englishman, Methwold: "Being children, they are taught to dance, and their bodies, then tender and flexible, screwed into such strange postures, that it is admirable to behold, impossible to express in words; as for a child of eight yeeres of age to stand upon one legge, raysing the other upright as I can my arme, then bringing it down, and laying her heele upon her head, yet all this while standing, looses the wonder in my imperfect relation, but to behold is truly strange: the like for their dancing and tumbling, which doth as farre in activity exceed our mercenary skip-jacks as the rope-dancing woman doth a capring curtezan, or an usher of a dancing schoole, a country ploughjogger."

Dancing-girls attached to the temple of Chockanātha were educated and drilled by a dancing-master. Since traditions of song, music and theatre were combined in the dance, this official could claim to be the artistic panjandrum of Madurai. He was learned not only in the *Nāṭya Śāstra*, the classic treatise on the divine art, but in theology and the humanities. One day this dancing-master heard about Christianity and the following night had a dream in which he was told that if he wanted salvation, he must go to such a place, near such a temple, where he would find a man of such a caste, who would take him to the right guru. Following these directions, the dancing-master arrived at Nobili's *retiro*. When he was ready for baptism, the question arose, how would he make his living in future? Formerly he had had charge of the dancing-girls of Chockanātha; now he supervised dance performances in Tirumala's palace.

Nobili had an ingenious solution to propose. The dancing-master agreed to it, and he who had formerly glorified Śiva the Dancing God through the beauty and gestures of his dancing-girls now spent his days praising Jesus Christ and His Mother in the measured beat of Tamil hymns.

The staple of Nobili's life continued to be theological discussion. One of his last recorded debates was with a Tiruchirāpalli pandaram, whose chief argument ran thus: "Why is it that God Who, according to you, is good, made men more inclined to evil than to virtue?" The pandaram's question was based on two generally held presuppositions which Nobili continued to combat, both orally and in writing, until the end of his life.

The first was fatalism—Nobili specifies that the pandaram denied freedom of the will. According to one of Nobili's colleagues "Fate is called the writing on the head, or the odour of past generation", and that man is driven by his fate followed from belief in transmigration. This, in turn, was intimately linked with a sense of physical evil. A single life might possess the attraction of a tale heard for the first time, but a tale repeated ten thousand million times! Hence the need to escape matter, change and the everyday world in the one thing which seemed to transcend change: knowledge.

The Tiruchirāpalli pandaram belonged to a sect which taught that those who knew the true God did not die. He claimed that there lived in the forests certain penitents of his sect who were several thousand years old, and that one of his disciples had decided to follow him precisely in order to escape death.

But how did one know the true God? Śankara said God is *neti*, *neti*—neither this, nor that. The importance of this "negative way" had been recognized by Aquinas in his dictum: "We know of God rather what He is not than what He is." But the negative way is not enough: it does not yield positive knowledge about God. "Since our intellect knows God from creatures," says Aquinas, "it knows Him to the extent that creatures represent Him." And because creatures derive their perfections from Him, we can predicate these perfections in an analogical sense of God. The school of Śankara denied the validity of analogical thinking about God. Hence, as Nobili had argued in the presence of the Nāyak of Salem, their knowledge led not to Eternal Life but to eternal death.

The pandaram's second presupposition was that moral evil is something positive. Nobili's position here was the scholastic one: that evil denotes the absence of good. And if evil is a privation, it is not something created by God as Creator of all things.

The pandaram's premises were like two ventricles forming the heart of Hinduism: preoccupation with physical and moral evil. It was evil, argued the Hindu, which glared from the earth and met the impartial eye. Useless to combat it—man lived in a tangled jungle, where in stepping back to escape a striking cobra, he would lay himself open to the predatory tiger.

Nobili says, "I discovered in my talks with the pandaram that he had no desire to learn, but was animated with a bad spirit." The fact is, Nobili here came face to face with a set view of the world which under other forms had already given him trouble. He had no way of countering it. Christian theological dogmas simply did not provide a solution to the problem of evil. At most, they put a good "construction" on the world. "Every being, considered as such, is good." But the Tiruchirāpalli pandaram, like many Hindus, would not accept this. Nobili's straight ranks of logical argument about the nature of God and His attributes, creation, avatārs, the relationship between God and the soul could all be outflanked on this weak left wing.

They had been outflanked even within the Church. Almost every important heresy, from Gnostics to Manichaeans, had been an attempt to solve the problem of evil. Some innovators, like the Christian Egyptian, Basilides, in the first century, had even gone

so far as to try to reconcile transmigration with Christian revelation as a way of explaining evil. Basilides's attempt had been
rejected as unorthodox and, ever since, the Church had set her
face against all attempts to probe too deeply into the problem of
evil—almost as though, in handling the pure black dye, man
would not only stain the world but stain himself for all eternity.
It is not surprising, then, that Nobili, on a rare note of exaspera-
tion, explains that he broke off his talks with the Tiruchirāpalli
pandaram, citing the passage from St Matthew: "Do not cast
your pearls . . ."

Nonetheless, in his writings Nobili continued to combat the
Hindu view that birth, personality and "thisness" are evils. His
olei manuscripts were widely circulated, but the question of print-
ing them raised difficulties. There was no such thing as an Indian
publisher. He could not borrow founts even from the Brahmins,
for they possessed none. Thomas Stephens had faced a similar
problem. Writing to Aquaviva, he said, "I have for many years
longed to see books printed in Indian types, as was done in the
Malabar Mission. The chief difficulty is that for such productions
one needs as many as 600 matrices (moulds) instead of twenty-
four, though, at a push, we could manage with only 200." However, no one could be found with the skill to cut the characters of
Devanāgāri—"town-script of the gods"—and Stephens's Purāṇa,
first published at Rachol in 1616, had to appear in Latin type.
Though Tamil characters were more easily cut than Devanāgāri,
none of Nobili's books was printed during his lifetime. This,
however, did not prove a serious obstacle to their popularity, since
the Indians had retentive memories and were accustomed to learn
by heart all important or favourite compositions.

While Nobili in his *retiro* continued to write and revise what he
had written, Baltazar da Costa and Alvarez, protected by Tirumala's licence, were reaping the fruits of their predecessor's
ploughing and sowing. Portuguese superiors back in Cochin were
delighted. "Their mode of life", writes one, "is more in keeping
with the example of Jesus Christ, who for the conversion of the
world chose not princes and scholars, but a few low-caste fisher-
men. He shows that this kind of life is more acceptable to Him

since he blesses it with greater success." Nobili might know
Sanskrit and have great experience, but what was the use of it all
if in forty years he could not give as many baptisms as a young
man ignorant of Sanskrit gave in three years? Were they really
worth the trouble, these Brahmin converts? They were employed
by the mission as catechists, schoolmasters, writers, sacristans and
so on, but those employments were few and without any prospect.
Those who had been trained for temple service or the courts of
princes had to be helped by the mission, and their conversion soon
came to be looked upon as an expensive luxury. And so gradually
interest in the old Brahmin sannyāsīs began to flag; it was commonly said that the future lay with the pandaraswamis.

Nobili foresaw what would happen and wrote to the General in
1644. Surely his father's old friend would grant a final wish. And
the General did grant it. In his last letter to Vitelleschi, Nobili
writes: "I am very grateful to your Paternity for ordering me to
remain in this mission till the end of my life", and he adds a
request for magnifying glasses, "for I have great difficulty in
reading the prayers of the Mass".

But the General's orders were disregarded. The provincial at
that time was Emmanuel Barradas, who, as Socius of Pero
Francisco, had been persistently opposed to Nobili. In 1654,
when Nobili was sixty-eight, Barradas ordered him out of the
mission. "It was deemed advisable to send him to some college
where he might take rest and receive all the attention he deserved."

Nobili did not want to rest, to leave his Indians. He asked only
one thing: to die in the Madurai Mission, where he had spent his
life and love. He had begun his work in the tumble-down *retiro*,
with its palm-leaf thatch, and there he wanted to end it: in India,
not on the hybrid coast which was neither Europe nor Asia.

However, weak and almost blind, Nobili was no longer able to
insist that Rome's will should be followed. This time his Portuguese superiors had the last word. And so, reluctantly, still wearing his red-ochre clothes, Nobili took up his bamboo staff and
gourd and said good-bye to the Christians of Madurai. Then he
walked out of the eastern gate, accompanied by a few Brahmin
converts who refused to leave him, even at the price of exile.

Nobili set out on the same coast-road by which he had first entered the city. Looking back, he could see Tirumala's palace and the nine tall gopurams of Chockanātha's enlarged temple, but of his own church and *retiro* nothing from a distance was visible. Yet his thirty-nine years in the city had surely not been wasted. High-caste converts in the care of the Brahmin sannyāsīs numbered 1,208 scattered in the districts of Madurai, Tirunelvelly, Tiruchirā-palli, Tanjore and Coimbatore, while low-caste converts adminis-tered by the pandaraswamis numbered 2,975. When Nobili first arrived, there had not been a single Christian belonging to the hinterland of South India. Now he left behind him 4,183.

"To open the door of India to Christ"—Nobili had imple-mented the motto on his banner. But the banner would not necessarily be furled at his own departure. The missionary methods he had evolved, his prose, his verse, his plans for a seminary could ensure that the door of India remained open.

He had been the first European to spend his life in the hinter-land of Hindu India since the Scyths had driven the Greeks from the Indus valley in the first century B.C. The Greeks had be-queathed a silver coinage, a few astrological theories and medical prescriptions, and the Gāndhāra school of sculpture. Nobili could claim to have left a more valuable legacy. But as far as official records went it was an anonymous legacy. The Indians of Nobili's day were not recorders of fact (since all facts belonged to the world of illusion), and the name of the Teacher of Reality, like the name of Alexander of Macedon, is absent from contemporary Indian documents and copper-plate inscriptions.

On his return to the Coast, Nobili was shipped across the straits to Jaffna, in north Ceylon. Here he was still surrounded by the culture he had come to love. The town was the capital of the Tamil kings, the Tamil name being Yazhppanam—from the word mean-ing lute-player: the original colony having been founded by a lute-player from the Kingdom of Pearls. Nobili also found the largest and best of all the missions of the Malabar province. Serious Jesuit work had begun only in 1602, yet already there were 40,000 Christians in the north of the island alone, the south being administered by Franciscans.

Practically the whole peninsula of Jaffna was Christian. Churches were plentiful and sturdily built of coral or brick. Near the well-endowed college stood a theatre where mystery plays in Tamil were performed. But the missionaries dressed and ate in Portuguese style: Ceylon was considered part of the Portuguese empire; and not far from every big church stood a barracks.

For two years, according to the Annual Letter, Nobili did much good by means of books which he wrote for children, who learned them by heart with the keenest interest. But he was still yearning after the Madurai Mission. Perhaps, too, he was thinking still of his Brahmin seminary. Despite a bequest of 1,000 florins from Vico's father, the seminary had never been realized for lack of money. Jaffna was rich enough, but not one Singhalese priest was working there or anywhere in the island. And already the Dutch hammered at the gates. In 1638 they had captured the important base of Batticaloa, and had sworn with the King of Kandy to drive every Portuguese from Ceylon. "Care must now be taken that the faith implanted among those peoples be rooted and propagated in such a way that in the event of the withdrawal or death of their first apostles, the faith may not perish, but be kept flourishing by an indigenous clergy." So Pope Pius V had written to the King of Portugal as long ago as 1571, and although Jaffna was to fall to the Dutch in a dozen years, still nothing had been done to ensure a self-supporting Christian community.

After two years in Jaffna, Nobili was again shipped back to the peninsula—not, as he would have liked, to Madurai, but to Mylapore: the birthplace of Tiruvalluvar, most famous of Tamil poets, and reputed to be intimately linked with St Thomas; hence its Portuguese name—San Thomé. The story current in Nobili's day was this. About A.D. 52 St Thomas landed at Maliankara near Cranganore, the Mouziris of the Greeks, a port much frequented in their early voyages by Phoenician and European pepper-traders of the Malabar coast. St Thomas founded seven churches in different parts of Cochin and Travancore and converted, among others, many Brahmins. Later he worked on the Coromandel Coast where, after making further converts, he was attacked by Brahmins and killed by a lance-thrust. His body was buried in Mylapore.

Only an oral tradition fostered by the Portuguese could be adduced in direct support of this legend with its morally appropriate death by a lance-thrust. St Thomas the empiricist might have had his doubts. But the fact remains that the legend was generally believed in the seventeenth century. Nobili had been sent to die in the burial-place of St Thomas.

Mylapore was a decent Christian town, and on Nobili's arrival a large crowd came to hear him speak about God. However, it was also a commercial port, carrying on trade in gold and sealing-wax with Pegu and in sugar with Bengal. To avoid the bustle Nobili retired with a few faithful disciples into a hut outside the city walls where he spent the last years of his life praying and dictating revisions of his books. He still wore his red-ochre clothes, and fasted more strictly than ever, eating each day only a handful of herbs, without rice.

From Mylapore one last letter was written, in Latin, to his sister Ludovica, then mistress of novices in her Roman convent. It was dated 23 September 1649, and Nobili distilled into it the essence of his own life: "Be careful that you teach nothing which is not, by God's grace, found doubly in you, for it would be a hateful thing if she who teaches the young brides of Christ did not prove her words by her deeds."

Nobili's last years were saddened by news of the Portuguese decline. Portugal had now lost to the Dutch her monopoly of cloves and nutmeg, lead and tin, retaining only those of Cochin pepper and Singhalese cinnamon. Discipline was collapsing: in 1653 the Viceroy was deposed at Goa by rebels under one Dom Braz de Castro. In 1656 Colombo fell to the Dutch, and Christians compelled to baptize, marry and bury according to the rites of the Dutch Kirk. So scarce had money become that much of the Malabar province was living on alms from Nobili's family in Rome.

Visitors from Madurai brought equally bad news. Tirumala continued friendly relations with the Portuguese. In 1648 he dutifully expelled the Dutch from Pattanam and the port called

Patariao dos Mouros, controlling the Coromandel Coast. But in the same year the Dutch retaliated by sending ten ships to capture the temple of Trichenden and fortify it, then to sack and partly burn Tuticorin.

The main threat to Tirumala came from the very Muslims it had now become his habit to summon on his own behalf. In 1656 a series of omens portended coming disaster. A child was born in Tiruchirāpalli with teeth; not far away a calf was born with two heads. Near Tanjore a pair of twins were born with a common stomach; they were worshipped like gods until, after a few days, they proved that they were mortal. Before the decade was out, the Sultan of Bījāpur, with twelve thousand horse, many chariots and camels, invaded and sacked the kingdoms of Madurai and Tanjore. Churches were destroyed, Christian children carried into slavery. When a Bījāpur soldier snatched an ear-ring from Baltazar da Costa, tearing the lobe in two, it was a sign of the end of the epoch Nobili knew. The Vijayanagar empire had collapsed, the Muslims had come to power.

Tirumala was retained as a puppet king, forced to pay a huge annual tribute to the Sultan of Bījāpur. One tradition has this to say of his death. Tirumala so nearly became converted to Christianity that he stopped all expenditure on temples. This angered the Brahmins, some of whom, headed by a *bhattan*—the officiating priest of the temple of Chockanātha—enticed the Nāyak into their temple under the pretext of disclosing a great treasure hidden underground. The *bhattan* induced Tirumala to enter the vault first, then slammed down its great stone trap-door, and announced to the people of Madurai that the goddess Mīnākṣi had translated her favourite to heaven.

Whatever the manner of Tirumala's death, two hundred of his wives loved the Nāyak enough to commit suttee. The flames of their funeral pyres symbolized more than the end of a reign, for with Tirumala there passed from Madurai many of the elements with which Nobili had had to contend: continual mobilization which had impoverished the kingdom and separated disciples from their guru, the influence of the Brahmins, the importance of Sanskrit and the Vedānta. "Thou art God": according to Śankara, the proper condition for realizing that proposition was the trance. But now the trance, which Nobili's reasoning had been unable to controvert, was invaded and shattered by scimitars whose sharp edge could not be shrugged away as illusion.

For some eight years Nobili lived on in Mylapore, known to Christians and Hindus alike as *o santo Padre*. Despite his age, his memory remained prodigious, his mind so orderly that he could visualize all he had written or intended to write, and he would amaze his copyists by referring not only to works he had composed, but even to those he intended composing, quoting chapter and verse.

At the beginning of January 1656 the last line of his twenty volumes of *oleis* was written. Then Nobili dictated this declaration: "It is my wish that all I have written in Tamil, Telugu and San-skrit should be in conformity with the mind of our Holy Mother the Roman Catholic Church. I beg that she deign to correct any-thing erroneous or objectionable or likely to give offence, which may have escaped me. And I most earnestly beg all who may copy or translate these books to place this protestation of mine at the end of each volume. San Thomé, 6th January 1656." Then, groping for his stylus, with the help of one of his disciples, he cut into the fibre the Tamil version of his Sanskrit name: Tattuva Bodhakar.

A few days later he fell ill. Since coming to India he had lived on the very brink of life, so that his friends found it difficult to tell how ill he was. Nevertheless, to increase his strength, they decided secretly to mix some meat extract with his single daily dish of herbs. Nobili guessed what they were up to, and quietly threw the mixture away without any remark. He was past all food now. For ten days he lingered on, with no great pain, perfectly at peace, aware that his heart-beats were growing fainter. And for one who had suffered so much during fifty years, it was a mercy not to expect a cycle of rebirths.

On 16th January 1656 Roberto de Nobili died. He was buried in Mylapore, at the meeting-point of the Portuguese and Vijay-anagar empires. No monument, no inscription marked his grave —he needed none, for every Christian in India would be a living memorial to the Teacher of Reality. One who had loved so much belonged to the whole peninsula, not to any one town or village, but for all that Mylapore could now justify her ancient boast. Whether or not St Thomas had died within her walls, Mylapore was made holy for all time as the burial-place of an Apostle of India.

Books by Roberto de Nobili

1. *Gnanopadesam* (Spiritual Teaching). Virtually a *Summa Theologica*, consisting of five parts (Kândam). The first and second kândam were printed in one volume, 1775. Second edition Madras, 1891. The third kândam was printed in Trichinopoly, 1907. The fourth kândam, the *Mantra-Vyakkyanam*, is in the press. The fifth kândam has not been certainly identified.

2. *Âttuma Nirunayam* (Disquisition on the Soul). Printed in Madras, 1889.

3. *Agnâna Nivâranam* (Dispelling of Ignorance). Printed in Trichinopoly, 1891.

4. *Tivviya Mādirigai* (The Divine Model). Printed in Pondicherry, 1870.

TAMIL TYPESCRIPTS IN THE SHEMBAGANUR ARCHIVES

5. *Tūshana Tikkāram* (Refutation of Blasphemies). About 470 pp.

6. *Punar Jenma Ácheba* (Refutation of Rebirth). Also known as *Nittiya Jivana Sallâbam* (Dialogue on Eternal Life). About 83 pp.

7. *Gnāna Sanchīvi* (Spiritual Medicine). About 100 pp.

OTHER BOOKS CREDITED TO NOBILI, BUT NOT FULLY IDENTIFIED

8. *Gnāna dakchanam.* The marks or foundations of the credibility of the religion which reveals God in order to lead men to salvation.

9. *Gnāna Vilakham.* The Spiritual Torch to distinguish truth from falsehood.

10. Talks about Eternal Life.
11. *Sangopanga murei anusāram.* Rules of Perfection.
12. Spiritual canticles and poems.
13. Dialogue on Faith for the instruction of children.

Bibliography

1. MANUSCRIPTS

ARSI=Archives of the Society of Jesus in Rome
ASSI=Archives of the Society of Jesus in Shembaganur,
South India.

ANNUAE LITTERAE Madura Miss. ARSI, Goa, vol. 53.

ANNUAE LITTERAE Provinciae Malabarensis 1603–1680. ARSI, Goa, vol. 55.

BESSE, L., S.J.—Histoire de la Province du Malabar, MS. ASSI.

BUCCERIO, A., S.J.—INFORMACAO DO MISSAO DE MADURE RE. O MTO. R. EM CHTO PATRE AO GERAL CLAUDIO ACQUAVIVA. 30 October 1610. ARSI, Goa, vol. 51.

CASTETS, J., S.J.—Histoire de l'Ancienne Mission du Maduré, MS. ASSI.

CATALOGI trien. Cochin et Malabar. ARSI, Goa, vol. 29.

CATALOGUS Provinciae Neapolitanae. ARSI, Goa, vol. 6.

CATALOGUS Provinciae Romanae. ARSI, vol. 14.

COMPENDIOSA INFORMATIO ISTARUM GENTIUM, ILLARUMQUE REIPUBLICAE LEGUM, MORUM ET RELIGIONIS (Memoir addressed to some Cardinals). Archives of Propaganda. Miscellanea Varie, vol. 6, f. 144.

DE TRIPLICI LINEA ET CINCINNO CAPILLORUM BRAMANU INDIAE ORIENTALIS, QUEM CURUMBY AUT SYNDI VOCANT. ARSI, Goa, vol. 51. Probably by Ros but based on "De Linea Brachmanum" of de Nobili.

EPISTOLAE Goanae et Malabaricae. ARSI, Goa, vols. 13–16.

EPISTOLAE Malabaricae. ARSI, vols. 17–23.

EPISTOLAE P. R. de Nobili et Controversia de illo. ARSI, Goa, vol. 51.

FRANCISCO, PERO, S.J.—Fourteen letters. ARSI, Goa, vol. 51.

GODINHO, N., S.J.—AN PROBARI DEBEAT MODUS QUEM SERVANT PATRES RUPERTUS DE NOBILI, ET ANTONIUS VICUS EJUS SOCIUS IN CONVERTS. BRACMAN URBIS MADUREI. ARSI, Goa, vol. 51.

INDIARUM MISCELLANEA. ARSI, Goa, vol. 38.

INDIPETAE. ARSI, Goa, vol. 2.

INFORMATIO CIRCA QUAEDAM ATTINENTIA AD CONVERSIONEM INFIDELIUM IN INDIA ORIENTALI (APOLOGIA DATA CARD. S. OFFICII: CARDINALES VERALLI, BENSII, ARA COELI, BELLARMINI). Written in Rome, author unknown. ARSI, Goa, vol. 51, ff. 82–7.

LAERZIO, A., S.J.—Thirty-five letters and Memoirs. ARSI, Goa, vol. 51.

MALABARICA HISTORIA. ARSI, Goa, vols. 47–50, 52, 54, 54a, and 55.

NOBILI, ROBERTO DE, S.J.—DE LINEA BRACHMANUM. ARSI, Goa, vol. 51, ff. 154–61.

— Letters (see Epistolae above).

— PROPOSITIONES 77 ET LIBRIS BRACHMANORUM SUMPTAE—14 TESTES MADURENSIS EXARRAVERUNT. ARCHEPISCOP CRANGANORENSI APPROBATAE. Archives of Propaganda. Miscellanea Varie, vol. 6, ff. 178–81.

— Tamil works written on Oleis. ASSI.

PARECERES E SENSURAS DOS PRES LETRADOS DE GOA, SOBRE A MISSAO DO PE ROBERTO. Under this title come the opinion and censures: (1) of Father A. Fernandez and Father F. Vergara, (2) of the Rector of St Paul, Goa, and four Theologians. ARSI, Goa, vol. 51, ff. 122–4.

PUBLICUM TESTIMONIUM DE MODO PROCEDENDI P. R. DE NOBILI IN MISSIONE MADURENSI, ITEM DE MODO INSTRUENDI NEOPHYTOS IN EADEM MISSIONE. ARSI, Goa, vol. 51, ff. 39–73.

RELACAO DE CONSULTA Q'O P. PROVINCIAL ALBERTO LAERZIO FES SOBRE A MISSAO DE MADURE COMFORME A ORDEM DO P. VISITATOR (COCHIN). ARSI, Goa, vol. 51, ff. 27–8.

ROS, DOM FRANCISCO, Archbishop of Cranganore.—DE LINEA ET CORUMBI BRAHMANORUM.

— Twenty Letters written between 1601 and 1620. Cf. EPISTOLAE.

UTRUM NOVUS ILLE RITUS QUO PATER ROBERTUS AD CONVERTENDOS INSTITUTENDOS IN FIDE BRACHMANSUT COEPIT SUPERSTITIOSUS SIT, AUT SUSPECTUS. ARSI, Goa, vol. 51, ff. 74–81.

VICO, A., S.J.—DE MODO QUO NOVA MISSIO MADURENSIS UTITUR AD ETHINICOS XTO CONVERTENDOS, 10 OCTOBER 1610.

— Thirty-four letters written between the years 1607 and 1632. ARSI, vol. 51.

— RESPONSA AD QUASDAM OBJECTIONES CONTRA LINEAM BRACHMANERAE. ARSI, vol. 51.

2. PRINTED WORKS

BAIAO, ANTONIO.—*A Inquisição de Goa*, vol. 1, 1949; vol. 11, 1930, Lisbon. (Vol. 1 appeared nineteen years after vol. 11.)

BASHAM, A. L.—*The Wonder that was India*, London, 1954.

BERTRAND, J., s.j.—*La Mission du Maduré*, 4 vols., Paris, 1847–1854.

BESSE, L., s.j.—*La Mission du Maduré*, Trichinopoly, 1914.

— *Liste Alphabétique des Missionaires du Carnatic de la Compagnie de Jésus au XVIIe siècle*, Pondicherry, 1918.

— *Researches on the Catalogues of the various Missions of the Malabar Province*, published as appendices to the Madurai Mission Catalogues, *circa* 400 pages. Trichinopoly, 1907–1918.

BESSE and HOSTEN, s.j.—"List of Portuguese Jesuit Missionaries in Bengal and Burma (1576–1742)." *Journal and Proceedings, Asiatic Society of Bengal*, Calcutta, New Series, vol. VII, no. 2, 1911.

BRANDOLINI.—*Riposta alle accuse date al praticao sin'ora da' Religiosi della Compagnie di Giesu*, Cologne, 1729.

— *Giustificazione del praticato sin "ora da" Religiosi della Compagna di Gesu nelle missioni del Madurei, Mayssur e Carnate . . .* Roma, 1724.

BRODRICK, J., s.j.—*The Life and Work of Blessed Robert Francis Bellarmine, 1542–1621*, 2 vols., London, 1928.

CALAND, W.—Robert de Nobili and Sanskrit language and Literature —*Acta Orientalia*, Leyden, vol. v, pp. 38–51.

CALEPINO, A.—*Dictionnarium*, 2 vols., Lyons, 1668.

CARDELIA, L.—*Memorie storiche de Cardinali della Santa Romana Chiesa . . .* Rome, 1893.

CASTETS, J., s.j.—*La Simple Vérité su la Querelle des Rites Malabares*, Trichinopoly, 1933.

— *The Madurai Mission*, Trichinopoly, 1924.

— " L'Eglise et le Problème des Castes." *Revue d'Histoire des Missions*, Paris, 1930–1.

Catalogus Patrum qui Congregationibus Provincialibus antiquae Provinciae Lusitanae Soc. Jes. interfuere 1572–1755, Lisbon, 1906.

CHANDLER, J. S.—*History of the Jesuit Mission in Madurai, South India, in the XVII and XVIII centuries*, Madras, 1909.

CORDARA, J. C., s.j.—*Historiae S.J. Pars Sexta*, Rome, 1849.

DAHMEN, P., s.j.—*Robert de Nobili S.J. Ein Beitrag zur Geschichte der Missionsmethode und der Indologie*, Münster, Aschendorffschen, 1924.

DAHMEN, P., S.J.—*Robert de Nobili, l'Apôtre des Brahmes, Première Apologie*, Paris, 1931. Translation of Father Robert's *Responsio* of October 10, 1610, with Introduction and Notes.

— *Un Jésuite Brahme, Robert de Nobili*, Museum Lessianum, Louvain, 1924.

— See LOMBARD.

FERROLI, D., S.J.—*The Jesuits in Malabar.* 2 vols., Bangalore, 1939 and 1951.

— *The Jesuits in Mysore*, Kozikode, 1955.

FONSECA, J. N. DE—*Historical and Archaeological Sketch of the City of Goa*, Bombay, 1878.

FORCELLA, V.—*Iscrizioni delle chiese e d'altri edifice di Roma dal secola XI, fino ai giorni nostri*, 14 vols., Rome, 1869–85.

FRANCESCHI, G. F.—*Selva Cedua Poliziana de Prete*, 1722.

FRANCIS, W.—*Madras District Gazetteers, Madura*, Madras, 1906.

FRANCO, A., S.J.—*Synopsis Annalium S.J. in Lusitania 1540–1725*, Augsburg, 1726.

GOYAU, G.—*Missions et Missionaires*, Paris, 1921.

HERAS, H., S.J.—*Conversion Policy of the Jesuits in India*, Bombay, 1933.

— *The Aravidu Dynasty of Vijayanagar*, vol. I, Madras, 1927.

LAUNAY, A.—*Histoire des Missions de l'Inde*, 4 vols., Paris, 1898.

LE BACHELET, S.J.—"Bellarmine et la Compagnie de Jésus," in *Gregorianum*, V, 1934.

LOMBARD, PETER.—Archbishop of Armagh's "Votum" in favour of Father Robert de Nobili, edited by Father P. Dahmen, S.J., in *Archivum Historicum S.I.*, IV, 1935.

LOPEZ, A., S.J.—*A short account of the Missions, 1644*, edited by L. Besse, S.J., 1907.

MACLAGAN, SIR EDWARD.—*The Jesuits and the Great Mogul*, London, 1932.

Memoria Historico-Ecclesiastica da Arquidiocese de Goa 1533–1933, Nova Goa, 1933.

MIRANDA, J. L., S.J.—*The Introduction of Christianity into the Heart of India, or Father Robert de Nobili's Mission*, Trichinopoly, 1923.

MORERI, L.—*Le Grand Dictionnaire Historique*, Amsterdam, 1740.

MÜLLBAUER, M.—*Geschichte der Katholischen Missionen in Ost-Indien*, Freiburg im Breisgau, 1852.

NAYAGAM, XAVIER S. THANI.—*Nature in Ancient Tamil Poetry*, Tuticorin, 1953.

NILAKANDA SASTRI, K. N.—*A History of South India*, Madras, 1955.

NILAKANDA SASTRI, K. N.—*Further Sources of Vijayanagar History*, Madras, 1946.

— *The Pandyan Kingdom*, London, 1929.

NOBILI, ROBERTO DE, S.J.—Letters: (*a*) found in Bertrand, fully or partly translated into French (16).

— (*b*) translated into French by P. Dahmen in *Revue d'Ascetique et de Mystique*, vol. XVI, Toulouse, 1935 (3).

— (*c*) translated into French by the same in *Un Jésuite Brahme*, Paris, 1924 (1).

— (*d*) translated into French by the same in *Revue d'Histoire des Missions*, vol. XIII, pp. 579–607, Paris, 1935 (5).

— *Responsio ad ea quae contra modum quo Nova Missio Madurensis utitur ad Ethnicos Christi convertendos objecta sunt*. The Latin text with a French translation was published by P. Dahmen, S.J., under the title: *Robert de Nobili, l'Apôtre des Brahmes, Première Apologie*, Paris, 1931.

PASTOR, L.—*History of the Popes*, London, 1891.

PATRIGNANI, G. A.—*Menologio d'Alcuni Religiosi della Compagnia di Gesù*, vol. I, Venice, 1730.

SCHINOSI, P., and SANTAGATHA, S.—*Istoria della Compagne di Giesu appertenente al regno di Napoli*, Naples, 1714.

SANTOS, A., S.J.—"Francisco Ros, S.J., Arzobisopo de Cranganore" in *Missionalis Hispanica*, Ano V, num. 14, Madrid, 1948.

TAMIL LEXICON published under the authority of the Madras University, 6 vols., Madras, 1924–34.

THOMAS, P.—*Christians and Christianity in India and Pakistan*, London, 1954.

XAVIER, M., S.J.—*Compendio Universal de todos as Viso-Reys Governadores, Capitaes Geraes*, etc., Nova Goa, 1917.

WICKI, JOSEF, S.J.—"Die Schrift des P. Gonçalo Fernandes, S.J., über die Brahmanen und Dharma-Sastra (Madura, 1616)" in *Zeitschrift für Missionswissenschaft und Religionwissenschaft*, 1957.

ZIEGENBALG, B.—*Genealogy of the South Indian Gods, a Manual of the Mythology and Religion of the People of Southern India*, Madras, 1869.

Notes

The chief sources for the Life of Nobili are his own few remaining letters, supplemented by the correspondence of other Madurai missionaries, documents such as the *Answer* defending the method of adaptation, Peter Lombard's *Votum* and triennial reports to Rome from Madurai. Many of Nobili's letters containing precious details were probably lost when the Dutch sacked Cochin. Most of the extant correspondence is to be found either in the archives of the Society of Jesus in Rome (abbreviated below to ARSI) or in the archives of Shembaganur, near Madurai. Other relevant MSS., Latin, Italian, Portuguese and Spanish, are in the British Museum; the archives of Propaganda, Rome; the National Library, Lisbon; and the archives of the Ajuda Palace, Lisbon.

The following notes provide source references, where these are likely to be needed, and supplementary material bearing on certain passages in the narrative.

CHAPTER 1

PAGE LINE

11 1 Rome. Proenza to the General, 20 September 1656.

12 5 saints. Pastor, *History of the Popes*, xiii, 328.

13 26 Terme. "la divota contessa nel 1598 fece fabricare a salvazione della sua anima et di suo figlio il cardinale Francesco Sforza, una chiesa in onore di S. Bernardo con un annesso monastero." Forcella, ix, 172.

16 34 us. Patrignani, *Menol.*, i, 295.

18 4 1596. In 1601 his name heads the list of Indipetae who belonged to the Province of Naples, and Fr Fabius states that he had been four years in the Society (i.e. 1597, 1598, 1599 and 1600, the fractions of 1596 and 1600 being omitted).

19 25 Japan. In a letter dated 31 July 1599 Aquaviva wrote of Nobili's "desire to go to Japan". ARSI Neap. 6 Epist. Gen. 1599–1602. ff. 51 et seq.

20 12 desire. ARSI, *loc. cit.*

21 10 different. ARSI, *loc. cit.*

CHAPTER 2

CHAPTER 3

CHAPTER 4

50   17 Ros. Sometimes spelt Roz, or in Latin Rozius, but the correct spelling is undoubtedly Ros; such, at least, is the opinion
of his Catalan countrymen. Consecrated Latin bishop of
Angamale (25 January 1601), he obtained from Paul V that his
see should be given back the archiepiscopal dignity of which
it had been deprived at the Council of Dampier (Udayam-
peroor) and be transferred to Cranganore, where the Apostle
St Thomas is said to have landed.

53   6 master. It has generally been assumed, rather than proved,
that the death of Muttu Krishnappa Nāyak took place in
1609, but in a letter dated Madurai, 6 December 1606,
Nobili states explicitly that the Nāyak had just died. Letter
to the Duchess of Sora, Archives of Prince Boncompagni,
Rome.

CHAPTER 5

61   5 respectful. Nobili to Aquaviva, Madurai, 1 December 1607.

62   4 God. Nobili gives a detailed account of the conversion to
Aquaviva. Madurai, 1 December 1607.

65   13 punishment. In *A Display of two forraigne sects in the East
Indies* (1630), Henry Lord, chaplain to the East India Company, puts foward yet another argument: "It is improbable
the soule should be enioyned to such a satisfaction for
sinne, as tendeth to its greater defilement." A form of the
same argument was employed by Matteo Ricci against the
Buddhists. In his *Solid Treatise on God*, an early presentation
of scholastic philosophy in Chinese (1603), Ricci asserts that
many vicious men would be glad to be changed into beasts,
the better to satisfy their brutal passions.

68   6 name. Fernandez gives his name in a letter to the Assistant,
Cochin, 12 December 1618.

68   29 done. Laerzio to Aquaviva, 20 November 1609.

69   14 shame. Laerzio, *ibid.*

70   9 request. "We know that our Fathers in China have obtained
great success by adopting the dress of the literati of that
country. Therefore I allowed him also to change his dress."
Laerzio, *ibid.*

CHAPTER 6

73   28 Chinaxauta. The name is given by Emmanuel Barradas in a report dated 1 November 1615. It has been suggested that Chinaxauta was the Portuguese way of writing *Cinna cavadi*, the small "choultry" or rest house; just as "choultry" is the English spelling of *cavadi*. According to that theory the rest house had, in its heyday, given its name to the locality. Now only a wretched hut was left and a name which in its turn soon fell into disuse.

74   2 hermitage. Fernandez and Nobili had continued to live together for a few weeks. In a letter of 7 May 1610, Fernandez says "for a few months", but since he left Madurai before the conversions began, he cannot have remained more than two months with Nobili.

75   6 glory. Nobili to Bellarmine, Madurai, 1 December 1607.

75   14 religion. Nobili to Aquaviva, Madurai, 1 December 1607.

75   22 Faith. *Ibid.*

75   26 turban. Pimenta, Goa, 2 December 1599. "Traduite du Latin en Français, à Anvers, chez Joachim Torgnese MDCI."

76   37 Frey. Possibly an abbreviation of Fernandez. An Englishman working in India would have been dubbed with a Portuguese surname. Ferroli, *The Jesuits in Malabar*, ii, 398. India at this time was hardly teeming with English painters, yet Brother Alexander is known to have at least one predecessor. James Story in the company of three friends, including Ralph Fitch, sailed from London for Aleppo in the *Tiger*, reaching Ormuz by the overland route in December 1583. The captain of that fortress had the four English merchant-adventurers arrested as spies and sent on to Goa, where they were thrown into jail. Thomas Stephens, the English Jesuit, heard about their plight, interceded for them with the Viceroy and secured their release on bail. Foreigners, other than religious, were forbidden to live in Portuguese India and all four would probably have been sent back to Lisbon by the next fleet, had not Fitch and two others fled to the interior, while Story for a short time entered the Society of Jesus as a lay-brother, where his talents were much in demand for the decoration of churches.

77   29 Christianity. For the Jesuit mission to Chandragiri, see Heras, *Aravidu Dynasty*.

NOTES

CHAPTER 7

NOTES

100   7 deserves. Nobili to Laerzio, 20 February 1609.

102 20 irons. *Ibid.*

CHAPTER 8

106 37 decision. In the *Responsio of* 1610, chapter 2.

109   6 seen. "As to my Brahmin master, I think it better to proceed slowly, not that I have any doubt about his perseverance, for I see clearly that God Our Lord is daily communicating to him more of His light, but to see what the other Brahmins will say when they see him wearing a crucifix hanging from his neck, and a new thread which I blessed and gave him. This was why I did not baptize him at Easter as I had intended." Nobili to Laerzio, Madurai, 22 April 1609; Bertrand, ii, 34.

109   7 Pentecost. Nobili to Laerzio, 15 May 1609. This letter is not given by Bertrand, though he inserts some of its contents in Nobili's letter of 22 April.

109 26 well-behaved. Nobili to Laerzio, Madurai, 7 June 1609.

109 36 baptism. In the early days of the Church Egyptians usually retained their heathen names after conversion, even though the name was taken from a god, e.g. Ammonius, Serapion, Pachomius.

111 36 riddance. Nobili to Laerzio, 31 December 1608.

112 18 conscience. *Ibid.*

114 23 Turk. A fair complexion was no proof that one was a Parangi but it raised suspicions tedious to allay. Antonio Proenza appealed to the professors of chemistry in Portugal to try and find a pigment which would allow him and his companions to pass as good-looking Indians, but he met with no response. Proenza to G. Nickel, Candelur, 20 September 1656.

CHAPTER 9

116 18 Dadamurti. Nobili mentions his conversion in a letter to Laerzio, 25 November 1608.

116 32 coming. Nobili to Laerzio, Madurai, 15 January 1609. In Bertrand, ii, 29, this letter is mis-dated 15 June, and *Ponghel* (Pongal) is translated by "banquet"; Pongal really means "boiling". See *Tamil Lexicon.*

PAGE LINE

120 25 Europe. Leitao notes that in Madurai God gives the grace of conversion not to the man with interested motives but to him who uses his reason and will. Leitao to Laerzio, 26 September 1609.

120 35 Christ. Buccerio's report to Aquaviva, 1610.

121 4 house. *Ibid.* Another proof that Nobili did not conceal from his converts that he was under the Provincial of Cochin.

121 26 Saturdays. *Ibid.*

122 22 medals, etc. Nobili to the Duchess of Sora, Madurai, 29 September 1615.

123 27 men. In the Sign of the Cross, Nobili changed the words *chutumana spiritu* (the second being a Latinism incomprehensible to Indians) to *Iruveral tondia nesam*. *Iruveral* is the ablative of the number two; *tondia* come from the verb *tonrukiradu*, to proceed; *nesam* means friendship, love. Hence the phrase means "the love proceeding from the two", that is from the Father and Son. In the Lord's Prayer Enriquez had translated "in heaven" by *vanangalil*, the locative plural of *vānam*, meaning air or firmament. Nobili replaced it be *moksha*, from Sanskrit. Its original meaning was "deliverance [from all evil]" and it had come to mean glory or place of glory. Again, Enriquez had rendered "hallowed by Thy name" as *naaman chutumana*. As *Chutumana* means clean, Nobili changed the phrase to *naamatei ellarum condara* —"may all bless and praise Thy name!"

124 32 feet. *Paripadal*, v, 77; xiii, 47. Nayagam, 12.

125 30 Muni. "There is a rumour spreading in Madurai that I am a Muni who has come to destroy idols and restore religion to its former purity." Nobili to Laerzio, 24 December 1608.

128 5 life. Nobili is still known by this name in Southern India.

CHAPTER 10

130 11 progress. Nobili to Laerzio, 22 April 1609.

130 25 Archdiocese. Nobili to Laerzio, in a letter which arrived 17 June 1609.

131 10 say. *Ibid.*

132 23 evening. Un hora di notte = not 1 a.m., as modern readers would understand it, but, according to the old Roman way of counting the hours, from sunset to sunset, 7 p.m.

132 37 Brahmins. Leitao to Laerzio, Madurai, 26 September 1609.

133   9 it. *Ibid.*

133 21 work. To Laerzio, 26 September; to Aquaviva, 24 October and 20 November 1609.

135 22 die. Laerzio's report to Aquaviva, Cochin, 8 September 1610.

138 14 love. Nobili's own text as reported by Vico in his letter of 27 May 1611. A summary of the earlier unrevised text is given by Laerzio in his report to Aquaviva, 8 September 1610.

138 21 congregation. Dahmen, *Apologie*, 76.

139 17 statement. "Primieramente mi dimandorno delle cose che appartegono a Dio, particolarmente de Unitate et Trinitate Dei (perche questi in molti libri et versi tengono che Iddio é Trino et Uno, ma non sanno i poveri come cio si sia)." Nobili to Laerzio, undated.

141 31 learned. *Ibid.*

143 37 plate. *Agnānā Nivāraṇam*, Second Dialogue.

144   8 wine. *Ibid.*

144 33 things. Nobili to Laerzio, undated. Probably end of April 1610.

145 18 difficulties. *Ibid.*

146 21 chalice. Buccerio's report to Aquaviva, 1610.

147 15 also. Besides Leitao, two priests, Antonio Dias and Francisco Suarez, were at different times sent to assist Nobili before 1610. *Apologie*, 70.

CHAPTER 11

148 22 him. Nobili to Aquaviva, Madurai, 21 October 1610. ARSI, Goa 51, f. 164.

148 28 reply. *Ibid.*

149   3 Goa. *Ibid.*

149   7 "innovations". Fernandez to Aquaviva, 7 May 1610. ARSI, Goa 51, f. 37s.

149 18 true. Theological Consultation, Goa 1610. Month and day unknown. ARSI, Goa 51, f. 122.

149 20 Cochin. The date is not given; probably June 1610. ARSI, Goa 51, f. 27.

149 29 palanquin. This is the first and last reference made to the palanquin in surviving documents. As the point was raised by

Luis Cardozo, whose sources of information are not reliable, it is a matter of conjecture whether Nobili's use of the palanquin was only occasional or habitual. Sannyāsīs of the *Māyāvāda* sect were carried in palanquins, according to Fernandez's report of 1616. Wicki, 113.

150 18 method. Pimenta's letter is no longer extant.

150 26 Portuguese. Publicum Testimonium de modo procedendi P.R. de Nobili in Missione Madurensi, item de modo instruendi Neophytos in eadem Missione. ARSI, Goa 51, ff. 39-50.

152 37 motive. *Ibid.*

155 30 all. Vico to Aquaviva, 25 October 1610. ARSI, Goa 42.

156 6 write. De modo quo nova Missio Madurensis utitur ad Ethnicos Christo convertendos. ARSI, Goa 51, ff. 88-109.
Rome. Responsio ad ea quae contra modum quo nova Missio Madurensis utitur ad Ethnicos Christo convertendos objecta sunt. See Chapter 16.

156 24 obstinacy. Nobili to Aquaviva, Madurai, 19 October 1610. ARSI, Goa 51, f. 162; Vico to Aquaviva, Madurai, 26 October 1610. ARSI, Goa 48, f. 178. Nobili and Vico were obliged to write a joint letter to the General, requesting him to obtain the Pope's sanction for a further step in accommodation. First, in view of Fernandez's attitude, was it necessary for converts to declare spontaneously that their religion was the same as that of the Parangis? Was it not enough to admit it when questioned? Secondly, was the reckless exhibition of the crucifix the best way of confessing Christ? It had now come to be misunderstood in Madurai, where it was regarded as a profession of Parangism rather than of Christianity. Nobili and Vico requested that converts should not be obliged to blazon it on their breast. Thirdly, Brahmins claimed that hanging a cross on their thread changed the nature of the thread from a mere indication of caste. Archibishop Ros had recently forbidden neophytes to tie anything to their thread. Could not his instructions be safely followed?

Nobili's fourth request was to be allowed to bless and administer ashes on every day of the year, as on Ash Wednesday, and in the same spirit. Admittedly the use of ashes in Madurai was superstitious—Śaivites wore them as a sign of their god, the Destroyer—but the Church had christianized many pagan practices of the old Romans. The matter was important, for Errama Setti was becoming less and less friendly, and it might be necessary to win the protection of another of the seventy-two poligars. One of these poligars was prepared to become a Christian if he could retain the habit of putting sacred ashes on his forehead: a practice, says Vico, "very common among men of rank and deemed so necessary that if they give it up they lose their social status." Nobili and Vico to Aquaviva, 12 November 1610.

The answer to this joint request is unknown. In future, new converts continued never to make a secret of their religion. The Archbishop's instructions regarding the thread were strictly followed, but the exhibition of crucifixes and medals continued. As for the use of ashes on the forehead, it was allowed by the Ordinaries of Cranganore and Mylapore, who had jurisdiction over the inland missions.

156 26 defence. Ros to Aquaviva, the Serra, 21 January 1611.

157 26 represented. Vico to Laerzio, 24 November 1610.

159 33 sannyāsī. *Ibid.*

159 35 Manamadurai. Laerzio's original gives "Re de Manamaduré" which Figueroa translates into Spanish as "Rey de Maduré". Heras, following Figueroa's wrong translation instead of Laerzio's original, concludes that "this monarch who is still called 'king of Madure' is the nominal Pandya King", Srivallaba of Tenkasi. It is doubtful whether the same conclusion can be drawn regarding a "king of Manamadurai". If Srivallaba is the man referred to by Laerzio, he must have been extremely old, since his accession took place in 1534. See also Nilakanda Sastri, *The Pandyan Kingdom,* 251–2.

160 2 hermitage. A letter of Laerzio, 1608; Vico to Laerzio, 24 November 1610.

160 9 him. Vico to Laerzio, 24 November 1610.

160 33 know. "Indian society (*respublica*) is divided according to four grades of social function and therefore of social standing, as is well known to all those who dwell among this people and is explained in the eighteen volumes of the Smruti in which all the ordinances of the Law with regard to the rank of the members of the social body, government and the characteristics of classes are set forth—and especially in the book called Manu, which is of the highest authority. The first grade is that of the wise men whom they call Brahmins

(Brachmanes) from the word, as they say *brahde*, i.e. to know."
From a Memoir sent to Rome by Nobili in 1615, quoted by
Brandolini. In his answer to Buccerio (1611) Nobili gives the
same etymology of Brahmin (Brachman): "either from the
root bruhum, which is said of knowledge or from the word
brumhiate, which means to know." The root referred to is
evidently *brh.*

162   19   pardaos. The theft and its aftermath are described by Vico,
Madurai, 27 May 1611.

164   16   Ciavarcovadim. Heras, followed Figueroa, reads Chavarco-
vadin, and interprets the word as Chakravartin. *Aravidu
Dynasty*, 392. The original of Laerzio runs "Fissando gli
occhi per quelle parte dove stanno li piedi de V.S. il suo
schiavo Ciavarcovadim, facendo riverenza scrive . . ."

165   7   path. Vico to Laerzio, Madurai, 31 August 1611.

165   13   door. Nobili to Fabiis, 27 October 1611.

165   15   Madurai. Vico to Laerzio, Madurai, 26 September 1611.

165   26   base. Responsio quibusdam a P. A. Buccerio objectis. ARSI,
Goa 51, ff. 213–18.

CHAPTER 12

168   11   needs. Vico to Vitelleschi, Madurai, 3 December 1617.

172   15   be. Nobili to Laerzio, 20 November 1610.

172   34   effect. In Dialogue ix of *Dispelling of Ignorance* Nobili writes:
"Erudite scholars have laid down that in an exact science
cause and effect are not only stated but their connection
cogently indicated in three unmistakable steps. Since even
the most learned scholars of this land are ignorant of these
facts, wherein lies their science?"

173   23   pagans. *Contra Gentiles*, i, 2. Cited by Dahmen.

174   1   Estevão. The most complete account of Thomas Stephens is
by G. Schurhammer in *The Month*, April 1955.

178   17   closely. P. D'Elia, *Galileo in Cina* (Analecta Gregoriana,
xxxvii).

181   27   Medicine. Proenza describes Nobili's literary works in a
letter to the General, 20 September 1656.

183   18   India. Questioned by the Portuguese as to their origin,
the St Thomas Christians replied with the following
tradition (for they had no written history). Long ago a
Syrian merchant—a certain Mar Thoma Cana—had arrived

on the Malabar coast and entered the port of Cranganore. The King of Malabar, Cheruman Perumal, gave the stranger an audience and granted him land at Cranganore, where Mar Thoma built a church and collected seventy-two Christian families. A copper-plate deed was still conserved in which the King granted to Mar Thoma on a date corresponding to A.D. 811 "seven kinds of musical instruments and all honours and the right of travelling in a palanquin; he conferred on him dignity and the privilege of spreading carpets on the ground and the use of sandals, and to erect a pavilion at his gate and ride on elephants." The King also gave the Christians a social status equal to the Nayars: that is, approximately midway in the caste system.

The Portuguese identified Mar Thoma with St Thomas. Similarly, the Spaniards in Peru identified a teacher called Tonapa with St Thomas the Apostle, who they believed had evangelized South America. See Juan de Santa Cruz, Pachacuti-yamqui Salcamayhua, *An Account of the Antiquities of Peru*.

CHAPTER 13

184   1   Francisco. Dahmen thought that Pero stood for Perez, and spoke of the Provincial as Francis Perez, but Pero is a diminutive of Pedro (Peter). The Provincial always signed Pero Francisco.

185   21   ceremonies. Francisco to Aquaviva, Cochin, 4 November 1612.

186   28   Jews. In 1607 the Dominican, Fray Gregorio Garcia, propounded the theory that America was populated by the lost tribes of Israel.

187   17   thigh. St Jerome on Jeremias, ch. 13. Responsio ad ea quae contra modum, quo nova Missio Madurensis utitur ad Ethnicos Christo convertendos, objecta sunt. Section relating to the thread.

188   26   kinship. Francisco to Aquaviva, Cochin, 4 November 1612.

188   35   university. *Ibid*.

189   26   mission. From the letter of Pero Francisco of 21 November 1613 we learn the date of Aquaviva's letter.

190   15   letter. Francisco to Nobili, Cochin, 11 August 1613.

190   35   modest. Francisco to Aquaviva, Cochin, 21 November 1613.

197 8 mission. This Portuguese document, though bearing no date nor signature, is evidently a copy of Nobili's statement written by the Provincial's order, and sent by him to the General. Certain expressions in it show that it was written in Cochin, probably in July 1613.

197 15 imitate. Ros to Aquaviva, 19 December 1613. ARSI, Goa 51, ff. 195-9.

CHAPTER 14

200 23 Coast. Vico to Laerzio, 24 November 1610.

201 6 experiment. Buccerio to Francisco, Madurai, 11 December 1614 and 8 February 1615.

202 18 Ros. ARSI, Goa 51, ff. 261-5.

203 8 Britto. In his letter to Vitelleschi, 4 December 1615, Britto speaks of the "glorious" Madurai Mission and the work done by Nobili "whose virtue is well known".

203 18 this. Laerzio to Aquaviva, 30 November 1615.

203 23 Roberto. Brodrick, *Bellarmine*, ii, 319 et seq.

205 34 Madurai. An probari debeat modus quem servant patres Rupertus de Nobili, et Antonius Viccus, eius Socius, in conversione Bracmanum urbis Madurae. Vico thanked Godinho profusely in a letter, 20 November 1616.

206 18 caste. Vico to the General, 10 December 1616. The Provincial did not allow them to minister to the castes that wore the thread. Cf. Vico's letter of 3 December 1617. The Annual Letter of 1616 refers to "the Aiyers who are dressed in white." Francisco may have compelled Nobili and Vico to wear white instead of the *kavi* dress he found indecent.

207 4 castes. Vico's second letter to Vitelleschi, Madurai, 3 December 1617.

CHAPTER 15

212 23 speak. The account of the conference is based on Nobili's letter to Pope Paul V, Goa, 15 February 1619.

216 14 head. "The whole affair ended in mere shouts on the part of the Archbishop of Goa. I could never have imagined that a man could shout so loud without bursting his head." Ros to Vitelleschi, 8 February 1619.

220 23 practices. *Ibid.*

CHAPTER 16

CHAPTER 17

Kingdom of Madurai, 14 October 1648, gives details of Tirumala.

242   35 two hundred. Rubino to Vitelleschi, 24 November 1627.

243   6 Madurai. Cordara, Partis VI, ii, 426 (A.C. 1630).

244   8 better. Martins to Vitelleschi, 2 October 1639.

244   34 Tirumala. For the war and preceding incidents I have drawn on transcripts of correspondence between the Viceroy and Lisbon in the India Office Library, London.

245   27 thirty-nine. Martins to Vitelleschi, 2 October 1639.

247   8 Tiruchirāpalli. Maya to the Provincial, 8 August 1640.

prison. That the missionaries of Madurai were arrested on the same day as Martins (22 July) follows from Maya's statement that at the moment of writing (8 August) they had been seventeen days in prison. Had the order for their arrest left Tiruchirāpalli on 22 July, it would have reached Madurai on the 26th, and 8 August would have been the thirteenth, not the seventeenth day after their imprisonment. Cf. Bertrand, ii, 311.

249   25 future. Maya to the Provincial, 8 August 1640.

CHAPTER 18

252   14 bored. B. da Costa's report of 29 October 1646.

252   16 tunic. The author of the Annual Letter of 1640 says that Fr Balthazar put on the dress of the "Brahmins of the Paraiyans"! officer. B. da Costa to Barreto, 14 October 1646.

254   9 results. Stanley Mayes, *An Organ for the Sultan*, London, 1956.

257   2 crowd. The account of the magician is given by Bertrand in what is supposed to be a letter of Costa dated Tiruchirāpalli, 1644. But this letter is a compilation of various scraps of information given by Costa and others at different dates. The incident of the magician belongs to the year 1630. Cf. Cordara ii, 426; Bertrand, ii, 354.

257   7 sick. Annual Letter of 1646 by B. da Costa.

258   3 pounce. *Ibid.*

258   10 strength. Bertrand, ii, 353.

261   10 pearls. Nobili to Mascarenhas, 27 November 1627.

262   1 success. Annual Letter of 1643.

262   19 Mass. Nobili to Vitelleschi, 7 April 1644.

262   25 deserved. B. da Costa to Barreto, 14 October 1646.

NOTES

263 11 4,183. Official report by A. Lopez, 1644.

263 29 Jaffna. Proenza, 27 September 1656.

264 10 interest. Annual Letter of 1648.

264 11 mission. B. da Costa, Kingdom of Madurai, 14 October 1646; Annual Letter of 1648.

265 10 God. Caldeira, Annual Letter of 1654, Cochin, 15 December 1654.

265 24 deeds. Nobili to Ludovica, San Thomé, 23 September 1649. Nobili had one surviving brother, Vincenzo de Nobili, Marquis of Civitella; Mgr. Sforza had died "in the flower of his manhood"; Nobili's other brother, the Knight of Jerusalem, had been killed in the war in Flanders.

266 18 power. Proenza to the General, Candelur, 20 September 1656.

266 31 suttee. Annual Letter of 1659.

267 34 died. Proenza to the General, 20 September 1656.

Index